AFTER DARKNESS
LIGHT

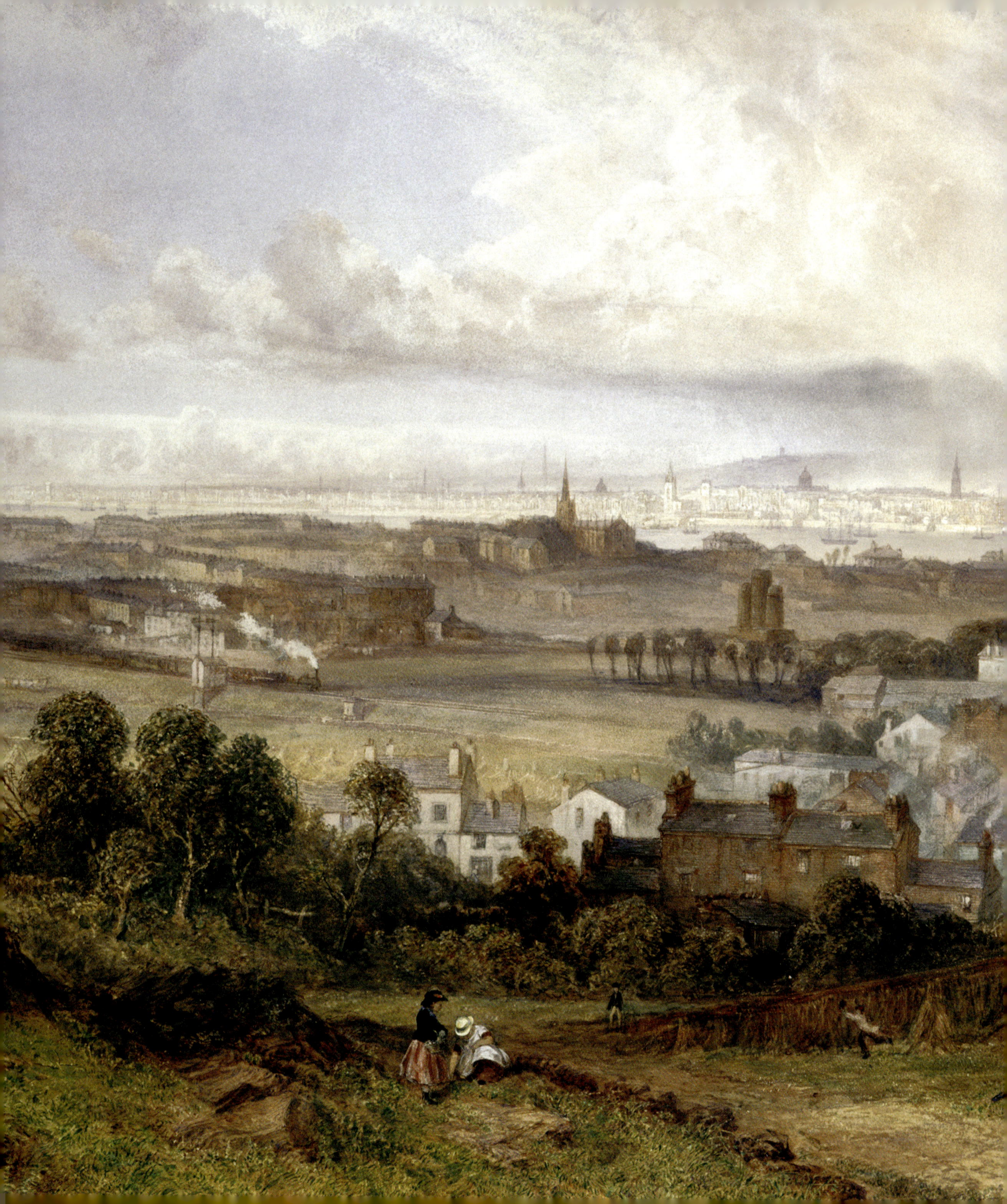

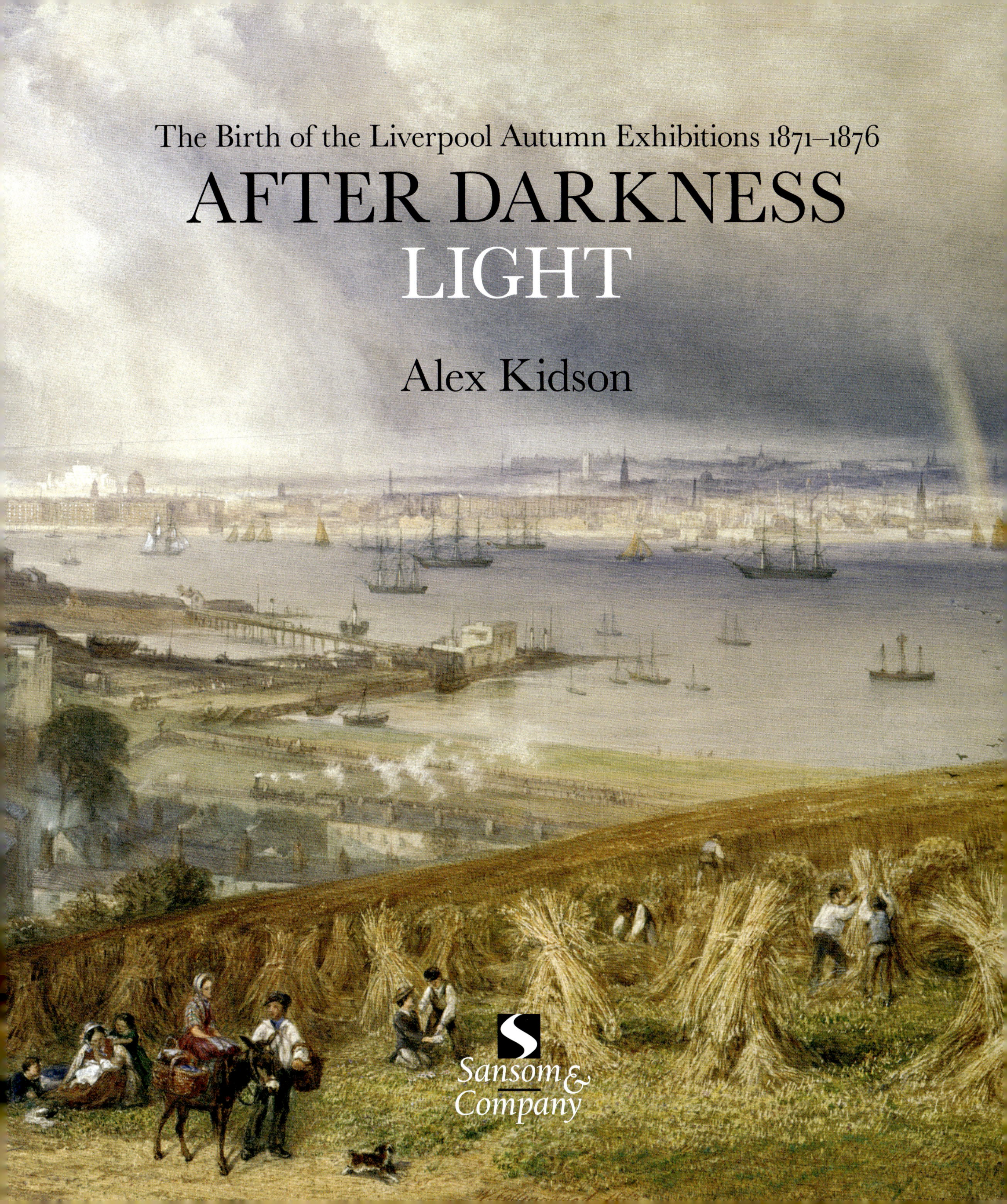

The Birth of the Liverpool Autumn Exhibitions 1871–1876

AFTER DARKNESS
LIGHT

Alex Kidson

Sansom &
Company

First published in 2020 by Sansom & Company,
a publishing imprint of Redcliffe Press Ltd.,
81G Pembroke Road, Bristol BS8 3EA
www.sansomandcompany.co.uk · info@sansomandcompany.co.uk

ISBN 978-1-911408-51-2

British Library Cataloguing-in-Publication Data:
a catalogue record for this book is available from the British Library.

Design and typesetting by E&P Design
Printed and bound by Cambrian Printers, Aberystwyth

Front cover: *Snowdon* · John Finnie · National Museums Liverpool (Walker Art Gallery)
Frontispiece: *Liverpool* · William Collingwood · National Museums Liverpool (Walker Art Gallery)

CONTENTS

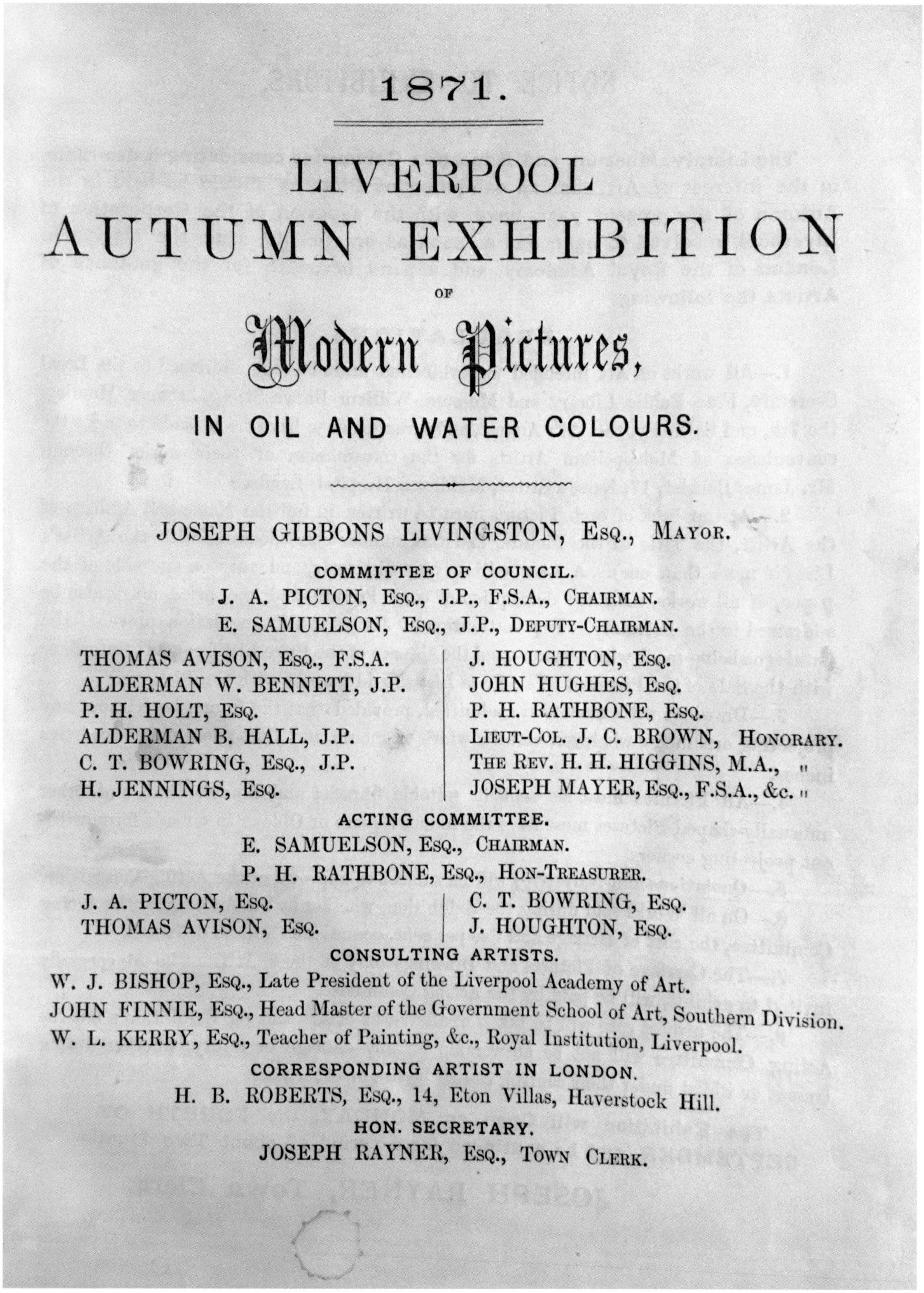

1871.

LIVERPOOL AUTUMN EXHIBITION

OF

𝕸𝖔𝖉𝖊𝖗𝖓 𝕻𝖎𝖈𝖙𝖚𝖗𝖊𝖘,

IN OIL AND WATER COLOURS.

JOSEPH GIBBONS LIVINGSTON, Esq., Mayor.

COMMITTEE OF COUNCIL.

J. A. PICTON, Esq., J.P., F.S.A., Chairman.

E. SAMUELSON, Esq., J.P., Deputy-Chairman.

THOMAS AVISON, Esq., F.S.A.	J. HOUGHTON, Esq.
ALDERMAN W. BENNETT, J.P.	JOHN HUGHES, Esq.
P. H. HOLT, Esq.	P. H. RATHBONE, Esq.
ALDERMAN B. HALL, J.P.	Lieut-Col. J. C. BROWN, Honorary.
C. T. BOWRING, Esq., J.P.	The Rev. H. H. HIGGINS, M.A., „
H. JENNINGS, Esq.	JOSEPH MAYER, Esq., F.S.A., &c. „

ACTING COMMITTEE.

E. SAMUELSON, Esq., Chairman.

P. H. RATHBONE, Esq., Hon-Treasurer.

J. A. PICTON, Esq.	C. T. BOWRING, Esq.
THOMAS AVISON, Esq.	J. HOUGHTON, Esq.

CONSULTING ARTISTS.

W. J. BISHOP, Esq., Late President of the Liverpool Academy of Art.

JOHN FINNIE, Esq., Head Master of the Government School of Art, Southern Division.

W. L. KERRY, Esq., Teacher of Painting, &c., Royal Institution, Liverpool.

CORRESPONDING ARTIST IN LONDON.

H. B. ROBERTS, Esq., 14, Eton Villas, Haverstock Hill.

HON. SECRETARY.

JOSEPH RAYNER, Esq., Town Clerk.

FIG. 1
Title page of the 1871 exhibition catalogue.

PREFACE

T his book has a long history. Years before it took concrete form it was prefigured during my time as curator of British paintings at the Walker Art Gallery in Liverpool, when responding to enquiries of all kinds about the Autumn Exhibitions was part of the daily routine. The lack of a Graves-type dictionary of the exhibits or indeed any kind of convenient written study of the history of the exhibition was an unwelcome and time-consuming fact of life.

Much later I was in a position to propose a project to remedy this, in the shape of an online dictionary of every work shown in the exhibitions. Still very much in progress, and at the time of writing not yet live, this project was kick-started by generous funding from the Paul Mellon Centre for Studies in British Art, and one of the conditions of their award was that I write an article about the exhibitions introducing them to a new generation of historians. This study is what has emerged. It is not an article, for try as I might in writing it, I could not achieve the necessary brevity. There were just too many paths to follow and issues that it seemed important to address. On the other hand, neither is it a proper history. While I was still thinking in terms of an article, I made the decision to confine my study to the first six years of the exhibition, and focus on the structure created by the organisers that proved to have such a long and healthy afterlife. The result is a hybrid text, but hopefully one that will be of interest and value to more dedicated scholars of Victorian exhibition culture.

One of the most enjoyable aspects of creating the dictionary has been trying to trace the present whereabouts of some of the exhibits. A handful were bought for Liverpool's infant permanent collection and are now in the Walker, while others were bought by local private collectors; but most were returned to their makers at the end of each show, their futures uncertain. I decided to represent this part of the project in the present book by bringing together, in the form of the plate sections, a selection of identified exhibits from each of the six years. Some of them are familiar masterpieces, others more representative of the type of works shown. Although pre-eminently shaped by the serendipitous process of searching on Google Images and the invaluable Art UK website, which has inevitably distorted the balance of works towards oil paintings, the choice has also sought to focus on such issues as the growth in the size of the exhibitions and their differing individual characters. It is perhaps necessary to add that in the case of a small number of the plates, the identifications cannot be called foolproof. Annie Beaumont's watercolour *Roses and Camellias* of the 1875 exhibition, for example, is here represented by an exhibition-size watercolour depicting roses and camellias that is signed and dated 1875, but evidently the possibility exists that she treated the subject more than once that year. Captions employ the titles given in the exhibition catalogues, which differ occasionally from those in use today.

For his initiative in identifying a number of the locations I would like to thank Martin Hopkinson, who in essence made this whole part of the book possible. Patrick Pinion of Pinion Creative was responsible for formatting the tables, and Lydia Miller helped to assemble the images with her customary skill and efficiency. Charlotte Keenan, Alex Patterson and Jessie Petheram at the Walker Art Gallery were unfailingly generous and helpful, as were Roger Hull and the staff at Liverpool City Archives. I am also deeply grateful to Mark Hallett, Director of Studies at the Paul Mellon Centre, to Paul Deaton and Clara Hudson at Sansom & Company, and to the book's editor, Ann Kay, and its designer, Ian Parfitt, with all of whom it has been a pleasure to work. Many other people have given me assistance, and I hope to be forgiven for not naming them all; they know who they are. Last but not least the support of my wife Suzanne May, who read the text and made many improvements, has been wonderful as always.

Alex Kidson

INTRODUCTION

The Autumn Exhibitions were a sequence of 63 exhibitions held in Liverpool more or less annually between 1871 and 1938.[1] From 1877 onwards they were an inextricable part of the history and growth of the city's Walker Art Gallery, whose *raison d'etre*, at least in part, lay in acting as a dedicated venue for them. Initially the gallery's permanent collection was shaped largely by purchases from the exhibitions, and its annual programme centred upon their delivery each year early in September. They were to some extent modelled, as earlier annual exhibitions in Liverpool had been, and as were the annual exhibitions in other provincial centres of the United Kingdom such as Birmingham, Manchester, Edinburgh and Glasgow, on the Royal Academy (RA) Summer Exhibitions in London; and it was a particular feature of the Autumn Exhibitions that they were scheduled to take place as soon as practicable after the RA closed in order that a number of pictures that had appeared in the London exhibition could, by arrangement with the artists, be sent directly on to Liverpool.

By 1877 the exhibition had caught on both with artists and the public. The opening in that year of the Walker Art Gallery, thanks to a gift to Liverpool in 1873 of £20,000 (rising to about £25,000) from Alderman Andrew Barclay Walker – in some quarters regarded as a controversial use of profits from the brewing industry – may be seen retrospectively as proof of the exhibition's success in its first six-year phase, as well as the trigger of its future growth. The Walker's annual attendance figure in 1880 of 610,779 has never been superseded and two years later the Council agreed to extend the building only five years after it had opened.[2] The Autumn Exhibition was a major factor in these developments and for decades to come it would remain a core feature not only of the cultural life of Liverpool but of the whole of the north of England.

In 1871, however, success was not necessarily guaranteed and for a variety of reasons, the first exhibition represented something of a gamble. The Town Councillors who undertook it were idealistic, aspirational men who took it for granted that Liverpool, already 'second city of the British Empire', needed to punch its weight as a centre of culture as well as commerce. More practically, they were confident that there was an existing demand for art in the city as a commodity for purchase, and they were also convinced of the value of art as a tool of social improvement.

On the other hand, there was a strongly entrenched and even majority body of opinion within the city that the arts were not what the penny rate should be spent on; as public meetings and some newspapers insisted, it was unfair to tax the working class to gratify the tastes of a wealthy elite, and the decision to risk the city's money on a venture that could well crash and burn was not one to be taken lightly.[3] Furthermore, it was a decision

1. No exhibition was held in the years 1917–18 and 1930–32. The planned 1939 exhibition was cancelled owing to the outbreak of World War II, and after the war the exhibitions were not resumed.
2. Edward Morris *et al.*: *The Walker Art Gallery*, 2nd edition (London, Scala, 2003), p. 11. The present text depends heavily on the research of the late Edward Morris and I should like to dedicate it to his memory. See also his *Victorian and Edwardian Paintings in the Walker Art Gallery and at Sudley House* (London, HMSO, 1996), pp. 1–11; his *Public Art Collections in North-West England: A History and Guide* (Liverpool, Liverpool University Press, 2001), pp. 88–9; and his (with Timothy Stevens) *The Walker Art Gallery Liverpool 1873–2000* (Bristol, Sansom & Co, 2013), pp. 15–24.
3. For discussion of the political divisions over building an art gallery in Liverpool in the 1870s see especially Suzanne Macleod: *Museum Architecture: A New Biography* (Abingdon, Routledge, 2013), ch. 2: 'Hobson's Choice: Art and Grog in Liverpool', pp. 36–71.

being made against the background of the recent collapse of the Liverpool Academy and its latterday rivals, the Liverpool Society of Fine Arts and the Liverpool Institution of Fine Arts, an episode calculated to indicate a potential fragility of the market for art in the city, as well as confirm the toxic polarisation and unreliability of its artists in general.[4] For the previous four years, since the final Liverpool Academy show of 1867, there had been no 'public' art exhibition in the city, only ones undertaken by commercial galleries; and it was to highlight this fact that the organisers adopted the motto *Post Tenebras Lux* – after darkness light – which they printed on the front cover of the exhibition catalogue.

The backdrop of ideological conflict and professional failure within the city's artistic community going back twenty years undoubtedly coloured the ways the organisers of the first Autumn Exhibition went about their task. Of the many policies enshrined in the exhibition, four can be seen as fundamental to its character from the outset. First, the exhibition was to be managed by themselves, city leaders and gentlemen-connoisseurs, not by artists. Even if Liverpool's artists would be delegated roles to play in the exhibition's organisation at a subsidiary level, they were nonetheless being punished for their former misdemeanours, with all that this entailed. Second, the exhibition was to be of a scale that immediately asserted its national significance; it was this (over and above even the quality of the exhibits) that would give it a jump over provincial rivals, as well as the raft of small (indeed some of them not so small) annual exhibitions that had established themselves in Liverpool in the second half of the 1860s. Third, an unusually close relationship was sought with the RA and other leading metropolitan exhibiting societies, above all in the efforts that were made to attract to Liverpool works that had recently been shown in London. At its simplest, this policy was a way of reducing the risk that the exhibition would be perceived as full of rubbish; but more broadly, it would imbue the show with a safe, academic character and guard against the excesses of local pride, independence and 'modernism' always to be feared from provincial artists and of which the Liverpool Academy's controversial embrace of Pre-Raphaelitism twenty years before had been a classic manifestation.

Fourth, and the most important of all in the minds of the organisers, was promoting sales. Not only were the commissions from sales a crucial factor in the profitability of the exhibition and thus of its future existence, but for those playing a longer game, a healthy sales record would be encouragement to good artists to send in their best work next time round, a process which, once begun, would take on a momentum of its own. It was chiefly the weakness of the last Liverpool Academy and Liverpool Institution of Fine Arts exhibitions in this regard, and not the quality of the art on display *per se*, which had led to their demise. It is not difficult to sense (although it is harder to demonstrate) that city leaders took good care, in their private clubs and smoking rooms, to whip their friends and colleagues into buying pictures from the first Autumn Exhibitions. That this would create the profits that would enable high-profile purchases for the Council's own growing art collection was merely an added bonus.

4. For a summary history of this episode see Edward Morris and Emma Roberts: *The Liverpool Academy and Other Exhibitions of Contemporary Art in Liverpool 1774–1867* (Liverpool, Liverpool University Press and National Museums and Galleries on Merseyside, 1998), pp. 10–15. The Liverpool Society of Fine Arts (1858–62), subsequently the Liverpool Institution of Fine Arts (1863–4), had been founded and supported by conservative artists dissatisfied with the pronounced bias within the Liverpool Academy during the 1850s towards Pre-Raphaelitism. Annually between 1858 and 1862 and again in 1864 these rival organisations held competing exhibitions, driving each other towards financial ruin.

THE 1871 EXHIBITION

The decision to go ahead with the first exhibition was taken at a special meeting of the Library, Museum and Arts Committee of the Town Council held on 14 December 1870.[1] A sub-committee was constituted, comprising six Councillor-members (all members of the parent committee), four 'consulting artists' and the Town Clerk, Joseph Rayner, and it was upon these 11 that the task of delivering the exhibition effectively devolved. Their names were duly printed, underneath the names of the Mayor and of the members of the Library Committee, on the title page of the 1871 catalogue (fig. 1).

The two key members of the 'Acting Committee' were its Chairman, Edward Samuelson (1823–1896; fig. 2), and its Treasurer, Philip Rathbone (1828–1895; fig. 3). That Samuelson was a Tory and Rathbone a Liberal no doubt helped minimise political fall-out from the project,[2] but both men already had a public image of cultivated independence (Samuelson's five brothers were all Liberals). So did the third major figure on the new committee, the older and more eminent James Allanson Picton (1805–1889). Picton, a marble bust of whom by J.A.P. Macbride was shown in the 1871 exhibition (pl. 14),[3] was an architect and an expert on the cultural history of Liverpool. He was celebrated for his role in the establishment of the Liverpool public library in the early 1850s, and had been Chairman of the Council's Library, Museum and Arts Committee since as far back as 1851. Having seen through the city's acquisition, successively, of handsome buildings to house the library and then the museum, he was now one of the most active backers of public funding for the still-missing art gallery. Many of the key features of the delivery of the exhibition depended upon the skill-set of these three men, including their experience as collectors, their familiarity with precedent and their energy in forging fresh contacts with artists and artistic institutions throughout Britain. As the *Liverpool Courier* was to write when the exhibition opened: 'the efforts of the indefatigable gentlemen who have been inviting artistic contributions … have been unexpectedly successful';[4] and these efforts included numerous visits to artists' studios, especially those of Royal Academicians, as well as to the 1871 exhibition of the RA and the other chief London exhibiting societies.

Of the four 'consulting artists' (a designation formally separate from the 'Acting Committee', who were confined to Councillors), three were familiar and respected figures within the Liverpool art scene. William James Bishop (1805–1888) had been President of the Liverpool Academy (which continued to exist, although it had ceased to hold exhibitions) since 1854; he had opposed the Pre-Raphaelite faction within the Academy and had shown only one work there between 1850 and 1863, although he returned to exhibiting in the mid-1860s. William Kerry (1818–1893), a watercolourist, was drawing master at the Liverpool Royal Institution; he sent nine works to the 1871 exhibition, Bishop six. The third consulting artist from Liverpool, the younger John Finnie (1829–1905), had arrived in the city in 1855 after

1. Morris 1996 [as at 'Introduction', note 2] p. 2.
2. As noted by James Moore: *High Culture and Tall Chimneys: Art Institutions and Urban Society in Lancashire, 1780–1914* (Manchester, Manchester University Press, 2018), p. 170.
3. Catalogue 901; the bust is now in the Picton Reading Room of Liverpool City Library.
4. *Liverpool Courier*, 2 September 1871, p. 6.

being appointed to teach art at the Mechanics Institute, and his association with the exhibition emphasised its intended appeal to students, amateurs and working men. He worked in a more progressive vein than Bishop and Kerry, and, having avoided partisanship in the political controversies of the late 1850s and 1860s by showing both at the Liverpool Academy and its rival organisations throughout the period (as well as being a regular at the RA), he now had a high profile of his own.

Arguably the chief function of these three men was to contribute to the exhibition's image by association, but the role of the fourth consultant must have been more active. This was Henry Benjamin Roberts (1831–1915), a genre painter who had been born in Liverpool and maintained close links with the city but who had moved to London in the late 1850s in order to further his career. Interestingly he had exhibited exclusively throughout the 1850s and 1860s with the Liverpool Academy – unlike Finnie – but the character of his work was uncontroversial and popular and at least by the 1860s it seems to have enjoyed some familiarity among Liverpool collectors.[5] Roberts had shown intermittently at the RA since 1859 – but every year since 1867 – and from 1868 he had lived in Adelaide Road on the edge of Haverstock Hill, an enclave of north-west London below Hampstead which was one of the capital's major artist colonies. The distinctively strong presence in the first Autumn Exhibitions of artists from Haverstock Hill and Hampstead (see below) surely reflects Roberts's role in networking, putting the word about and soliciting possible exhibits from artists who may have lost sight of Liverpool with the demise of its Academy exhibitions four years earlier.

The logistics of assembling the exhibition were the responsibility of the Town Clerk, Joseph Rayner. Something of the practicalities, which were obviously based largely on precedent, may be deduced from the 'Notice to Exhibitors' and 'Regulations' printed at the front of the catalogue (fig. 4). The send-in week was that of 7–12 August, and submissions had to be sent either directly to the 'Local Secretary' in Liverpool (Rayner himself, although there is evidence that he delegated this function)[6] or else, 'for the convenience of Metropolitan Artists', the firm of James Bourlet in London. That left a mere two and a half weeks for transporting the London pictures to Liverpool, unpacking, laying out, numbering and hanging the exhibits, correlating the physical items with the artists' own lists of works sent, together with their prices (which had to be 'written very distinctly, and only on one side of the paper'), and then assembling and printing the catalogue in perfect numerical order, error-free. The 1871 catalogue is not error-free,[7] but it is remarkably accurate given that it must have been produced in only a few days.

THE EXHIBITION SPACE

One advantage enjoyed by the Acting Committee was that they could call upon galleries in the Free Public Library and Museum on William Brown Street. This magnificent and relatively new addition to the cluster of public buildings around St George's Hall had opened in 1860 and was under the jurisdiction of the Library, Museum and Arts Committee. Although the galleries concerned may not have been ideal, in that they required their normal exhibits to be stripped out, the historical issues of finding a room in the city large enough to hold a major art exhibition, and absorbing the costs of renting it, were avoided.

As the opening report on the exhibition in the *Liverpool Courier* noted, four rooms in the building (which was generally referred to by press and public alike as the Free Library)

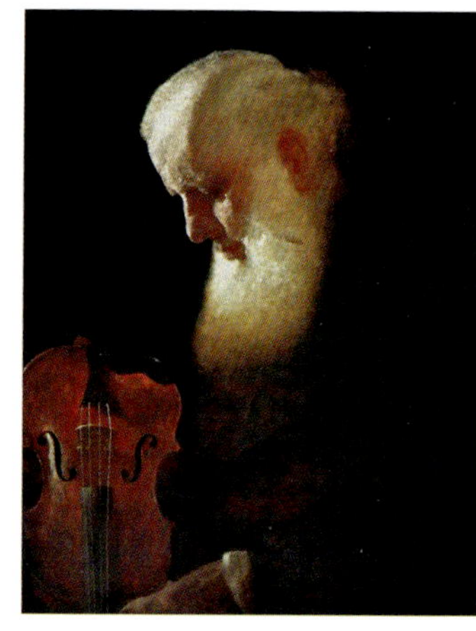

FIG. 2
Edward Samuelson in later life, with his Amati violin (*An Old Acquaintance* by David Woodlock, exhibited at the Liverpool Autumn Exhibition in 1883, no. 469).
National Museums Liverpool (Walker Art Gallery)

5. All three oils by Roberts in the Walker Art Gallery today were painted in the 1860s and seem to have been in the city until they later passed into the gallery's collection; one may have been owned by Alderman Andrew Barclay Walker and certainly was by his son, Lord Wavertree; another, the *Oliver Twist – First Introduction to Fagin* of 1868 which was one of Roberts's seven contributions to the 1871 LAE (pl. 11), was certainly owned by Samuelson by 1886 and since it was unpriced in the 1871 catalogue, may already have been his by that date and perhaps the basis of friendship between the two men.
6. *Liverpool Courier*, 2 September 1872, p. 5. In 1875 the *Daily Post* wrote of the exhibition 'the general business machinery has been perfectly organised by the practised hands of Mr. B.H. Grindley' (4 September 1875, p. 5).
7. The most obvious errors are that catalogue number 300, and again numbers 644 and 645, were inserted out of sequence.

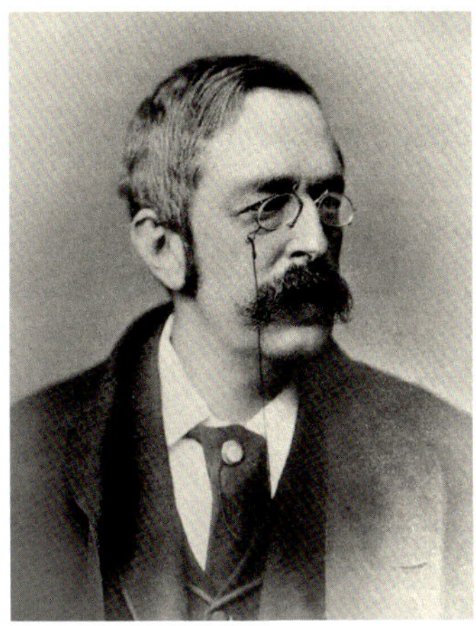

NOTICE TO EXHIBITORS.

The Library, Museum, and Education Committee considering it desirable, in the interest of Art, that an exhibition of Pictures should be held in the Autumn of the present year, have, with the sanction of the Corporation of Liverpool, resolved to open one as soon as practicable, after the closing in London of the Royal Academy, and append herewith for the guidance of Artists the following

REGULATIONS.

1.—All works of Art intended for exhibition must be sent addressed to the Local Secretary, Free Public Library and Museum, William Brown Street, between Monday, the 7th, and Saturday, the 12th August, and arrangements have been made to meet the convenience of Metropolitan Artists for the transmission of their works through Mr. James Bourlet, 17, Nassau Street, Middlesex Hospital, London.

2.—At the back of each Picture must be written in full the Name and Address of the Artist, the Title of the Picture, and the number corresponding with the Artist's List (if more than one). A List written very distinctly, and only on one side of the paper, of all works, with the description of each Picture, and the price, must also be addressed to the Secretary. The inattention of Artists to this regulation prevents the Catalogue being made with accuracy, and the absence of the Price List frequently interferes with the Sale of the Pictures. The Price List should be sent with the Pictures.

3.—Drawings with mounts are admitted, provided that the frames be without any projecting ornaments whatever, and the width of mount and frame does not exceed five inches.

4.—All Pictures must be sent in suitable frames ; and Round, Oval, and other unusually-shaped Pictures must have the frames Square or Oblong in outside form, without projecting corners.

5.—Quotations and Narratives will be subject to approval of the Acting Committee.

6.—On all Works sold during the Exhibition, whether by the Artist or by the Acting Committee, the cost of carriage and five per cent. commission will be deducted.

7.—The Carriage of Pictures and Drawings only of those Artists who are specially invited to exhibit, will be paid by the Acting Committee.

8.—The utmost care will be taken of all Works of Art sent for Exhibition ; but the Acting Committee will not be answerable for any damage or injury, whether during transit or whilst under their control, caused by fire or otherwise.

The Exhibition will Open on MONDAY, the FOURTH OF SEPTEMBER, and be continued for a period of about Two Months.

JOSEPH RAYNER, Town Clerk,

Hon. Secretary.

were devoted to the exhibition, namely 'an upper room of the library proper, the room usually devoted to paintings [the Council's existing permanent collection of pictures] and a bird and a fish-room from the museum portion of the building'.[8] An annotated plan of the space appended to the minutes of the Acting Committee meeting of 28 June 1871 (fig. 5) reveals that at that date it was still unclear to Committee members whether four rooms would be needed or only three. In addition to the four main galleries, of which two were

8. *Liverpool Courier* [as at note 6].

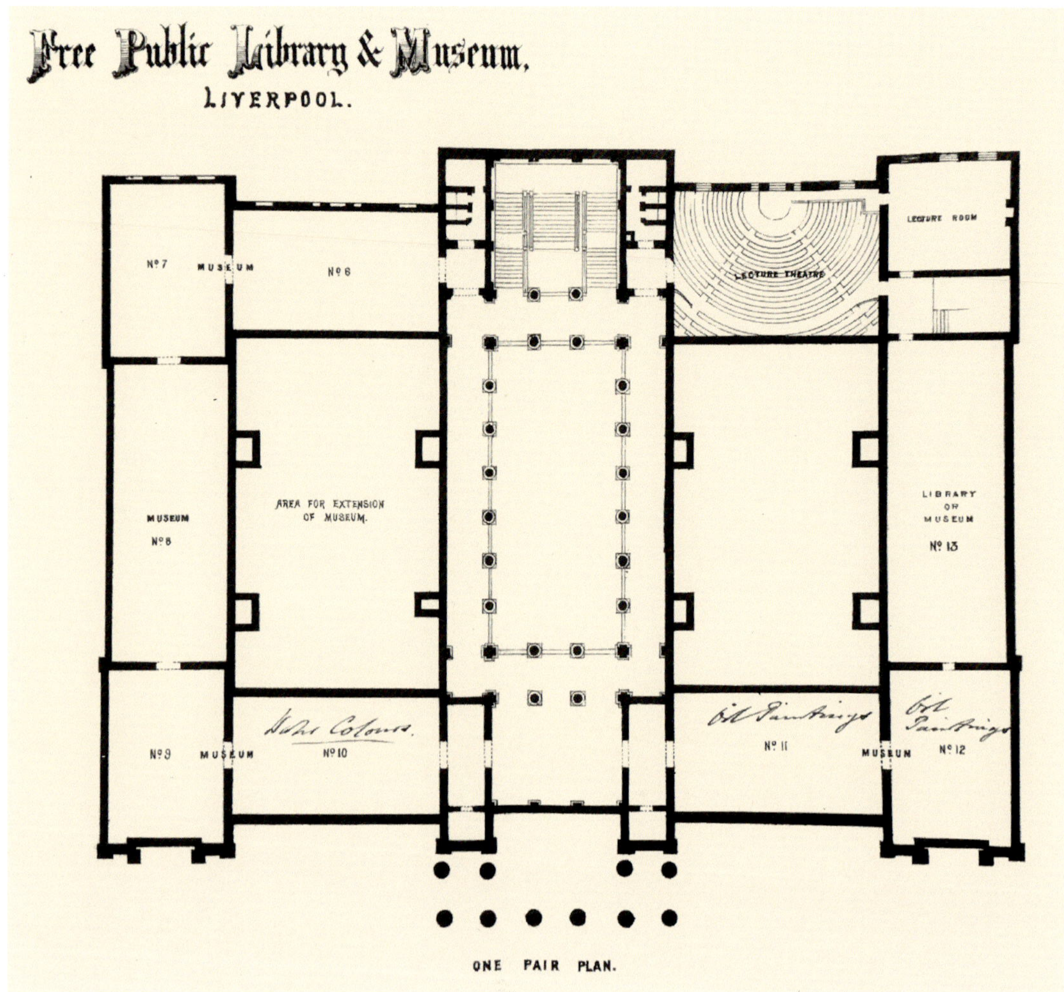

FIG. 5
Upper-floor plan of the Free
Public Library and Museum,
with manuscript annotations
of the intended exhibition layout
(from the minutes of the 1871
Acting Committee).
Walker Art Gallery Archives

given over to oil paintings and – eventually – two to works on paper, there were also, as is deducible from the exhibition catalogue, a 'small vestibule on the left' at the start of the exhibition, a corridor 'entering the watercolour rooms' (which was hung with oils) and another corridor between the two watercolour rooms that was hung with watercolours. There was also a refreshment-room adjoining the galleries and a ladies' cloakroom.[9] Not all of this is clear from the floor plan. According to the critic from the *Daily Post*, who confirmed that the two galleries on the left of the exhibition entrance were those hung with the oils, and those on the right the watercolours, 'the suite of rooms … is admirably suited for the purpose … the light is excellent, and … it would not be possible to see the pictures to better advantage'.[10] Not everybody agreed with the last remark. A group of local artists persuaded the *Liverpool Mercury* to write, at the very end of its long series of articles on the exhibition:

> we have received numerous complaints – indeed requests to notice the very great injustice that has been done to the Liverpool artists in the hanging. Most of our best men who have contributed to the exhibition, have either been put on the floor, placed in passages or dark recesses, or skied. We do not know whom the hanging was deputed to, but it has been most unfairly accomplished; though we should not have noticed it had we not been requested to do so.[11]

9. *Liverpool Albion*, 4 September 1871, p. 5.
10. *Liverpool Daily Post*, 2 September 1871, p. 5. This opinion was reformulated in the *Nineteenth Annual Report of the Free Public Library, Museums and Schools …* (Liverpool, Liverpool Printing and Stationery Company, 1871), p. 5: 'It is satisfactory to state that in point of light and arrangement, the rooms were everything which could be desired.' The report technically covered the year September 1870–August 1871, but evidently it was felt consideration of the Autumn Exhibition could not be postponed.
11. *Liverpool Mercury*, 9 November 1871, p. 3.

CONTENTS OF THE EXHIBITION

The total number of catalogued items in the 1871 exhibition was 908.[12] Of these, 433 were oil paintings (47.7%), 446 drawings and watercolours (49.1%), 21 sculptures and carvings (2.3%) and eight miniatures and miscellanea (0.9%). They were by 451 different artists.

Compared with the totals for the previous public exhibition in Liverpool, the 1867 Liverpool Academy, these figures were impressive. The 1867 Academy had comprised only 215 works, and of these, 20 of the most noteworthy had been borrowed from local collectors, so that the total of send-in items was only 195. But this exhibition had been an anomaly, the last twitch of a dying organism; and observers with slightly longer memories might have recalled that its predecessor, the 1865 exhibition of the combined Liverpool Academy and 'Liverpool Art Institute' (presumably the Liverpool Institution of Fine Arts), had contained 1,090 works (by 543 artists). These were the numbers that would have most likely been targeted by the Acting Committee during the first months of 1871, and in their light the final totals for the new exhibition were by no means spectacular. That certain people saw it that way is clear from complaints in press reviews of the exhibition about the quality of some of the works included and assertions that the Committee had been so desperate to fill the rooms that they had allowed their aesthetic judgement to take a back seat. Others took a more generous view, but perhaps a surer indicator is the number of artists in the exhibition who were represented by a large body of work. In 1871 no fewer than 11 artists showed six works or more, and the total number of works included by these 11 was 81 (8.9% of the whole exhibition). By only the following year the equivalent totals were eight and 50 (out of 959) and by 1876 they were five and 33 (out of 1,186 – a figure that in itself revealed much about the potential capacity of the rooms).

But the 1865 exhibition in Liverpool was not the only comparator of interest to the Acting Committee. In the immediate context, the most direct competition for the exhibition came from two provincial rivals, the Royal Manchester Institution and the Royal Society of Artists in Birmingham. These organisations (both directed by connoisseurs, not artists) had coincidentally held their first exhibition in the same year, 1827, and having mounted essentially unbroken sequences of shows ever since, were now ingrained in the artistic culture of their regions. In 1870 the Royal Manchester Institution's exhibition had consisted of 555 catalogued items by 366 artists (smaller totals than usual; the 1869 equivalents had been 643 and 396 and in 1871 they would be 671 and 436); while in 1870 the Birmingham exhibition had contained 664 catalogued items by 349 artists, figures close to its average. That the new Liverpool exhibition had surpassed these totals easily must have put a rosier complexion on its achievement.

Comparisons with the RA Summer Exhibition itself, even though this was more of a model than a rival, are also of considerable interest. In fact the 1871 Summer Exhibition was smaller than average, consisting of only 1,338 catalogued items (over the following five years the mean figure would be 1,547). Of these items 758 were oils (56.7%) and 160 were sculptures (11.9%); actual watercolours, which comprised virtually half the exhibition in Liverpool, numbered only 198 (14.8%). Thus the make-up of the exhibitions was significantly different. The presence of the human figure made itself felt much more at the RA, not only through the strong showing of sculpture, mostly of an Academic character,[13] but also because of the far greater incidence of portraits, especially among the oils. At the 1871 RA 114 portraits in oils were shown (15% of all the oils); and on top of this portraits also made up 104 of the sculptures, 29 of the 36 enamels and miniatures, 25 of the 75 crayons

12. Henceforward totals refer to catalogue numbers, not to objects, as the totals of the latter cannot be calculated with exactitude. This is because in a few cases unspecified numbers of works are included under one catalogue number. In fact in 1871 the discrepancy between catalogue numbers and objects is only two (908:910) as only one catalogue number, 243, is of more than one work (three landscapes in one frame). In later exhibitions the gap is mostly considerably larger.

13. The inadequate representation of sculpture was an endemic problem for all the provincial exhibitions, not just in Liverpool; the 1870 Birmingham exhibition contained only five sculptures out of 664 works. There are indications that the Autumn Exhibition Committee became conscious of this issue in future years and made specific efforts to address it.

and prints, and even five of the watercolours. In Liverpool only 11 of the 433 oils were portraits (2.5%), and although 12 of the sculptures were, there were only two among the watercolours. As portraiture was just as much a staple of artistic practice in Liverpool as it was elsewhere in Britain, it can only be supposed that the Autumn Exhibition Acting Committee deliberately adopted a stance of excluding portraits in a spirit of aesthetic idealism; and where exceptions were made, this was mostly because of the local social pre-eminence of the sitters, not on artistic grounds. On the other hand, the Liverpool equivalent of portraits was evidently landscapes of North Wales. At the RA there were 28 of these (2.1% of the total); at the Autumn Exhibition there were 90, virtually 10% of the whole exhibition.

The fact that the Acting Committee had a policy from the outset of soliciting works for Liverpool that had appeared at the RA earlier in the year might encourage the supposition that there was considerable overlap in content between the two. According to Edward Morris the Autumn Exhibitions, 'although often selected with great care and imagination, were in effect travelling versions of the principal London summer exhibitions, particularly the Royal Academy'.[14] It is true that 310 of the exhibits at the 1871 Autumn Exhibition were by artists who had appeared at that year's RA, but only 61 had actually been exhibited there (to which should be added a handful more that had appeared in earlier years). Of course, many of these works were among the most prominent, and by many of the leading artists;[15] yet the fact that so many were different might seem to imply a commendable concern with 'originality' on the Acting Committee's part. As the *Daily Post* noted in its overview of the show: 'Many of the pictures have never been exhibited before, and have been specially painted for this exhibition – a compliment rarely paid to a provincial exhibition.'[16]

THE ARTISTS

Of the 451 artists[17] included in the first Autumn Exhibition, 47 (10.4%) had shown at both the previous public exhibitions in Liverpool, those of 1865 and 1867.[18] One might be tempted to classify these as the core Liverpool supporters: professional senders-in little affected by art politics. Of the 107 exhibitors in 1867, 62 returned in 1871 and of the 543 exhibitors in 1865, 156 did. Put one way, that meant that 28.7% of all the exhibitors in 1865 were loyal enough to return six years later; but put another it meant that 65.4% of the 1871 artists had not been represented in Liverpool's last major public art exhibition, perhaps a more telling indicator of 'the efforts of the indefatigable gentlemen who have been inviting artistic contributions'.

Twenty-nine of the 451 artists did not send an address with their entries, but of the 422 who did 61 (14.4%) came from Liverpool, and a total of 237 (56.2%) were from London;[19] figures proportionally very close to those of 1865, which were respectively 74 (14.6%) and 281 (55.4%) out of the 507 who gave addresses. In 1871, 119 artists (28%) were from the provinces of Britain, with healthy contributions from the Home Counties and southern England, Birmingham and Edinburgh, but weak showings from Manchester, the north-east and Ireland, and a non-existent one from all parts of Scotland except its capital.

The table on p. 61 attempts to break down the geographical distribution of the artists in greater detail. Within London itself, six enclaves particularly rich in contributors (Hampstead, Haverstock Hill, St John's Wood, Kensington, Regent's Park and Fitzrovia, which provided over 42% of the London total) are separated out from the rest of the

14. Morris and Roberts 1998 [as at 'Introduction', note 4], p. 31, n. 79.
15. The number of artists who in 1871 showed at both the RA Summer Exhibition and the Liverpool Autumn Exhibition was 148, of whom 115 were from London.
16. *Daily Post*, 13 September 1871, Supplement, p. 1. The writer did point out representation also from 'the Old and New Watercolour Societies, the Dudley Gallery, and the Suffolk Street Gallery'. The theme of many of the works being painted specially for the exhibition recurs several times in both press coverage and Committee Reports during the years 1872–6.
17. The Liverpool sculptural firm Allen and Clotworthy is here counted as one artist.
18. Of these 14 were from Liverpool and five were women artists. The 14 from Liverpool were W.J.J.C. Bond, William Collingwood, Thomas Daniels, John Finnie, Miss Hunt, W.L. Kerry, the sculptor J.A.P. Macbride, Ephraim Pugh, R.P. Richards, John Robertson, James Smith, Jacob Stone, Richard Swainson and J.E. Worrall. The five women artists were Miss Hunt, Mrs Sophie Anderson, Mrs Mary Ensor, Miss Fanny Jolly and Mrs C. Rossiter.
19. The 1871 totals exclude, for Liverpool, artists from Birkenhead, the rest of the Wirral and other Liverpool suburbs in Lancashire; and for London, outer suburbs and places in the inner Home Counties.

capital. Outside London the selected zones, although covering the whole country, conform less to rigorous geographical criteria than reflect plausible catchment areas (thus Birkenhead, the Wirral, Manchester, and the rest of Lancashire have all been taken to merit separate consideration, whilst 'the London suburbs' merge unsatisfactorily with the rest of Inner London on the one hand, the south of England on the other; other 'borders' are necessarily equally ambiguous). The 1871 table also charts the number of works received from each of the given zones, divided between oils, 'works on paper' and sculpture; and finally it makes an attempt to provide some very rough breakdown of the gender of the artists of the works concerned. This is inevitably a doomed enterprise, since in many cases the gender of artists has been lost to view; yet even allowing for method-ological shortcomings (exhaustive biographical research has not been carried out) and for the opacity of the results, the exercise has seemed worthwhile: especially because in their first years, the Autumn Exhibitions appeared to demonstrate an element of partiality towards women artists (see below). Of the 1871 exhibition's 273 artists whose gender has been defined as 'known', 63 (23%) were certainly female; applying the same proportion to the remaining 178 whose gender has not been identified would add another 41 female artists to the total and yield a grand total of 104.[20]

According to the table, a total of four artists submitted five works from foreign addresses. Here however 'foreign addresses' includes those of native artists temporarily abroad, and the table cannot be used to calculate the presence in the exhibition of the 10 genuinely foreign artists, that is, those born and working abroad (some of whom submitted to the exhibition without giving any address at all).[21] The presence of foreign artists – which was also a little-noticed part of many, although not all, RA Summer Exhibitions – continued a tradition established at the Liverpool Academy and the Liverpool Society of Fine Arts in the 1850s, especially the latter which at great cost had employed agents to encourage submissions in five European cities: Paris, Brussels, Antwerp, Düsseldorf and Munich. In 1865, when participation from abroad was dominated by artists from Germany, Belgium and Holland, no fewer than 39 had been included, 27 from Düsseldorf alone.[22] It is clear that the Acting Committee consciously decided to retain this feature of the old exhibitions, no doubt aware of the considerable presence in Liverpool of foreign businessmen whose record, or potential, as patrons may at least in part have resided in the availability of works by their countrymen. It is less clear whether the old networks that facilitated the selection, transportation and delivery of foreign pictures were still in place: the sharp reduction in actual numbers from 39 to 10 in 1871 implies a degree of atrophy, but the identities of the artists concerned suggests not only that some elements of continuity survived but also that the new exhibition carried its own appeal for younger artists. Five of the 10 artists were under 40, none of them had previously shown either in Liverpool or at the RA, and two of them were Americans: William Dana (1833–1927) and Alexander Wust (1837–1876).[23] Of the five older artists, one, the Frenchman Philibert Léon Couturier (1823–1901) had also not shown formerly at Liverpool or the RA, but the remaining four all had some previous: the Dutchman Mari Ten Kate (1831–1910; pl. 10) and the Düsseldorf artist Adolf Schreyer (1828–1899) had both shown at the Liverpool Society of Fine Arts as far back as 1860; a second German, Ludwig Hermann (1812–1881) from Berlin, had showed at both the Liverpool Academy and the Liverpool Society of Fine Arts in 1862 and at the versions of the latter in subsequent years; while the Belgian-born Director of the Weimar Art School, Charles Verlat (1824–1890), had shown in Liverpool between 1861 and 1864. Pleasingly and perhaps even symbolically, although no doubt coincidentally, this gave a representation from five different foreign nations of two artists each.

20. For a different calculation see Jane Sellars: *Women's Works* (Liverpool, National Museums and Galleries on Merseyside, 1988), p. 1.
21. Foreign-born artists domiciled in Britain, of whom there were much larger numbers, are not considered in this section.
22. Morris and Roberts 1998 [as at 'Introduction', note 4] pp. 12–13.
23. Dutch-born, Wust had joined the even younger Dutch artist Willem Maris (1844–1910) on a trip to Norway some months previously and they submitted a joint work. Of the two remaining younger artists, one, Joseph Van Luppen (1834–1891), was Belgian; the other, Tony Robert-Fleury (1837–1911), was French.

ATTENDANCES, PRICES AND SALES

The exhibition opened on Monday 4 September 1871 and ran until Saturday 18 November, a total of 76 days. During that period, excluding visits on season tickets, of which 313 were sold, the recorded attendance was 22,725,[24] an average of 299 walk-up visitors a day. The figure would have been considerably lower but for the decision – perhaps prompted by an eloquent letter published in the *Daily Courier* on 11 September from 'A Clerk'[25] – to open the exhibition from 16 October in the evening, from 6–9 p.m., when the day entry fee of 1 shilling was reduced to 6d.[26] The result was 'largely-increased attendances',[27] and these prompted a further decision to extend the exhibition by a week from its original planned closing date of 11 November.

Attendances made up the highest proportion of the exhibition's total income, £990 10s 6d of the total of £1,522 18s 8d. Of this, season ticket sales to 131 gentlemen, 132 ladies and 50 students, charged at different rates, contributed £62 2s. Sales of catalogues, which were available in sixpenny or threepenny editions, accounted for £165 10s, and excluding a few miscellanies, the remaining income was made up of commission from the sales of 235 pictures to the value of £6,395 2s 6d, which amounted to £320 18s 6d.

The total surplus enjoyed by the exhibition was £615 16s 8d,[28] of which the Committee set aside £500 for purchases for the Council's permanent collection, with the hubristic promise 'to devote a larger sum for the same purpose next year'.[29] In the event the £500, increased to £600, was held over for two purchases from the 1872 exhibition, of paintings by J.W. Oakes and F.W.W. Topham (pls. 24, 25), both at a price of £300.[30] The purchases by the Council from the 1871 exhibition (see below) were not officially reported and do not show up in the exhibition accounts.

Exact details of which pictures were sold to whom do not appear to have survived in the 1871 exhibition records, but we know the names of the 94 buyers and the amounts that each of them spent.[31] Many of them are well-known Liverpool civic leaders and businessmen. The exhibition's main men – P.H. Rathbone (who spent £438), Edward Samuelson (£50 3s) and James Allanson Picton (£32 6s) – are all among them, as is Andrew Barclay Walker, whose patronage of art would set the city by the ears two years later, and who on this occasion spent £1 2s. Other members of the Samuelson clan also feature, one of them being Edward's older brother Bernhard, who at the private view, in what was obviously a carefully staged *coup de théâtre* guaranteed at a stroke to put the exhibition on the national map, splashed out 1,250 guineas, the full undiscounted price, for Frederic Leighton's great *Hercules Wrestling with Death for the Body of Alcestis* (pl. 2). This transaction – which was probably sealed privately well in advance – inevitably from the viewpoint of statistical analysis skewed the playing field. The price of Leighton's picture was far in excess of any other work in the exhibition (the next most expensive, W.Q. Orchardson's *In St Mark's Venice*, had a price-tag of £800, and only 12 oils in the exhibition cost £300 or more); and the total value of sales thereby achieved would be hard for following exhibitions to match. Taking the Leighton out of the equation, the remaining 93 purchasers spent £5,583 (an average of £60 each), on 234 works (2.5 works per buyer, at an average of roughly £23 17s per work after discount had been negotiated). Since the catalogue reveals that a significant proportion of the oils – 189 of the 386 that were priced – cost between £5 and 30 guineas, and that 250 out of the 414 watercolours that were priced cost between £2 and 15 guineas, it seems clear at what end of the range most of the buying took place.

24. *Nineteenth Annual Report* [as at note 10], p. 6. The figure appears to include educational visits, which were calculated separately in later reports.

25. 'Thousands of persons, clerks in offices, assistants, male and female, in shops, and those employed in work-rooms, would be delighted to be enabled to pay [the exhibition] a visit were it open at such times as they could conveniently attend without neglecting their business …'; *Daily Courier*, 11 September 1871, p. 5.

26. *Daily Post*, 14 October 1871, p. 5.

27. Notice in, for example, the *Porcupine*, 11 November 1871, p. 525. The total of 'morning visits' [i.e. between 10 a.m. and 4 p.m.] was 14,416 and that of the evening visits 8,309; *Statement of the Accounts of the* [1871] *Autumn Exhibition* in *Liverpool Autumn Exhibition Accounts 1871–1926*, Ms. volume, Walker Art Gallery Archives.

28. *Statement of the Accounts* [as at note 27].

29. *Nineteenth Annual Report* [as at note 10], p. 6.

30. *Twentieth Annual Report of the Free Public Library, Museum and Gallery of Art …* (Liverpool, Liverpool Printing and Stationery Company, 1872), p. 5.

31. *Statement of the Accounts* [as at note 27]. Ten days after the exhibition opened, the *Daily Post* [as at note 16] noted that 105 works had already been sold, and gave a list of 18 prominent buyers together with the works they had bought.

Almost all the most expensive works in the exhibition came from London. All the water-colours priced at over £150, of which there were eight, and all the sculptures costing more than £200, of which there were three, were by London artists. Of the 12 oils costing over £300, eight were by artists from London, and the other four all lived in the south. The most expensive oil by a Liverpool artist – Richard Norbury's *Glyn Crafnant* – was priced at 80 guineas, and of the local watercolours (the artist was in fact from Birkenhead) the priciest was R.G. Kelly's *Delphi, County Mayo* at £50. The most expensive painting from Edinburgh was Otto Leyde's *Sheep Shearing in Upper Clydesdale*, which cost £75. Predictably, virtually all these top-end works were by men. Women may have been reasonably well represented in the exhibition as a whole, but this was not reflected in their prices. Only one of the 31 oils by women in the exhibition was priced at over £50, and many of them cost less than £15.

The exception that proved the rule was *Elaine* (pl. 3), a large composition based on lines from Tennyson's *Idylls of the King* by Mrs Sophie Anderson, which was priced at £420. The work had been shown at the RA in 1870[32] and had been greeted with criticism as well as praise, a fate that it would also encounter in Liverpool. In a second grand publicity-seeking gesture on the part of the Acting Committee, this was by some distance the most expensive of the three works in the exhibition to be selected for purchase for the Liverpool permanent collection;[33] and if the Leighton *coup* had been engineered by Samuelson, this one can surely be ascribed to Rathbone. He came from a distinguished family of Liverpool social reformers (he was the son of the fifth William Rathbone and brother of the sixth, as well as the uncle of Eleanor Rathbone) and that he should have sought to use the Autumn Exhibition as a vehicle for articulating issues of gender equality would have been entirely in keeping with family tradition. Even if the nature of Rathbone's involvement in the purchase of Anderson's picture remains opaque (there is some suggestion that the money came out of his own pocket)[34] – the decision to go ahead must have been much discussed privately and justifying arguments found to overcome potential public opposition. The size of the discount – at 25% proportionally larger than many of those negotiated for sales from the exhibition – may well have been one of them. But the artist ticked other boxes. She was Parisian by birth and upbringing, as though to underline the wide horizons of the Liverpool exhibition. Now in her late forties, she was demonstrably experienced, had shown at the RA since the mid-1850s and had been one of the most loyal of artists in support of the Liverpool exhibitions during their years of schism. This picture was unusually elevated for her in terms of its subject matter and illustrated a famous passage from England's most celebrated poet. Moreover, the moment was opportune: earlier that year the Liverpool artist Jessie Macgregor (1847–1919) had been only the second woman to be awarded the RA's gold medal for history painting, after Louisa Starr in 1867; both awards had been controversial and there is no doubt the choice of Anderson's picture for the collection tapped into a topical cause.

PRESS REVIEWS

The Liverpool critics' reactions to Sophie Anderson's picture[35] provide a telling case study within their response to the exhibition as a whole. As with their reception of the latter, their view of *Elaine* was generally favourable, but enshrined a surprising variety of shades of opinion (there is no hint of syndication). Among the shorter notices, probably the most favourable was that of the *Courier*, which wrote that the picture was 'one of the finest conception[s] in the collection … a striking realisation of Tennyson's lines', and revealed 'unexpected strength in a female artist'.[36] The *Daily Post* promoted the picture into its

---

32. Although it was omitted by Algernon Graves from volume 1 of his *Dictionary of Royal Academy Exhibitors 1769–1904* (London, Henry Graves and George Bell, 1905) p. 33.

33. £315 was paid for Anderson's picture; the other two were John Finnie's oil *Snowdon* (pl. 1) and J.M. Jopling's watercolour *"Sweet eyes of starry tenderness"* (now known as *Starry Eyes*; pl. 12) for which £80 and £100 were paid respectively.

34. The painting mentioned by the *Daily Post* in its report of 13 September (see note 16) as having been bought by Rathbone was F.W.W. Topham's *The Pope's Rebellious Children*, whose catalogue price was £210. If Rathbone had acquired this for a negotiated price of £123 and also paid £315 for Anderson's picture, that would bring the sum of his spending to £438, the figure given for him in the exhibition accounts (as at note 27). In 1872 Rathbone bought Alphonse Legros's *The Pilgrimage* (pl. 18) from the exhibition and gave it to the Liverpool permanent collection, and in 1873 he combined with George Holt to do the same thing for Val Prinsep's *Leonora di Mantua* (pl. 30).

35. Discussion of press coverage here is confined to six leading Liverpool journals (although there were more newspapers in the city), namely the *Albion*, the *Courier*, the *Mail*, the *Mercury*, the *Porcupine* and the *Post*; the exhibition itself also attracted coverage from several national journals.

36. *Liverpool Courier*, 2 September 1871, p. 6.

initial overview of the exhibition rather than taking it in numerical sequence, but noted only that it was 'ambitious, and in most respects successfully ambitious', adding slightly snidely: 'the barge bearing the body of Elaine is a fine piece of drawing'.[37] The critic of the *Porcupine* took as his central theme the lack of 'elevation of aim' in contemporary art and found *Elaine* too realistic: in going too close to 'literal truth' Mrs Anderson's picture lost in 'poetic feeling' and the accessories were too prominent and overwhelmed the central idea.[38]

The *Albion* did not include the picture among the oils singled out for notice in its initial overview of the exhibition, as the *Daily Post* had, but in a later review described the work as 'a grand representation of the poet's thought' and praised the pains taken in working out the details: the figure of Elaine herself, the coverlet ('a marvel of careful work'), the boat and its pilot 'are all admirably depicted'. Only the 'rather hard' treatment of the foliage prevented the painting from equalling 'any of Millais's best efforts'.[39] It was left to the *Mercury* to provide the longest and most conflicted reaction. In his initial overview of the exhibition, its critic, who was none other than the stalwart Liverpool topographical painter William Gavin Herdman (1805–1882; fig. 6), called it 'scarcely one whit inferior' to Leighton's *Hercules*; a 'noble picture … we can well imagine the crowds of admirers this great work will attract'.[40] But by the time that Herdman came back to *Elaine*, in his eighth notice of the exhibition seven weeks later,

> we have had opportunities of listening to the general criticisms of the public, and also of more carefully examining this important picture … we do not think in all our experience we ever heard such wide and conflicting opinions … Some say we have now a lady artist whom we can name with Angelica Kauffmann, R.A., and Rosa Bonheur, that Mrs Carpenter is left in the shade, and that the Royal Academy could not do a more gallant and graceful act than elect the lady at once amongst the privileged forty of the notables of the day, whilst on the other hand it is stated that the picture is only fit and good enough to be placed as a panel to one of Busby's hearses, and that all the town council have to do, having given £420 for this picture, is to present Messrs. Busby's with it for that purpose, ordering another to match for the other side of the hearse. Without endorsing either of these extremes, we may state our opinion at once, that passing at present a few defects which will be enlarged upon, it is on the whole a very fine picture, though, in consequence of those defects, not one we should have purchased for a permanent gallery of art in Liverpool …

Herdman then proceeded to devote a large number of column inches to his effortfully phrased reservations, before winding up repeating his view that it was a very fine work.[41]

A sixth journal, the *Liverpool Mail*, did not mention Sophie Anderson at all. This was because it ostentatiously declined to print any review of the Autumn Exhibition, instead covering the rival exhibition taking place at the same time at Agnew's Liverpool Exchange Galleries, which consisted of no fewer than 187 pictures drawn extensively from the recent RA exhibition, including Millais's magnificent *Chill October* (fig. 7) and several other pictures by him.[42] The existence of this exhibition, which was not the first but only the latest in a sequence of such shows mounted by Agnew's over the previous few years, puts a new complexion upon the Council's motto *Post Tenebras Lux*. Given that many leading London artists appeared in both shows, the tangible differences between them could be said to be, firstly, that Agnew's exhibition, despite containing nearly 200 works, was 'small' – and indeed this term was employed to describe it by the *Porcupine*[43] – and secondly that Agnew's

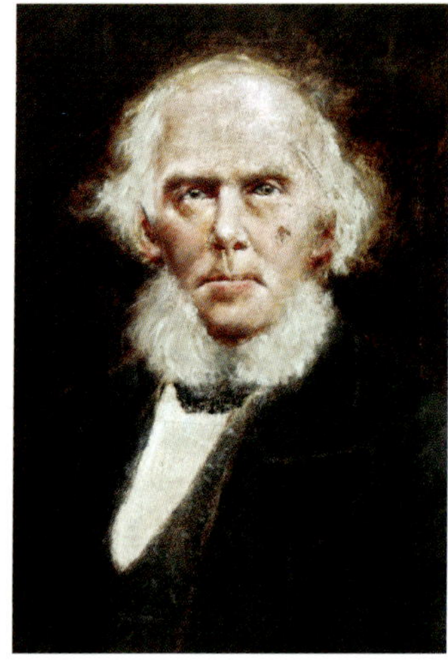

FIG. 6
W.G. Herdman in later life; from a posthumous painting by Henry E. Kidson, exhibited at the Liverpool Autumn Exhibition 1896.
National Museums Liverpool (Walker Art Gallery)

37. *Daily Post*, 2 September 1871, p. 5. As the newspaper most favourable towards the Committee (see below) the *Post* may have been putting up a smokescreen here.
38. *Porcupine*, 16 September 1871, p. 390.
39. *Albion*, 25 September 1871, p. 5. The reference to Millais was probably doffing a cap at his *Chill October*, then on display in Liverpool at Agnew's (see below).
40. *Liverpool Mercury*, 2 September 1871, p. 6.
41. *Liverpool Mercury*, 25 October 1871, p. 6.
42. *Liverpool Mail*, 16 September 1871, p. 11. The *Mail* enjoined its readers to pay Agnew's exhibition *several* visits, and pointedly observed that 'the majority [of works] are far above the average of those usually to be seen at a public exhibition'. The *Mail* also published advertisements for Agnew's exhibition, but none for the Autumn Exhibition.
43. *Porcupine*, 14 October 1871, p. 454.

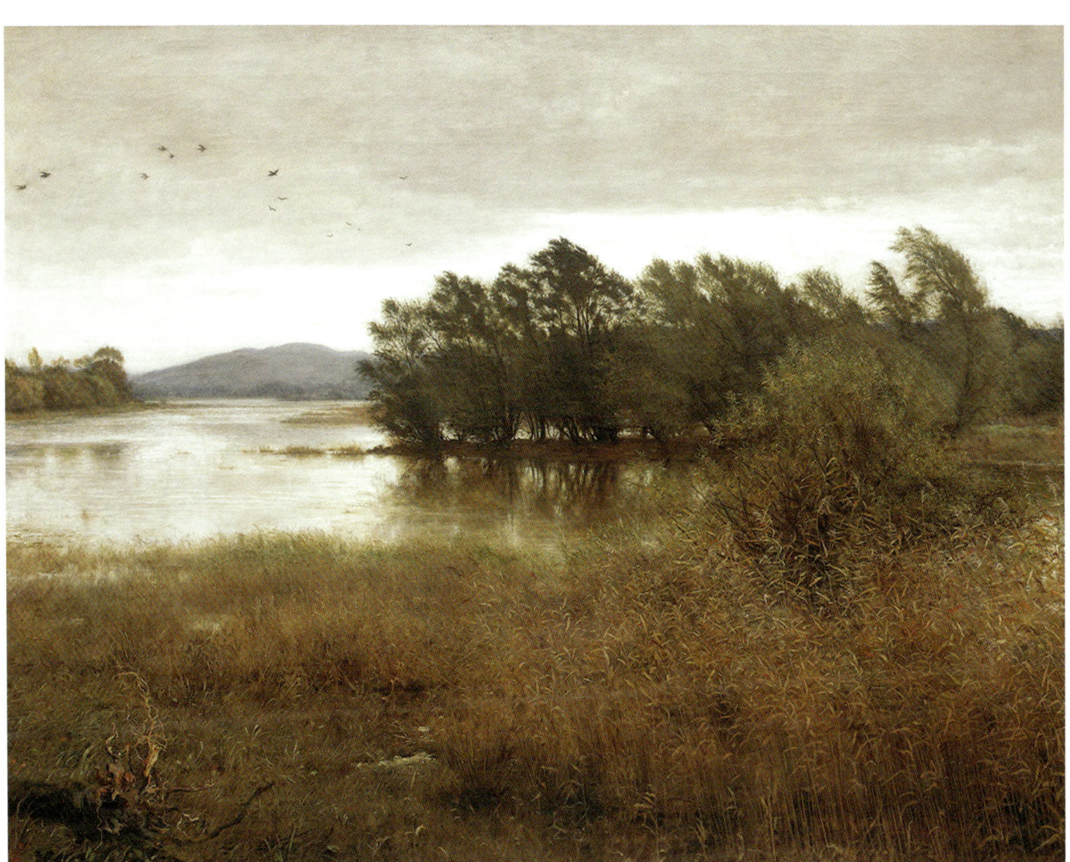

motives were avowedly commercial whereas those of the Council were essentially altruistic. Both these differences, of course, were more apparent than real. As the *Porcupine* put it:

> It shows the rapid advance made of late years in the business of picture-dealing, when a private firm like that of Messrs. Agnew can enter into successful competition with a wealthy Corporation in securing a large proportion of the most prominent paintings of the London season. In other respects, of course, it would be unfair to enter into any elaborate comparison of Agnews' collection with that at the Free Library. They have been brought together with a different design, and selected on an entirely different principle in each of these cases. Nevertheless, the fact ought to be noted that Agnews' exhibition contains, in proportion to its size, a very much larger number of high-class pictures than the more extensive collection in William Brown-street. There is neither credit nor discredit on one side or the other in this position of affairs, as far as the activity of the two organisations is concerned. It simply shows, what everyone must recognise, the superiority of trade enterprise over amateur enthusiasm in all matters of business detail.[44]

The issues articulated in this deft paragraph were essentially those which the gentlemen of the Autumn Exhibition Committee had faced from the outset: Agnew's exhibition represented only another facet of the argument that art patronage in Liverpool ought to remain a private sphere and not involve public finances. The decision by the *Liverpool Mail* explicitly to support Agnew's and to ignore the Autumn Exhibition was just one way of saying this. The other leading journals adopted a less drastic approach, but the same political dimension was present in each of their responses.

43. *Porcupine*, 14 October 1871, p. 454.
44. *Porcupine*, 23 September 1871, p. 411.

If column inches were the sole measure of their enthusiasm towards the Autumn Exhibition, then the Liverpool papers would rank in the following order: *Mercury, Porcupine, Albion, Post* and (coolest) *Courier*. The *Courier* carried only one notice, admittedly a long one, at the outset of the exhibition, in their issue of 2 September. It is in this that we encounter the jibe that the members of the Committee have been 'unexpectedly' successful in their efforts to assemble pictures, and throughout, underlying a pretence of objectivity, there is a tone of hostile bias. Of all the papers it is the *Courier* that makes the most of the unevenness of the exhibits:

> There are some – nay, a great many – very fine pictures, but there are also, alas, a still greater number of "specimens" as to which it is a source of endless wonder and amazement how anyone professing to be an artist could have painted them, and still more, how any committee of selection could have accepted such freaks of genius, or such impositions in the name of art. If these are the accepted contributions, we should like exceedingly to have a peep into the limbo of the rejected. Perhaps there was no selection after all, and the management being anxious to escape the dreary aspect of bare walls, took whatever was offered.[45]

The comments of the *Courier* on the hanging of the pictures are also the most colourful:

> On the whole it may be said that the pictures are judiciously displayed, but no hanging committee ever yet escaped criticism, and no hanging committee ever will. It will probably be felt by most visitors to the Exhibition that one glaring blunder has been committed in the treatment of Mr F. Leighton's great picture. It is certainly neither skied nor floored, unless the latter term apply to the manner in which it is completely overwhelmed by Mr Webb's immense picture, "Folkestone 50 years ago" (193) hung immediately over it. The incongruity of thus placing two such pictures so totally different in conception, in style of treatment as to light and shadow, is excessively painful … No greater injustice could have been done to either artist than to place these pictures in such juxtaposition. On inquiring from a gentleman of official position why Mr Leighton's work had been overhung in such a manner, the naïve reply was that "no other picture would fit so well," and to this complexion of art appreciation we have come at last.[46]

With such observations, the *Courier* is closer to the knuckle than the other journals (some but not all of which offer blander versions of the same criticisms). Three days after publishing this piece it offered a long and politically astute review of Agnew's exhibition; and the following week it published the letter from 'A Clerk' that was implicitly strongly critical of the Autumn Exhibition's restrictive and socially divisive opening times.

The *Daily Post* printed four articles whose tone was much more favourable towards the Committee. The terms in which they, and especially Samuelson and Rathbone, are congratulated in the initial survey piece are genuine and fulsome; and so far from being full of 'freaks of genius', the exhibition 'is characterised … by an equality of excellence very rarely achieved'. The view of the hang is wholly positive: 'the line has been very spiritedly and independently composed … and the arrangement of pictures in reference to colour has been so careful and agreeable that neither the general effect nor individual pictures suffer from inappropriate juxtaposition'; whilst (as noted above) 'it would not be possible to see the pictures to better advantage'.[47] Uniquely, the *Post* offered a progress report eleven days after the private view in order to report positively on the high attendances and at length on the number of sales, as well as on the complimentary reaction to

45. *Liverpool Courier*, 2 September 1871, p. 6.
46. *Ibid.*
47. See note 10.

the exhibition of London artists,[48] all matters of great significance to the Committee. The most curious feature of its treatment of the exhibition is that its sequence of notices of individual pictures breaks off after 20 September, before its intended reviews of the landscapes in oil and works on paper had appeared; and its only further mention of the show is a brief paragraph on 14 October commending the wise decision of the Committee to open the exhibition in the evening.

The notices in the *Albion* (which appeared weekly) register as those of a newspaper of record rather than of criticism. It produced an introductory survey followed in successive issues by six polite and methodical reviews of selected exhibits in numerical order. The *Albion* declined to notice the Agnew's exhibition, probably less because it was following the Committee's line than because it wished to avoid controversy. Typically, even in its overall assessment of the quality of the exhibits, the *Albion* took a milktoast view:

> that there may be, amongst a collection of nearly 900, some that critics might think should have been left out, was only to be expected, but these few ought not to be grudged a place, when so many productions of undoubted merit and celebrity are to be met with.[49]

Of all the Liverpool papers, the *Mercury* devoted the most column inches to the Autumn Exhibition. It did give the Agnew's exhibition one review, but surrounded this by eleven pieces on its larger rival: an introductory survey, nine regular reviews, all lengthy, and, midway through the exhibition, a more satirical piece titled *Who Are the Patrons of Art?*[50] This was not signed, as others were, W.G.H., but it clearly related thematically to Herdman's remarks, in his first article, which described at length Liverpool's lack of a public educated in the higher forms of art and the absence in the recent past of resources calculated to improve this situation. Despite this gloomy prognosis, Herdman seems to have viewed the Autumn Exhibition essentially with optimism, taking his task to mean giving as many artists honourable mentions as possible. He covered many more exhibits than any of the other papers did, even if in a telegraphic and often rather bland manner, and he was still reviewing the watercolours and sculptures on 9 November, long after the other papers had wound up their coverage and only two days before the exhibition's original closing date. Herdman also seems to have regarded it as part of his brief to relay the opinions of others, not just his own. The result was a coverage, which, while bearing the most general structural resemblance to that of the *Albion,* had greater density and, even if with a sense of detachment from political issues, personality.[51]

At the furthest extremity from the listing-by-numbers approach of the *Mercury* and the *Albion* was that of the weekly journal, *The Porcupine*. It printed one brief introductory announcement, four reviews, a piece consisting of four sonnets inspired by pictures,[52] and a humorous piece at the close of the exhibition about a concert in the galleries being given by the police band; plus, even-handedly, two reviews of Agnew's exhibition, one of which, titled *The Beautiful and the True,*[53] was an in-depth look at only three pictures. Such discursiveness was also characteristic of its coverage of the Autumn Exhibition: its first review proper, dated 9 September, essentially concentrated on only two works: Leighton's *Hercules Wrestling with Death* and Albert Moore's *A Venus* (pl. 4). As befitted the journal's title, the basic tone was spiky irreverence, applied to topics – whether individual pictures, or artists, or salient artistic trends – worthy of extended treatment. But (as was mostly true also of the *Mercury*) the *Porcupine* concentrated on the art; issues of the selection, the hang and the presentation were of little concern.

48. *Daily Post*, 13 September 1871, Supplement, p. 1.
49. *Albion*, 4 September 1871, p. 5.
50. *Liverpool Mercury*, 3 October 1871, p. 6.
51. Herdman's annual criticism of the exhibition in the *Mercury* was eventually the subject of an article, 'W.G.H.' in the *Porcupine* which observed sardonically that it 'deserved to be immortalised'; *Porcupine*, 16 September 1876, pp. 396–7.
52. The four pictures concerned were Prinsep's *Odin, the Northern God of War*, Frederick Sandys's *Ysulte* (pl. 5), Pettie's *The Love Song* and Albert Moore's *A Venus*; *Porcupine*, 30 September 1871, p. 428.
53. *Porcupine*, 14 October 1871, p. 454.

Ultimately, all the newspapers (except the *Liverpool Mail*) can be said to have regarded the exhibition positively, as good for the town and good for local artists. Their criticisms could be viewed in the light of teething troubles which with attentive management on the part of the Committee could be put right in future. That the organisers themselves saw it in this light is reflected in their annual report published several months later, where they stated that 'the success of the Exhibition has been beyond their most sanguine expectations'.[54]

54. *Nineteenth Annual Report …* [as at note 10], p. 5. The full text of the report as it relates to the Autumn Exhibition is quoted in Morris 1996 [as at 'Introduction', note 2], pp. 2–3.

THE EXHIBITIONS 1872–76

The 1871 Autumn Exhibition created a blueprint for future shows, its success ensuring that many of the policies and solutions that its organisers had adopted would be retained with little or no need felt for change. The same suite of rooms in the Free Library continued to be used for each of the following five exhibitions, with, as far as can be inferred, no variation in the categories of work hung in each of the rooms and corridors. The same regulations were printed on the second page of the 1872 catalogue as in 1871, the only difference being that the send-in period in early August was altered from a Monday to Saturday to a Wednesday to Wednesday, and hence extended from six days to eight (including a Sunday, so presumably in practice seven). Further changes were made in 1873 and 1874, after which the arrangements remained identical for the following two years.

Much the most significant change occurred in 1874 when the organisers gave themselves an extra week to unpack and hang the show and prepare the catalogue: the send-in days that year were Wednesday 5 to Wednesday 12 August and the exhibition opened on Monday 7 September.[1] The obvious explanation for this, namely that the increasing number of works being submitted was creating intolerable logistical pressure, may in fact not be the correct one. The 1873 exhibition had opened on Monday 1 September and in 1874 the organisers may simply have felt that rather than move back into August, the 'first Monday in September' opening date was by that time set in stone. Throughout all six exhibitions the catalogue itself remained consistent in appearance and page size (8⅞ x 6⅝ inches), its style reminiscent of but not slavishly imitating the catalogues of the RA. The quality of the editing of the information remained remarkably accurate although errors continued to occur.[2] At this stage there were no advertisements padding out the catalogue, as became the norm later in the exhibition's history.

Two additions were made in 1872 to the body of the exhibition's organisers. Significantly, a second London 'consulting artist' was included in the shape of Alfred D. Fripp (1822–1895). Fripp was a watercolourist well-known to local audiences, having shown at the Liverpool Academy (and, in 1858, the Liverpool Society of Fine Arts) over a period of twenty years from 1841; but his claim to the present honour was that he was Secretary of the Old Watercolour Society, and thus in a position to solicit submissions from a wider range of watercolour artists than Henry B. Roberts, who painted as much in oils as in watercolours (and may well have pleaded an excessive workload from being the only London artist on board in 1871).[3] Fripp remained until 1876 (and beyond), with the original four consulting artists. The second new member was a Liberal Councillor colleague of Rathbone's, F.G. Prange, whose selection was almost certainly not a reflection of his politics, but rather his known reputation as an art-lover.[4] Joined in 1873 by the Conservative Joseph Armstrong (perhaps a genuinely political counterweight appointment), Prange himself remained only

1. The changes made in 1873 included strengthening the wording governing the submission of the artists' lists of works and prices (which were evidently continuing to create problems with making the catalogue) and a new regulation that works by Royal Academicians and Associate RAs were sold at Liverpool on condition that the buyer made them available for potential loan to the following year's RA Summer Exhibition.

2. In both the 1873 and 1874 catalogues there were numbering errors which led to multiple works being given the same catalogue number; see table overleaf.

3. Roberts had been gently criticised in the *Porcupine* during the 1871 exhibition for sending too many of his own pictures (*Porcupine*, 16 September 1871, p. 391) and may have wished to take a lower profile. He sent only two pictures to the 1872 exhibition.

4. After his term on the Acting Committee, Prange wrote at least one review of the Autumn Exhibition for a London journal: *Academy*, 4 September 1875.

until that year, being replaced for the 1874 exhibition by William Bower Forwood (1840–1928), a young Conservative Councillor who was at the outset of a distinguished public career in Liverpool. Forwood was on the Committee only one year and was replaced for 1875 by Andrew Barclay Walker, who, having by then made his promised gift of an art gallery to the city, could presumably not be overlooked.

For 1876 two more new members joined. One, Arthur Hornby Lewis, was a replacement for one of the original members of the Acting Committee, Councillor James Houghton, who had died in 1875. The other was Charles Millward, who held the title Corresponding Hon. Secretary in London. Thus the total number of Acting Committee and Consulting Artists, which had been 11 in 1871, rose to 13 in 1872, 14 for the following three years, and 15 in 1876. At no point were any of these men termed the Hanging Committee, but the date when this term was substituted in the catalogue for 'Acting Committee' (used in 1871–3) or 'Exhibition Committee' (used in 1874–6) was not far off.[5]

CONTENTS OF THE EXHIBITIONS

In 1872 there were 959 catalogued items,[6] as against 908 the previous year. All this increase, perhaps owing in part to the efforts of Fripp, was accounted for by the growth of the number of works on paper,[7] whose tally rose from 454 in 1871 to 514. According to a report in the *Courier*, the Committee for 1872 rejected 500 submissions 'for want of space',[8] and it seems likely that most of the rejects were also watercolours – evidence perhaps that the 1871 exhibition had been generally perceived as heavily biased in their favour within the artistic community – since the 1872 totals for both oils (430) and sculpture (15) actually went down, a result that the Committee can scarcely have desired. The figure for the latter was evidently of concern to the Committee and deemed as requiring their attention. Already in that year, in order to beef up the representation of ideal sculpture, they requisitioned one of the collection of works in plaster by the late Benjamin Spence which had been presented to the Free Museum in 1870 by his widow (fig. 8). In 1873 the total number of sculptures rose to 35, a gain difficult to account for through chance.[9] Of all the five exhibitions, the one of 1873 saw the largest overall rise in the total number of catalogued items, 99, and again most of this rise was in the 'works on paper' category, where the figure rose to 569. After 1873, on the other hand, the figures for both sculpture and 'works on paper' were held steady and efforts switched to securing a bigger proportion of oils. In 1874 the number of oils topped 500, and by the 1876 exhibition the 'oils' figure was larger than the watercolours for the first time and close to 600, out of a total of 1,186 catalogued items.

Works in the 1871–76 exhibitions

	1871	1872	1873	1874	1875	1876
Oils	433	430	454	511	520	582
Works on paper etc	454	514	569	573	580	574
Sculpture	21	15	35	36	36	30
Total (catalogued)	908	959	1,058*	1,120†	1,136	1,186
Total (estimated)	910	966	1,060	1,139	1,139	1,192

** The last work in the catalogue is number 1,057 but two different works were given number 967*

† The last work in the catalogue is number 1,118 but two works were given number 507 and two 1,110

The figure of 1,186 works was still nearly 350 shy of the total for that year's RA exhibition (1,523), but in 1871 the difference had been 430 in a year when the RA figure was unusually small. The gap was closing. Indeed, in 1876 the Liverpool total of oils and watercolours

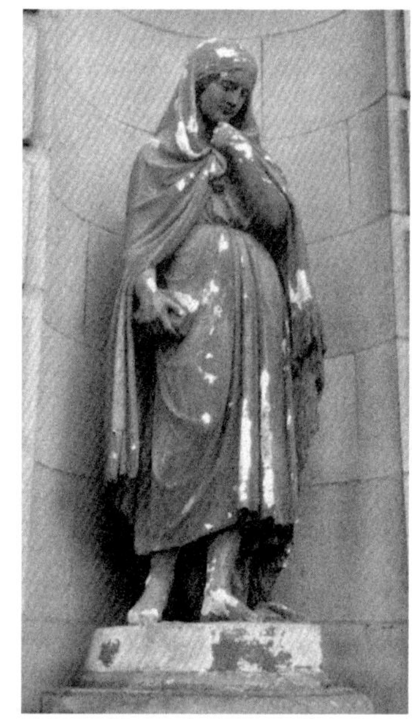

FIG. 8
Highland Mary by Benjamin E. Spence. Plaster. 1872 Autumn Exhibition no. 957.
formerly Liverpool City Council

5. The term Hanging Committee was first used in the catalogue of 1878, when its Chairman was Rathbone and Arthur Hornby Lewis its Deputy Chairman and Treasurer.
6. But 966 estimated actual items, i.e. including multiple works under one catalogue number. See the table (left) for this figure for other years.
7. As used here, this term includes prints, 'black and white', architectural drawings and miniatures, as well as watercolours.
8. *Liverpool Courier*, 5 September 1872, p. 4. The figure of 500 may be an exaggeration but the report is valuable in confirming that the Committee were now acting as a jury, for which there is no positive evidence the previous year.
9. Highly unusually, one sculptor, Albert Bruce-Joy, contributed 15 works.

was over 1,120; at the RA it was only 1,070. It was the far larger totals at the RA for prints, architectural drawings, enamels and miniatures, and above all sculpture that accounted for the difference. Yet despite the evidence of changing statistics, there was arguably little perceptible alteration in the contrasting character of the shows. Between 1872 and 1875, out of the total of 4,500 exhibits in Liverpool only 46 were portraits in oil and watercolour, plus a further 68 in sculpture. In the 1876 Autumn Exhibition, admittedly, something of a shift was perceptible, with unusually large figures of 18 portraits in oils and six among the 'works on paper', plus nine in sculpture. But the figures for portraits at the 1876 RA were 127 in oils and watercolours, plus 54 miniatures, plus 97 among the sculptures. Liverpool meanwhile continued to be inundated with scenes of North Wales – even if the number of 89 in 1876 was lower than average.[10] The equivalent figure at the RA was 17.

THE ARTISTS

In keeping with the year-by-year growth in the number of exhibits, the figure for the artists mostly also rose. In 1872 the number was 486, a rise of 35; in 1873 it was 530, and in 1874 it shot up to 607. In 1875, when the total number of exhibits showed the smallest rise in the period of only 16, the number of artists actually dipped by 20. However, in 1876 it recovered sharply, reaching 647. In terms of the ratio of exhibits to artist, these figures work out at: for 1871, 2.01 works per artist; for 1872, 1.97; for 1873, 1.99; for 1874, 1.84; for 1875, 1.93; and for 1876, 1.83. Whether the trend of gradual reduction in this figure is truly an indicator of the exhibition's gathering strength may be arguable, but in the context of rising numbers of works and artists overall, it could suggest that some artists felt increasing pressure to deliver quality rather than quantity in the works that they submitted.

The tables for 1872–76 (pp. 77, 95, 113, 133 and 155) plot the geographical distribution and gender of the artists and their works for each of the five exhibitions. The internal patterns that they reveal are often of more than passing interest even if few of them are startling. There was clearly a deterioration of relations with Birmingham artists after the 1873 exhibition, when their figure dropped from 14 to only two in 1874, three in 1875 and seven in 1876. The figure for Edinburgh artists, which reached a peak of 18 in 1872, also declined in the following years, although less dramatically, but they were compensated for by arrivals from elsewhere in Scotland, chiefly Glasgow, especially in 1876. Manchester artists, similarly, began sending to Liverpool in greater numbers from 1875. The figure for the north-east (Northumberland, Durham and Yorkshire), only four artists in 1871, jumped to nine the following year but made no further advance thereafter. The Irish presence also remained disappointing.

The figures for Liverpool artists may at first sight appear relatively stable against the 1871 total of 61, which had represented 14.4% of all the artists in the exhibition for whom addresses are available.[11] From 1872 to 1876 the artist totals range from between 64 (1872) and 86 (1876) and the percentages from 13.2% (1872) to 16.6% (1873). But these figures need to be read against others for their true significance to become apparent. The rise from 61 artists to 64 between 1871 and 1872, and especially the ensuing spike from 64 to 80 between 1872 and 1873, coincide with emphatic falls in the number of oil paintings submitted by Liverpool artists – from 61 (coincidentally) in 1871 to 45 in 1872 and 42 in 1873. The locals were sending in watercolours instead: from 71 in 1871 their totals rose in 1872 to 102 and to no fewer than 128 the following year. These were the *anni mirabiles* for such Liverpool artists as Sam Pride (15 exhibits, nine sales) and Albert Hartland (11 exhibits, nine sales, including all seven of the

10. The figures for earlier years were: 1872, 109; 1873, 101; 1874, 86; 1875, 94.
11. All the percentage calculations presented in this paragraph exclude artists who did not give their address.

watercolours he submitted in 1873). Against this pattern a complementary one may be read in the figures for London artists. In 1871 the numbers had been 237/56.2%; these figures fell in 1872 to 233/53.2%, and although in 1873 the artist total crept up to 240, the percentage went down to 50%. That the Committee had mixed feelings about this trend may be inferred from the figures for 1874, when the number of artists from London jumped dramatically to 315 and the percentage returned to over 55%, coinciding with an unmistakeable pendulum swing away from watercolour exhibits towards oils (1873: 569/454; 1874: 573/511). Over 1874 and 1875, more than 67% of the exhibitors of known address came from London and Liverpool, but by 1876 the pattern was reversing, and in a show where the overall numbers of artists and exhibits had swelled perceptibly, London and Liverpool together comprised only 65.8%.

Insofar as the figures for women artists can be calculated with any accuracy, they reveal a trend of gradual numerical growth but no proportional gain. Against the 1871 baseline of 63 definite women artists, there were 66 in 1872. This amounted to a slight drop in the percentage of women to the combined total of artists of known gender, from 23% to 21.4%, but if this is extrapolated against the figure for artists of uncertain gender, the total of women artists emerges as identical with the previous year, 104. In 1873 the equivalent figures are 74, (23.6%) and 128; in 1874 they are 85 (21.1%) and 128; in 1875, 95 (22.8%) and 133; and in 1876, 95 (21.4%) and 138. The year 1876, the only one when the figure of women-definites does not rise, and where the proportional total is one of the lowest, may perhaps be identified as a defining moment when the Autumn Exhibition's initial 'encouragement' of women artists slackens. Arguably women artists' best performance came in 1873 – another reason for identifying the exhibition of this year as, of the six, the one with the most distinctive profile.[12]

Thirteen women were among the 83 artists who showed in all six of the exhibitions from 1871 to 1876 (for a complete listing of these see Appendix 1, p. 156). Two of them were from Liverpool: Annie Beaumont, who chiefly painted flowers and fruit in watercolours (pl. 77) and contributed 19 works, and the young subject-painter Jessie Macgregor who contributed 16. Two more, Mrs Pauline Walker (18 works) and Mrs Mary Ensor (20), who had shown in Liverpool at every opportunity since 1861, were from Southport and Birkenhead respectively. Of the 83, 24 were from Liverpool, with the three local 'consulting artists' prominent among them: W.J. Bishop contributed 25 works to the six exhibitions, John Finnie 30 and William Kerry 31, only one behind the most prolific of all the 83 artists, Albert Durer Lucas. Henry B. Roberts, the fourth of the original consulting artists, was also among the 83, showing a total of 23 works. At the other end of the scale, the one artist who showed only six works in six years, one faithfully per year, was the only one of the 83 who can safely be termed a household name. This was Frederic Leighton, whose collusion with the organisers in 1871 had already marked him as a true friend of the Autumn Exhibition, and who seems to have continued to work informally behind the scenes on its behalf. In his youth Leighton had spent some years in Italy (where, among other things, he had become a friend of Alfred Fripp), and he was well connected with foreign artists, especially Italian ones. The appearance of a work by Giovanni Costa in Liverpool in 1874, for example, was no doubt at Leighton's suggestion.[13]

FOREIGN ARTISTS

As an indicator of the Autumn Exhibition's image and appeal in cities abroad, as well as of the organisers' ability to network on a European as well as a national basis, the presence

12. It may be significant that the *Daily Post*, in its review of the exhibition, 1 September 1873, p. 5, devoted a paragraph to the advance of women artists: 'No less than 163 pictures, about 17% of the whole Exhibition, are painted by women; ten years ago there would not have been 16 …'. The figure of 163 works calculated by the *Post* compares closely to that of 164 arrived at in the table for 1873 (p. 95), but it should be noted that this figure is obtained from the 74 'definitely female' artists and not from the putative figure of 128 artists reached by adding a proportion of the 'unknown gender' ones. Whether the critic of the *Post* knew that every 'unknown gender' artist was male is not clear.

13. Costa had exhibited three works at the RA in 1869 and 1870 and showed there again in 1874.

of works by foreign artists arguably offered valuable 'state of the nation' type evidence for each exhibition's relative health. By this measure, the jump in the numbers of foreigners from 10 in 1871 to 19 the following year was a distinctly rosy sign for the 1872 exhibition. To be sure, mere numbers might be viewed as something of a two-edged statistic. Would it be good for the exhibition to be flooded with foreign pictures of a banal, conservative kind, or by young Americans studying in Europe? Was there value in seeking a more rounded representation of foreign countries, rather than being content with the kind of Belgian-German hegemony that had dominated the Liverpool exhibitions of the early 1860s? Was it better if the same loyal artists returned to exhibit year after year (five of the 19 in 1872 had showed the previous year) or was it preferable to have new faces? Potentially these were, or might become, issues of genuine concern for the Acting Committee. At no point in the sequence of the first six exhibitions is there a sense that the foreign works were hand-picked examples of key trends in European art centres; but nor is it obvious that they were simply whatever had happened to turn up on the day.

Of the 19 foreign artists in 1872 (who contributed a total of 24 works), seven were Belgian, including Charles Verlat and Joseph Van Luppen, both of whom had showed in 1871. Among the five Belgian newcomers were two relatively senior figures, the *animalier* Eugène Verboeckhoven, now aged 74, who contributed *A Pastoral* painted jointly with the much younger Düsseldorf-based landscapist Fritz Ebel, and Josef Van Lerius of the Antwerp Academy, who contributed a major work priced at £350, *The First Sail* (pl. 15).[14] Both he and Verboeckhoven had first shown at an exhibition in Liverpool as far back as 1855.[15] There were four Dutch artists (including Mari Ten Kate, who had shown the previous year, but also Hendrik Mesdag and Willem Koekkoek, whose father and elder brothers had been Liverpool regulars in the 1860s). Of the other foreign artists, three were German (including the returning Ludwig Hermann), three American (including Alexander Wust)[16] and two French.[17] Newcomers to the Autumn Exhibition numbered 14, of whom seven had shown in Liverpool in the 1850s and 1860s. It is striking that the nationalities represented in this group of artists are precisely the same as in the previous year, and also that the proportion of the artists who had shown in Liverpool before 1871 actually rose (from 40% to 52.5%). This gives a strong idea of the Committee, in their approach to foreign admissions, seeking to reconnect with tried precedent as a way of prioritising growth of numbers.

From 1873, however, the pattern changes. The totals of foreign artists stabilise – 19 again in that year, 21 in 1874 and 17 in 1875[18] – and there is a sense instead of a widening of horizons becoming the chief priority. The proportion of artists who had shown in Liverpool before 1871 begins to dwindle: six out of 19 in 1873; seven out of 21 in 1874; four out of 17 in 1875. The 'traditional' bias towards artists from Germany and Belgium repeated in 1872 (10 artists out of 19) also begins to evaporate in 1873 when there were seven out of 19.[19] Instead – and reflecting the city's rebirth as an artistic centre since the devastating days of the Franco-Prussian War and Commune of 1870–71 – the most prominent grouping came from Paris. They included a young American student of Jean-Léon Gérôme's, Frederick Bridgman, but also, strikingly, Jean-Baptiste-Camille Corot, who sent his *Joinville-sur-Marne*, Charles-François Daubigny (who had shown one work at the Liverpool Academy in 1860) with his *Sunset in Holland*, and perhaps most remarkably of all, Johan Jongkind, with his *Seaport in Holland*, which was available for sale at £150 but found no takers.[20] The Autumn Exhibition's first Italian painter, Achille Vertunni (1826–1897), was represented by an expensive *Bay of Naples* (possibly thanks to Leighton, who many years before had frequented Vertunni's

14. Recently this painting has been titled *Catching the Breeze* but it is identifiable as *The First Sail* from the extended critique in the *Porcupine*, 9 November 1872, p. 502.

15. Fritz Ebel had shown at the Liverpool Society of Fine Arts in 1862–3.

16. A further significant American-born contributor in 1872, although by now resident in England, was J.A.M. Whistler, who sent his *Arrangement in Grey and Black – Portrait of the Painter's Mother* (pl. 19).

17. One of these was the Danish-born August Friedrich Schenck (1828–1901), who however had long lived and worked in Paris; the other was Edmond Castan (1817–1892), probably the 'G. Castan' who had shown two paintings in Liverpool in 1863.

18. Of these totals returning artists made up four in 1873 and 1874, and three in 1875. The 1874 total of 21 includes Antonio Zona (1814–1892), who happened to be visiting England in that year but was essentially based in Venice/Milan. The total number of works contributed by foreign artists was 26 in 1873, 29 in 1874 and 24 in 1875.

19. Four were first-timers: the *animaliers* Friedrich Voltz from Munich and Isidore Verheyden from Brussels, and the latter's compatriots Henri Bource and Jean-Baptiste Van Moer; the two latter had shown previously in Liverpool, most recently in 1864. Ludwig Hermann had shown at both the preceding Autumn Exhibitions; C.J. Grips and Adolf Oberlander in 1872.

20. The paintings by Corot and Daubigny were not for sale. All three artists, Corot especially, had been featured in the bi-annual London exhibitions of the Society of French Artists organised by Paul Durand-Ruel from the beginning of the 1870s, even if none of this trio of paintings can be traced among the exhibits. Alphonse Legros, the purchase of whose *Pilgrimage* by Philip Rathbone in 1872 (see 'The 1871 Exhibition', note 34) helped cement the artist's loyalty towards Liverpool, was on the Committee of the SFA and may have been instrumental in obtaining the loan of the three works, none of which can today be identified with certainty.

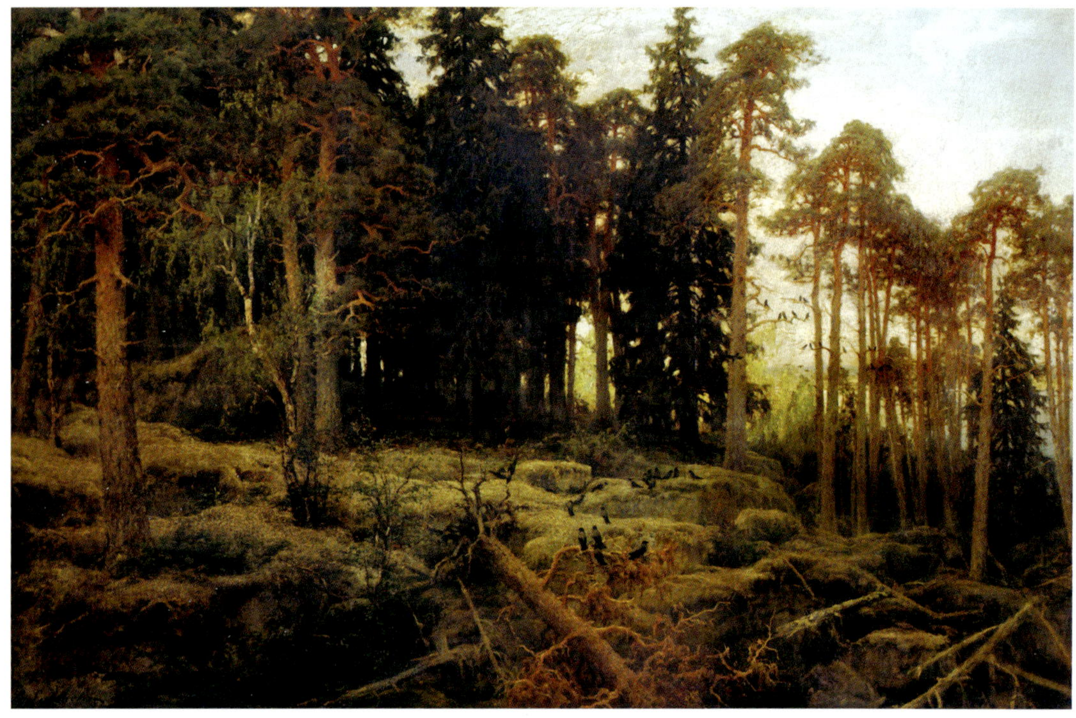

well-known studio in Rome at 53 Via Margutta), and also from Rome – the first works by a foreign artist that were not oil paintings – came two etchings by a further member of Vertunni's circle, the Spanish artist Mariano Fortuny (pl. 44).

The trend which had started in 1873 continued the following year when, of 21 artists, four were Italian (including Giovanni Costa) and three French, together with four non-French nationals living in Paris: August Schenck (see note 17), Frederick Bridgman, whose colourful contribution *The Diligence* (pl. 51) was purchased for the Liverpool permanent collection, and two Finnish-born artists, Thorsten Waenerberg (1846–1917) and Berndt Adolf Lindholm (1841–1914; fig. 9), who had both been in Paris since the previous year and were presumably invited together.[21] Among the native French artists was the 24-year-old Jean-François Raffaëlli, whose *A Beggar* was priced at 100 guineas. Three further Americans, making their Autumn Exhibition debuts,[22] and Josef Israels from The Hague brought the total up to 15, leaving the Belgian and German contingent at just six. Of these only two were Germans and even one of these, Oswald Achenbach, gave his address as Rome.

In 1875, of the 14 foreign newcomers to the exhibition eight were French, three were Italian, only one was German, one Dutch and there were no Belgians at all (although the returning Henri Bource and Adolf Oberlander[23] brought the figure to three Germans and Belgians out of a total of 17 for all foreign artists). There was a new nationality in the shape of Fritz Thaulow (1847–1906), who from Christiania sent *A Summer Night in Norway* priced at 75 guineas. Of the three Italian artists one was Carlo Nicoli, whose four works (pl. 78) constituted the Autumn Exhibition's first foreign sculptures; and among the French contingent were its first foreign women artists: Henriette Browne (1829–1901), whose politically charged *Alsace 1870* (fig. 10) was widely noticed and described in one paper as '*the* picture of the Exhibition',[24] and Léonide Bourges (1838–1909). Bourges, a former pupil of Daubigny, had already showed in Liverpool in 1863 and 1864.

21. It is tempting to wonder whether behind this was the Liverpool sugar beet importer Arnold Baruchson (1807–1876). Baruchson had been Chairman of the Liverpool Society of Fine Arts in the 1860s and collected continental art (E. Morris: *French Art in Nineteenth-Century Britain* [New Haven and London, Yale University Press, 2005], p. 190). In 1864 he had given to Liverpool Council for its art collection Louis Daguerre's remarkable Diorama painting *The Ruins of Holyrood Chapel*, which he is stated to have bought 'on the Continent' (likely in Paris, given the work's Parisian inception) shortly before donating it to the Council. In 1875 Baruchson made another donation to Liverpool, this time of Lindholm's large *Forest in Finland*, and although the possibility exists that he acquired this on seeing Lindholm's exhibits at the 1874 Autumn Exhibition, it seems more likely that he had already bought it from Lindholm and on the basis of this recommended to colleagues the artist's inclusion the following year.
22. Eugene Benson, Charles Rosenberg and Frederick Sammons.
23. Oberlander was unique among the Autumn Exhibition's first foreign artists in sending three or more pictures in four successive years: a total of 16 over the years 1872–5, of which seven sold: all three in 1872, two out of six in 1873 and two out of four in 1874.

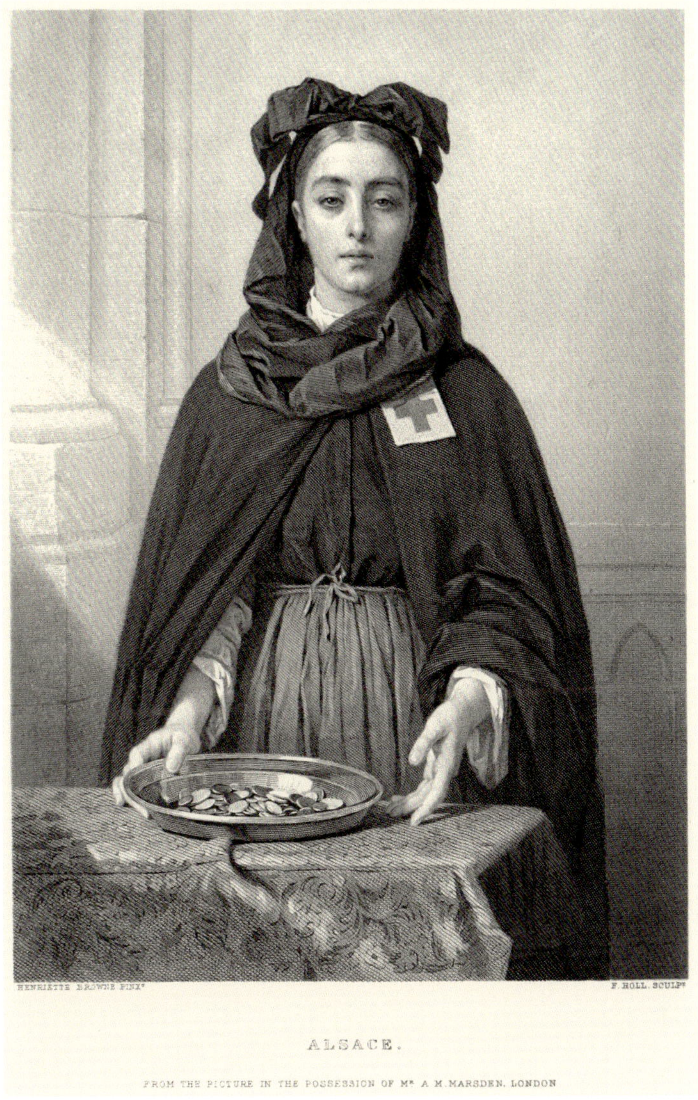

FIG. 10
Alsace engraving by Frank Holl
after the painting by Henriette
Browne.

24. *Albion*, 4 September 1875, p. 4.
The *Liverpool Courier* (4 September
1875, p. 5) observed that it was
a picture about which a whole
column could be written. The
striking incidence of works in the
early Autumn Exhibitions with
Franco-Prussian War subjects
or overtones – even Corot's 1873
Joinville-sur-Marne could have been
viewed in this light – is a topic
beyond the scope of this study.
25. A fifth American, Frederick
Sammons, sent from Florence.

No doubt the Exhibition Committee considered
the slight fall in numbers of foreign artists in 1875
disappointing and determined to redress the situation,
since in 1876 the figure jumped to 28, of whom no fewer
than 24 were showing for the first time. Of the 28, 10 were
French nationals (including another woman artist, Marie
Cazin), and four Americans also sent in from France (out
of six in total).[25] There were six Belgians (a seventh, Dutch-
born, was the female animal painter Henriette Ronner),
two Spaniards (both working in France), one German,
one Hungarian-born artist working in Germany (Gyula
Benczur, a professor at the Munich Academy) and
finally one Italian. The representation of nine different
nationalities, together with the rise in the percentage
of foreigners to total artists – over 4% for the first time
– arguably gave the exhibition a more cosmopolitan air,
complementing the sight of the city's new art gallery now
rising on the site next door.

ATTENDANCES, PRICES AND SALES

If the participation of foreign artists was the icing on
the cake, the exhibition's bread and butter, as far as the
Committee was concerned, were the attendances and
sales that guaranteed its continuing viability. Figures for
these, drawn from the annual reports of the Free Library
Committee together with the exhibition accounts,[26]
are shown in the table overleaf; and of all the statistics
available, they shed the most valuable light on the internal
history of the exhibition in these years, especially when
taken in conjunction with the reports themselves.

In many key areas the 1872 exhibition did less well than its predecessor: daytime attendances
and revenue in most categories (especially from attendances) were down, resulting in a
reduction in total income from visits of over £150. However, the overall attendance figure
was slightly up, thanks to improved figures for the evenings, when the tickets were cheaper;
and also thanks to the fact that the exhibition was open for considerably longer (it was this
that meant that the daily average for walk-up attendances was lower).[27] The total value of
the works sold went down, unsurprisingly (the Leighton effect) but their number actually
rose, and the average price of each sold work went up to £25 13s from (minus Leighton)
£23 17s. Copies of the exhibition catalogue in which individual sales are marked with
the buyer's name and the price paid survive for this year (as well as for 1873 and 1874),[28]
and predictably they reveal a strong bias towards inexpensive and in many cases local
watercolours. However, Leighton again found a purchaser for his blue-chip submission
Weaving the Wreath (pl. 16), in the shape of the Liverpool ship-owner George Holt,[29]
whilst Jessie Macgregor sold both of her works, *Oft times Old Songs awaken Memories*, which was
bought by the noted local collector William Sproston Caine for the undiscounted price of
50 guineas, and *Prattling*, which was offered at 20 guineas and bought for 15 by Lieut. Col.
Richard Steble – one of the 17 purchases made this year by this public-spirited individual.

Income and profit from the 1871–76 exhibitions

	1871	1872	1873	1874	1875	1876
Exhibition dates	4 Sept–18 Dec	2 Sept–14 Dec	1 Sept–29 Nov	7 Sept–5 Dec	6 Sept–4 Dec	4 Sept –2 Dec
Days open (excluding open days)	76	104	90	90	90	90
Charge for entry (day)	1s	1s	1s	1s	1s or 6d	1s or 6d
Charge for entry (evening)	6d	6d	3d	3d	6d or 3d	6d or 3d
No. of visitors (days)	14,416	13,276	13,318	16,524	19,453[*]	22,360[*]
No. of visitors (evenings)	8,309	9,618	18,361	19,905	22,131[†]	22,049[†]
*1s visits / †6d and 3d day and evening visits						
Total visitors	22,725	22,894	31,679[‡]	36,429[‡]	41,584	44,409
‡Excluding 'about 10,000' (1873) and 'about 16,000' (1874) free educational visits (source: Library Committee Reports); no figures for free educational visits were given for 1871–2 or 1875–6						
Average daily attendance	299	220	352	405	462	493
Income from attendances (excluding season tickets)	£928 8s 6d	£824 17s	£895 8s 2d	£1096 9s 3d	£1288 4s 6d	£1436 17s
Season ticket sales	313	332	523	795	1099	1161
Income from season tickets	£62 2s	£59 6s 6d	£96 8s 6d	£151 16s 6d	£210 7s	£221 1s
No. of works sold	235	242	271	338	345	255
Value of sales	£6395 2s 6d	£6214 4s 6d	£7402 17s 6d	£9558 5s	£12319 6s 6d	£8803 10s
Income from works sold	£320 18s 6d	£312 6s	£371 17s	£479 0s 3d	£616 1s 3d	£440 15s 3d
Income from catalogue sales	£165 10s	£168 0s 6d	£199 17s 6d	£247 0s 6d	£279 14s 3d	£301 12s
Total income (including further small sums not tabulated above)	**£1522 18s 6d**	**£1368 8s 3d**	**£1566 1s 3d**	**£1976 13s 6d**	**£2406 17s 11d**	**£2409 15s 10d**
Exhibition profit	**£615 16s 8d**	**£309 8s 5d**	**£466 1s**	**£588 14s 11d**	**£1002 9s 10d**	**£1017 19s 3d**

In their 1872 report, the Library Committee allowed themselves to note that 'at the close of the Exhibition a very pleasing tribute was paid by a number of the exhibiting artists to the Mayor, Edward Samuelson, Esq,[30] and Mr Philip Rathbone, to whose exertions a large portion of the success of the exhibition was due';[31] but otherwise the report was considerably briefer and its tone less hubristic than that of the year before. The results had been 'very satisfactory', and there was an expectation that 'after the payment of all expenses a considerable surplus [unspecified] will remain for the future purchase of pictures from the next Exhibition'.[32] In fact the profit was barely half that of the previous year, just over £300.

The figures for 1873 show gains across the board, some minor, some healthy, and in two areas spectacular: cheap or free admissions and season ticket sales. Evening attendances rocketed from 9,618 to 18,361, and there were also 'about 10,000' free educational visits (it is not clear whether these were introduced this year or had existed in previous years, under the radar). Season ticket sales rose from 332 to 523. These figures provoked a lyrical outpouring in the 1873 Committee report:

> The large increase in the number of season tickets … demonstrates the existence of a rapidly increasing section of the public, who return again and again to study the pictures carefully,

26. *Liverpool Autumn Exhibition Accounts 1871–1926*, Ms. volume, Walker Art Gallery Archives [as at 'The 1871 Exhibition', note 27].
27. Shortly before the official closing date of 30 November the Committee extended the duration of the exhibition by a fortnight, to 14 December.
28. Walker Art Gallery Archives. The exhibition accounts do not record buyers and the amounts they spent after 1871.
29. As in the previous year, the price paid for Leighton's picture was the full, undiscounted one, suggesting that the purchase had been negotiated some time in advance; a notion reinforced by the fact that Leighton had not sent the work to the 1872 RA Summer Exhibition. See L. and R. Ormond, *Lord Leighton* (New Haven and London, Yale University Press, 1975), pp. 108, 119; also Morris 1996 [as at 'Introduction', note 2], pp. 255–6, note 7. The new regulation *Contributions from R.A.'s and A.R.A.'s* added to the Notice to Artists at the front of the 1873 catalogue (see note 1) may have reflected a stipulation on Leighton's part that the work would be available for exhibition at the 1873 RA.
30. John Pearson was Mayor during the 1872 exhibition; Samuelson succeeded him.
31. *Twentieth Annual Report of the Free Public Library, Museum and Gallery of Art, of the Borough of Liverpool, for the year 1872* (Liverpool, Liverpool Printing Company, 1872), pp. 5–6.
32. *Ibid.*, p. 5.

and who will in time form a body of independent and cultivated art opinion, the effects of which must be most advantageous to the town.

Hitherto the Committee have been somewhat disappointed at the comparative apathy of the artizan class, but this year the attendance in the evenings has been very hopeful, so much so, indeed, as to warrant the expectation that an interest in Art may be thoroughly excited, and a knowledge diffused among that class which may be productive of valuable industrial results. The presence of Art Galleries and Museums in Paris has enabled that city, in the absence of most material advantages, to become a large manufacturing centre, owing solely to the educated taste of her artizans. London has, within the last few years, become the seat of art manufactures, which have in several instances been the direct outgrowth of South Kensington, and which in most cases owe their success to the interest in art it has excited, and the opportunity of study it affords. If Liverpool is to become eventually more than a mere warehousing port, any means of attracting such manufactures into her midst should be most anxiously improved. In the last century Wedgwood sent large quantities of his earthenware to be decorated by transfer in Liverpool. At present considerable quantities of Staffordshire china goes to London for decoration; and in stained glass and other artistic glass manufactures, it is more than competing with Munich and Venice. The attendance of the artizan class at these Exhibitions is, therefore, a most important element from an industrial point of view.[33]

The report went on to draw attention to the high proportion of sales achieved by local artists in comparison to metropolitan ones:

Out of £7,402 17s 6d. the local sales amounted to no less than £1,704 17s 6d., and, as might be expected, if the numbers of works are compared, the proportion is very much larger. London artists sold 129 out of 545 sent; local artists 87 out of 213 sent … There seems, therefore, no indisposition to encourage native talent as soon as is recognised; and if these Exhibitions had been successfully initiated some years previously, it seems probable we might have retained in our midst artists who were driven away elsewhere to seek encouragement which their own townsmen would gladly have afforded them.[34]

In hindsight these remarks read as a statement of the Committee's intent with the 1873 exhibition all along, but despite their upbeat tone, the exhibition's overall profit remained well below that of 1871 (even if larger than 1872). The Committee may belatedly have realised the dangers of crowing about disproportion between local artists and Londoners, since (as was noted above) the outstanding feature of the 1874 exhibition, and one which must have been engineered, was a large influx of London artists. This was a pattern which continued in 1875 and it must be at least partially responsible for the strongly improved figures in these years in the 'total value of sales' category (and hence 'income from sales' also). The remarkable figure for 'total value of sales' in 1875, £12,319 6s 6d, which represents a virtual doubling of the same figure in 1872, was partly responsible for the leap in the figure for the profit made by the exhibition this year: not only the first time that this had exceeded that of 1871, but also the first time that it was more than £1,000. It was too much to hope that this rise in the value of sales would extend to 1876, when a retrenchment occurred to well below 1874 levels; but the Committee in their report shrugged this off: 'this is easily to be accounted for from the depression of trade'.[35] The 1875 exhibition had at least given proof of potential.

Perhaps unsurprisingly, there is a close correspondence between the figures for sales given in the table opposite and the patterns of artists' prices as revealed in the catalogues: slow

33. *Twenty-First Annual Report of the Committee of the Free Public Library, Museum and Gallery of Art, of the Borough of Liverpool, for the year 1873* (Liverpool, Henry Greenwood, 1873), pp. 6–7.
34. *Ibid.*, p. 7.
35. *Twenty-Fourth Annual Report of the Committee of the Free Public Library, Museum and Gallery of Art, of the Borough of Liverpool, for the year 1876* (Liverpool, Henry Greenwood, 1877), p. 17.

growth in 1872, greater expansion in 1873, effusion in 1874–5 and even (most strikingly) contraction in 1876. Thus for example the number of oils priced at £300 or more, 12 in 1871, rose to 16 the following year and 24 in 1873; while in both 1874 and 1875 the figure was 34, before returning to 20 in 1876.[36] Up to and including 1873 no artist from Liverpool charged more than £175 for an oil but in 1874 and 1875 there were two costing more than £300 – Richard Norbury's *King Lear and Cordelia* was priced at 350 guineas in the former year and R.P. Richards's *The Silver Cloud* (fig. 12) £425 in the latter. In 1876 the most expensive was John Finnie's *An Autumn Flood* (£250). Similarly with Scottish artists: before 1874 no oil was priced at more than £200, but in that year Sam Bough's *Crossthwaite Bridge, near Keswick* (pl. 55) had a price-tag of £500 and in 1875 James Docharty's *Falls of the Dochart, Killin, Perthshire* the same. The most expensive Scottish picture in 1876 was W.E. Lockhart's *A Skate on the Garry* at £100. A comparable trend is visible with watercolours: the figure for 1871 of eight costing more than £150 fell to six the following year and only two in 1873, but rose to 11 in 1874 and 15 in 1875 before dropping to 10 in 1876.

The record of purchases for the city's permanent collection in these years (see Appendix 2, p. 156) suggests that there was no systematic policy on the Committee's part, but rather that they adopted an *ad hoc* approach. Notionally their plan – as implied in several of their early reports[37] – was to use the profits of one year's exhibition as spending money for purchases from the next. This did not of course guarantee that there would be acquisitions every year, for an exhibition might fail to make sufficient profit to expend on a worthwhile picture. However, in 1872 the Committee had £615 to play with from the previous year and they duly spent it on two paintings (pls 24, 25) whose exact same price and extremely contrasted characters suggest that issues of accountability, transparency and aesthetic balance were uppermost in their minds. Acute sensitivity to potential public criticism, as well as reaction to their experiences in the previous year, when their choices, although they had leaked into the press during the exhibition, had not been officially reported or accounted, are detectible in their selection.

In 1873, nominally with only £310 profit available, the Committee spent £787 10s on pictures, making up the shortfall through a grant from the Library Fund.[38] Several possible explanations for this hubristic gesture suggest themselves. It would be tempting to imagine that the Committee already knew of Andrew Barclay Walker's (fig. 11) impending gift of money for the city's new art gallery, which was announced in the middle of November, yet this seems not to have been the case.[39] But they undoubtedly did believe that the 1873 exhibition had been of higher artistic quality than its predecessors.[40] Perhaps too there was some disagreement between Committee members about which pictures were the most deserving. No doubt Rathbone stood out for the acquisition of Louisa Starr's *Sintram* (pl. 33), perhaps less on grounds of its artistic merits (the picture had previously received considerable criticism at the RA) than as a way of reinforcing the impact made by Mrs Anderson's *Elaine* and to prevent that acquisition of two years earlier coming to appear a beached whale.

Over the next two exhibitions the Committee's policy went into reverse. In 1874, with £466 profit from the previous exhibition theoretically available, they spent only £205. Again they chose three works, but these were individually much cheaper than before. The statement made by the choice of the two oils, both of which were by younger artists and the more expensive of which was by an American (pls 51, 54), are of considerable interest from their progressive and experimental nature, but again the whiff of sensitivity

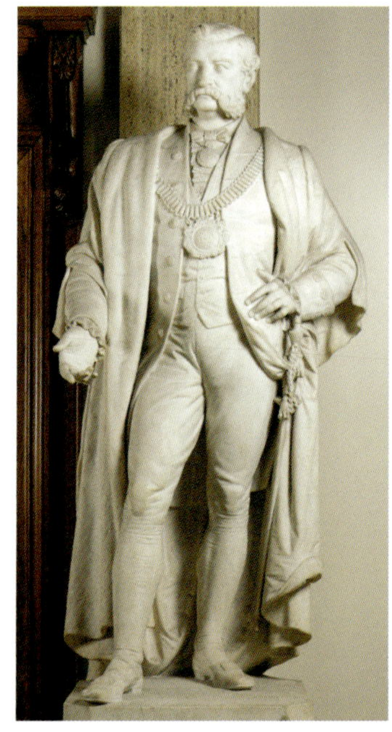

36. The numbers for artists from outside London (four in 1871) were one in 1872 and 1873 (both foreigners), but eight in 1874 and five in 1875 before declining to three in 1876.
37. See e.g. 'The 1871 Exhibition', note 10; note 31.
38. *Twenty-First Annual Report of the Committee* [as at note 33], pp. 6, 8. The figure followed here is that of the report, and not the sum of the figures given in Morris 1996 [as at 'Introduction', note 2], where the £153 10s for E.A. Goodall's *Pescheria* [p. 178] should probably be £157 10s (i.e. 150 guineas).
39. To ensure that there was no hint that he had bought his election as Mayor by promising the gift, Walker deferred announcing it until after the event; see the *Daily Courier*, 11 November 1873, p. 4.
40. *Twenty-First Annual Report of the Committee* … [as at note 33], p. 7.

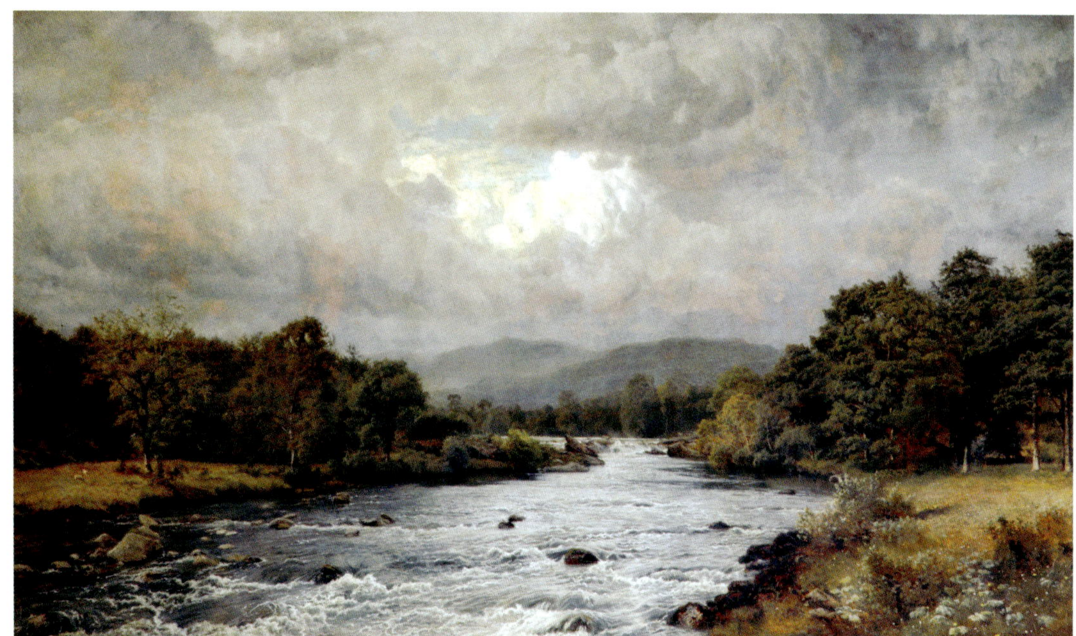

to criticism is detectible, as well as a further strand of thought. With the city's new art gallery now more than a gleam in Councillors' eyes, it was tempting to argue that they would be prudent to shepherd available financial resources against the possibility of over-spend on the building. This viewpoint had been aired in the press in September 1872 – just after the Committee had announced its purchases from that year's Autumn Exhibition, but at a time when the art gallery, soon to be the focus of a doomed public appeal led by Picton, was still apparently as far away as ever. In an article titled 'Room and No Room', the *Courier* had commented:

> We quite agree [with Picton] that the profits of the exhibitions should be used for art purposes; but we are not sure that, under the circumstances, it is wise to purchase the pictures … would it not be better for the committee to husband their resources? The proposed art gallery will involve a considerable expenditure, and those who profess to have the scheme at heart would do well to practise economy for a time. Unless Mr Picton and his associates have made some real bargains, the purchase sanctioned yesterday is simply unjustifiable. If they have picked up some priceless specimens of art for a "mere song," the town will be indebted to them; but what is the use of pictures if the owners have no place to hang them? Being unacquainted with the pictures intended to be bought, we can express no opinions on the merits of the bargain. But that the expenditure is ill-timed is beyond a doubt. Till the new gallery is erected the committee should devote all their energies and the accumulation of funds for the grander scheme. They should take Alderman Livingston's advice and not purchase horses till they have provided a stable.[41]

It seems likely that by 1874 some of this thinking had rubbed off: no doubt it was politic in the early stages of the gallery's delivery to appear to be practising economy. In 1875 the need for even greater caution may have been felt, for this year the Committee made no official purchases from the exhibition at all.[42] It is true that Edward Armitage's *Julian the Apostate Presiding at a Conference of Sectarians* (pl. 63), at £1,500 the most expensive picture yet to be shown in the Autumn Exhibitions, did enter the permanent collection, thanks to the iron-founder Alderman William Bennett, who bought the work privately and immediately presented it to the city (a gesture which had its precedents earlier in the decade, especially where getting 'difficult' pictures into the collection was concerned).[43] Conceivably, however, part of the explanation for inaction lay elsewhere. In this year of unprecedented sales, it is possible that all the Committee's preferred choices were pre-empted by private buyers.

Of course, caution over purchases became increasingly counter-intuitive: with a new gallery in the offing there was an urgent need for pictures to fill it. In 1876 for the first time the Committee bought as many as four works, spending over £1,420, which was all the profit from the 1875 exhibition, plus the left-over from 1874, and more besides. Their choices (pls 82, 86, 89, 94) again covered widely ranging genres, yet noticeably they were all in a relatively middle-of-the-road vein. Art that was obviously 'advanced' or potentially controversial, most notably anything with visible Pre-Raphaelite tendencies, was conspicuously avoided. Naturally that did not prevent press criticism of the works that were selected.

PRESS COVERAGE

The potential for the Committee's purchases to court controversy in the press had been largely dodged in the first year of the exhibition's existence. Even though, as we have seen, Sophie Anderson's *Elaine* had attracted criticism, relatively little of this was concentrated on its suitability as an acquisition for the city's collection (at least in the columns of the press, although there are signs that the choice had prompted a good deal of chatter). In essence, the Committee had avoided publicising their selections and had been rewarded by the newspapers failing to focus on the issue. This changed in 1872. The Committee were clearly proud of their choices, Oakes's *A North Devon Glen* and Topham's *Fall of Rienzi*, as well as of the quick and efficient way they in which they had conducted the selection process; and they seem to have issued an official, rose-tinted press release (printed *verbatim* by both the *Mail* and the *Post*).[44] A few days later the *Courier*, the paper that to date had shown the greatest hostility towards the Committee and which had already that month, in its article 'Room and No Room' argued against purchasing at all while there was no gallery to put the pictures in, published a long letter from an anonymous correspondent, 'S', in which the mediocrity of the purchases to date was lambasted with an eloquent fervour unmatched in any other piece written in the early years of the exhibition's history. The considerations that applied to the Committee's dilution of their exhibitions with too many mediocre pictures, 'S' argued, were redoubled when it came to selecting pictures for the city's permanent collection:

> The selection for such a purpose cannot be too carefully made, for a work so placed is pretty sure to have a permanent influence for good or ill. And what would seem to be required in pictures which are to be so selected is, first, that there should be distinctly original thought evinced in the selection and treatment of the subject; that it should have that impress of the mind and individuality of its author which will give it an intellectual interest, beyond the question of its being well or ill painted; for what is the use of a picture, however "well painted," that leaves no impression on the mind distinguishable from that produced by fifty other equally well-painted works? Secondly, that the execution should be such as to render the work, to some extent at least, a study and a model of its kind; and thirdly, in laying the first foundation of a new collection, it is certainly desirable that the works selected should be as far as possible typical each of a certain class or school – that they should be to some extent representative works. Put in a negative form, all these conditions might perhaps be summed up into the

43. See 'The 1871 Exhibition', note 34.
44. *Liverpool Mail*, 21 September 1872, p. 11; *Daily Post*, 19 September 1872, Supplement, p. 1.

one great commandment of art, "Thou shalt have nothing commonplace." For the very object of art is to raise us above the commonplace; and there is nothing so deadening to the mind, so contrary to all the real ends of art, as tameness and mediocrity, even where no special faults exist.[45]

Looking back at the 1871 purchases, 'S' observed that Jopling's works 'seldom show much feeling or thought apart from mere brilliancy of execution'; Finnie's landscape was unmemorable, whilst *Elaine* (perish any thought of consistency from one year to the next on the part of the *Courier*) 'was tame and feeble to a degree, and added nothing to anyone's idea of the poem … To buy such a work for the Gallery of Art was *an utter and absolute waste of money*, about which at the time astonishment was expressed on all sides by those who knew anything of the artistic value of pictures'. As for the present year's acquisitions, the *Rienzi* 'is a work totally devoid of that power in art which we call *genius*. There is no intensity of conception in it – no imaginative power – nothing to differentiate it from fifty other "historical paintings" of the ordinary type'; while Oakes's picture,

> attractive as it may seem at first sight, is a picture belonging to an essentially false school of landscape painting … Works of this type have exactly the same kind of merit which belongs to good scene-painting; they give neither the facts of nature, nor the poetry which underlies the facts; but they furnish a striking visual effect, obtained by a kind of adroit artificial manipulation of sunlight, which takes the popular taste, and is cried up accordingly … The constant placing of good things before people leads them insensibly to learn wherein the goodness consists, and to distinguish between what is intrinsically excellent and what is merely ephemeral and sensational. But the Liverpool public will get no such education from their promised "Gallery of Art" if the choice is conducted on the principles which seem to have been followed hitherto. So far from the gallery becoming, as we are told, "of importance as to be a credit to the town," it will in that case only end in being a collection of large commonplace works, affording no instruction to anyone, and no great pleasure, except to those whose education in matters of art has been of a very limited description.[46]

The fall-out from this diatribe, the last contribution of the season from the *Courier*, may not have been instantly obvious, yet there is an almost tangible sense that the paper's editorial offices subsequently received a quiet visit from on high. From 1873, its approach completely changed: its reviews were polite and deferential, and its previously even-handed approach to rival exhibitions gave way to a pronounced bias in favour of the 'Corporation Exhibition', with regular titbits and updates about it being provided in a column called 'Literary and Fine Art Notes', of which there were eight instances in 1873, 11 in 1874 and eight in 1875.

Again from 1873 on, it would be fair to claim that all the local newspapers, not just the *Courier*, adopted a tone of caution in broaching the issue of purchases for the city. While the topic was not wholly neglected, at no point did it again receive the level of engagement shown by 'S' in 1872. Although Fripp's watercolour *Dinner Time at the Quarries – Purbeck* (pl. 94) was roughly handled by the *Daily Post* and the *Porcupine* in 1876,[47] most of the purchases were judged favourably, and the failure of the Committee to buy anything in 1875, potentially an easy target, was ignored. For their part, the Committee seem to have learnt their lesson from issuing hubristic press releases about their acquisitions, and although there are strong traces of a syndicated announcement of Alderman Bennett's 'munificent' donation of Armitage's *Julian the Apostate* in 1875,[48] for the rest the release of information seems to have been low-key and designed not to draw attention to itself. From

45. *Liverpool Courier*, 24 September 1872, p. 7.

46. *Ibid*. 'S' conceded that the only two worthwhile large pictures in the 1872 exhibition, Millais's *Marquis of Westminster* (pl. 17) and Whistler's [as 'S' titled it] *Study in Black and Grey* (pl. 19), were not for sale, as well as 'somewhat deficient in general interest'.

47. *Daily Post*, 24 November 1876, p. 6. The *Porcupine*, 9 September 1876, p. 377, commented that 'three hundred guineas is rather too much public money to be laid out in the purchase of a work that has little but prettiness to recommend it. The drawing throughout is weak, and the colour, though agreeable, totally false, and the design paltry'. It was also tepid about the purchase of Sir John Gilbert's work, wondering if it had been executed by an assistant.

48. The word 'munificent' appeared in the headline of the reports in: the *Courier*, 11 October 1875, p. 5; the *Mercury*, 11 October 1875, p. 6; and the *Daily Post*, 11 October 1875, p. 6.

1873 on, a sense of the Committee seeking to work with the local press and guide them towards a positive and constructive approach towards the exhibitions is much stronger than in the years 1871–2.

The *Courier* was not the only Liverpool newspaper to perform a *volte-face* towards the exhibition. The *Liverpool Mail*, which in 1871 had ignored the exhibition in favour of Agnew's, the following year published a short notice reporting early sales and visitor numbers,[49] as well as the Committee's prepared report on purchases for the permanent collection.[50] Although it continued to be grudging towards the exhibition for another year, the *Mail* did gradually thaw, until in 1876 it printed five substantial reviews, the same number as the *Post* and three more than the *Albion*.[51] In its way, the 'conversion' of the *Mail* can be viewed as quiet evidence for the triumph of the Autumn Exhibition, its metamorphosis into a civic institution from the plaything of a handful of Councillors. The same might equally be said for the trajectory of the coverage from the *Porcupine*. In the period 1871–4 it printed four or five pieces a year; but this went up to seven in 1875 and 10 in 1876, not counting its extra humorous contributions.

In the period 1871–4 the *Porcupine* conscientiously afforded the rival Agnew's exhibition two notices each year, but in 1875 and 1876 only one, in each case much shorter than its Autumn Exhibition pieces, and in 1875 describing the Agnew's show as 'below the standard of certain other years'.[52] This might seem to tell its own story – especially in conjunction with Agnew's experimentation in some of these years with the launch date of their show, to avoid competing with the opening of the Autumn Exhibition. Yet if the tally of column inches devoted to the two exhibitions by the Liverpool press between 1872 and 1876 swung decisively in William Brown Street's favour, it would be premature to view this in the nature of a 'victory'. The character of the reviews and indeed the whole editorial policy towards reporting the visual arts differs not only from journal to journal but also within each journal from year to year. Some years a newspaper would review Agnew's exhibitions – or indeed those of the dealers Grindley's (which had also been going on annually since the late 1860s and which achieved a notable *coup* in 1874 by displaying Elizabeth Thompson's RA sensation of the year, *The Roll Call*; fig. 13), of the Bebington Library, of the emergent Liverpool Art Club, or even of the Manchester Royal Institution[53] – while in other years they would neglect them altogether. The same goes for the number of pieces devoted to the exhibitions each year. The randomness of the overall pattern offers no suggestion of a political dimension, but simply the arrival of a new phenomenon that tested the existing structure of local journalism.

That two Liverpool newspapers should decide, within four days of each other, to carry a review of the 'rival' Manchester exhibition is, to be sure, evidence for the existence of shared journalistic tropes. This was a particularly whimsical one; others which surfaced in different newspapers at different times included, for example, devoting special reviews to the works of local artists in the exhibition;[54] quoting the reviews that had appeared in London journals;[55] noticing the number of pictures rejected by the Committee;[56] or featuring, more or less positively, the difficulty of the task they faced in hanging the exhibition.[57] But the two most common topics, which appeared with variants in most of the papers in most years – and which clearly reflected the Committee's chief preoccupations – were the progress of sales (interim figures were frequently reported as well as end-of-season ones) and the assertion that this year's exhibition marked an advance upon the previous ones. Thus the *Albion* in 1874, even before the exhibition had opened:

49. *Liverpool Mail*, 14 September 1872, p. 9.
50. See note 44.
51. The history of the *Albion* at this period is complicated by its attempt from November 1871 to run a daily as well as a weekly issue. Reviews of the Autumn Exhibition in the 1872 weekly were suspended abruptly after 14 September and may have been transferred to the daily thereafter. The 1873 daily *Albion* did carry reviews of that year's exhibition, but from 1874 coverage reverted to the weekly. It has not been possible to trace any copies of the 1872 daily or 1873 weekly *Albion*.
52. *Porcupine*, 9 October 1875, p. 443.
53. Reviews of the Manchester exhibition appeared in the *Albion*, 19 September 1875, p. 3, and in the *Liverpool Courier*, 15 September 1875, p. 7, in both of which the dangers and pitfalls of a prevalent Manchester school of 'Corotism' were noticed.
54. E.g. *Albion*, 25 September 1875, p. 4; *Daily Post*, 13 September 1876, p. 6.
55. *Liverpool Mail*, 7 November 1874, p. 9; *Porcupine*, 11 September 1875, p. 372; *Courier*, 11 October 1875, p. 5; *Daily Post*, 11 October 1875, p. 6. The last two articles quoted the same London reviews of Armitage's *Julian the Apostate* in their articles about Alderman Bennett's 'munificent' gift (see note 48).
56. See note 8; also *Albion*, 7 September 1872, p. 2; *Albion*, 5 September 1874, p. 4.
57. E.g. *Albion*, 29 August 1874, p. 7; *Liverpool Mercury*, 24 September 1874, p. 8.

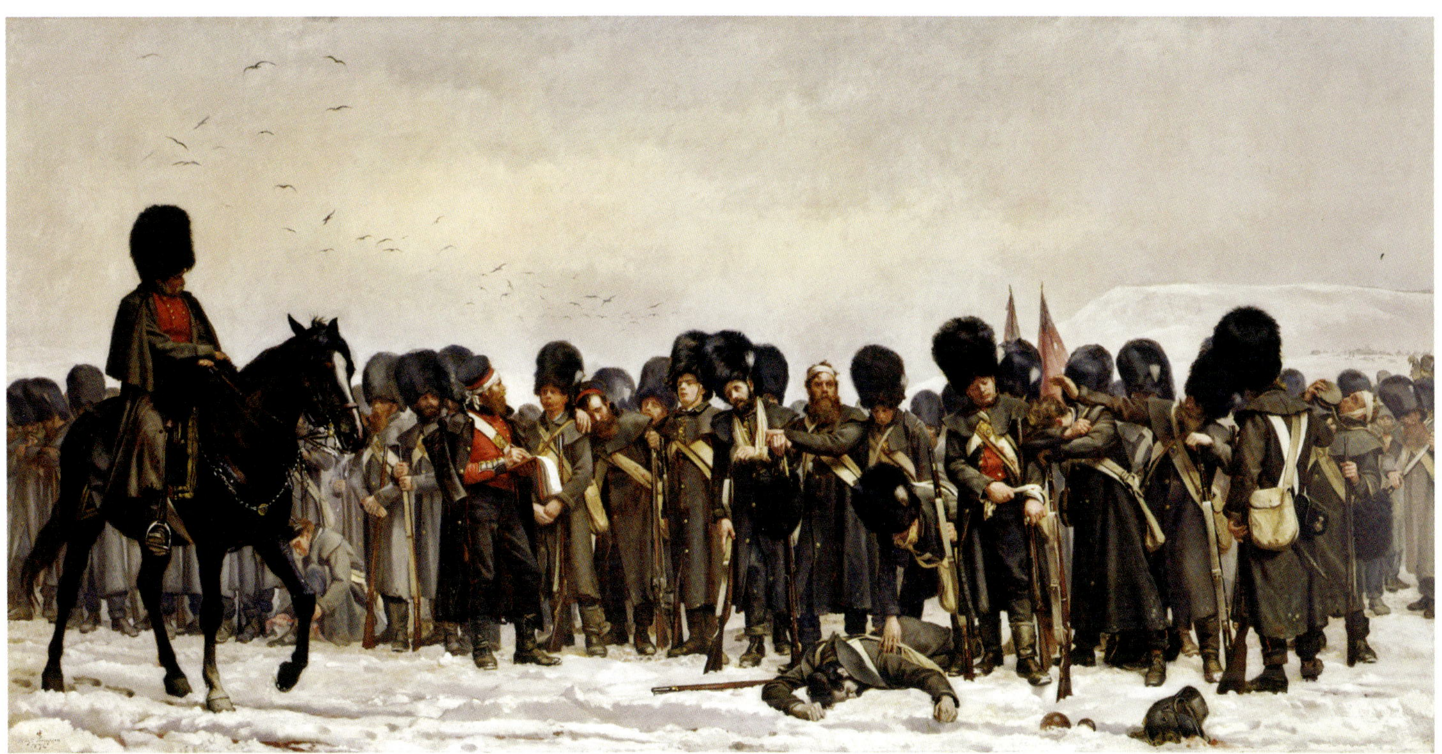

year after year the talent, quality and tone of the exhibition has advanced. Last year's show was thought to transcend anything of the kind held previously in the town, but if report be true the forthcoming one will eclipse all former ones. Certainly the goodly array of names which from time to time have been found recorded in these columns as probable senders naturally excited expectations which we have good reason to believe will not be disappointed.[58]

The 1874 exhibition, with its pronounced change of direction towards a greater metropolitan bias, was the *annus mirabilis* for the 'best ever' comments, closely followed by 1876 (which, naturally, marked an advance on 1875, which in turn had topped 1874). In the words of the *Mail*, on 2 September 1876:

> That the Corporation Exhibition of Modern Pictures is growing in favour year by year
> is evidenced by the greater success which attends each succeeding one, not only as regards
> pecuniary results, but in the higher standards of excellence attained, and it is no exaggeration
> to say that the present exhibition, the press view of which took place yesterday, is far superior
> in this latter respect to any of its predecessors.[59]

On the same day the *Albion*, *Courier* and *Mercury* all said the same thing, in slightly different words. Yet even within the 'best ever' trope, it was possible to find variations of opinion, such as that the present year's improvement consisted chiefly in the reduction of bad pictures rather than a greater number of good ones;[60] or that the improvement was confined to the oils, and did not extend to the watercolours.[61]

In the last resort the chief impression conveyed by the Babel of press criticism is that there was room for all. The showing of *The Roll Call* and even the 1875 exhibition of the Manchester Royal Institution come across in the newspapers not as competing concerns so much as

58. *Albion, Ibid.*
59. *Liverpool Mail*, 2 September 1876, p. 9.
60. *Daily Post*, 1 September 1873, p. 5; *Porcupine*, 9 September 1875, p. 377.
61. *Daily Post*, 4 September 1875, p. 4.

partners in a single local enterprise. The trigger of this atmosphere of goodwill was undoubtedly the pervading sense that the Autumn Exhibition was bedding down and here to stay. It was widely talked about, and most importantly, it was increasingly visited by all sections of the community, developments in which the press played an important part. As the *Porcupine* wrote at the end of the 1876 exhibition:

> The dry bones of criticism are scarcely a fit dish to serve up for breakfast on a day that will joyfully close a successful chapter of local history. The present exhibition has been a success. If the sales have not equalled former years, the crowded evenings are abundant proof of the wisdom of the directorate. Thousands of men hitherto indifferent have been brought under the elevating influence of art, and have been in consequence lured from base occupations. This is exactly what is wanted in money-grubbing Liverpool, and we rejoice that there is still sufficient life in our Corporation to carry to a glorious climax so beneficial a result.[62]

Over the past six years in Liverpool art had become cool.

62. *Porcupine*, 2 December 1876, p. 567.

THE 1877 EXHIBITION

The Autumn Exhibitions of 1871–6 have the character of precursors to those that took place in the Walker from 1877. The opening of the seventh show in the series, on 6 September 1877, was bound to represent – especially in the minds of some of the dignitaries present – the culmination and fulfilment of a process designed to procure for the city the permanent 'Gallery of Art' in which the exhibition was now displayed; the closure of one era and the opening of a new one of expansion and possibility. The somewhat limited spaces in the Free Library and Museum which had been sacrificed for long spells over the past six years could return to housing books, fish and birds full-time, and regular visitors to the Autumn Exhibition could absorb the unfamiliar sensations afforded by the new building dedicated to art, the juxtaposition of temporary exhibition and permanent collection – and even such little things as the new catalogue design.[1]

The biggest difference between the 1877 exhibition and its predecessor was its enlarged size. The jump of 134 works from 1,186 to 1,320 was the largest so far in the exhibition's history (and liable to raise the old issue of whether quality had been sacrificed to numbers).[2] Obviously, this increase was enabled by the availability of extra space. The exhibition occupied eight rooms on the upper floor of the gallery, plus the vestibule space or landing first reached by the visitor on climbing the stairs which was largely reserved (at least in 1877)[3] for sculpture. From this vestibule, doors to the right and left led to two suites of three connected galleries. Rooms one to three were on the right and four to six were on the left,[4] with Rooms one and four being large show galleries in which the major oils were mostly featured, while beyond these Rooms two to three and five to six offered more modest spaces which held small oils and works on paper. Smaller still were two rooms, seven and eight, opening off the vestibule beyond the entrances to Rooms one and four, which were reserved for works on paper, each holding about 100 pieces. In 1877 Rooms one and four contained 130 and 156 oils respectively, two and five each a larger number of smaller oils, and three and six each around 200 watercolours.

Whether this represented a very different experience from that of the Free Library may be questioned. By the time the Free Library's corridors and vestibule are factored in as well as its four main rooms, its number of actual spaces is not far short of what was available at the new gallery, whilst theoretically the latter's left-and-right configuration of galleries replicated the situation at the Free Library where there were two main spaces on each side of the entrance. What was different was that instead of the oils being hung on the visitor's left and watercolours on the right, now the oils occupied the first two rooms on both sides of the central vestibule, with the watercolours being relegated to the four farthest-flung spaces that the visitor encountered. Given that the 1877 exhibition's growth in overall numbers had failed to yield any fresh bias in favour of oils *per se* – their number rose from

1. The new catalogue – smaller, perhaps with pockets in mind – was not a success, with many more misprints (or misreadings of artists' handwriting) than in previous years.
2. A striking feature of the first five years of the exhibitions in the Walker Art Gallery was the see-sawing of the total number of works. In 1878 the figure dropped to 1,062; in 1879 it rose to 1,356 (a leap of 294 that made the rise of 1877 seem positively puny); in 1880 it fell to 1,080; and in 1881 it rose again to 1,435. This phenomenon is beyond the scope of the present survey.
3. Late-arriving large oils colonised the wall spaces in the vestibule in succeeding years.
4. This numbering appears to have been reversed in 1878, to judge from the plan (fig. 14) in George R. Halkett, *The Walker Art Gallery Notes Liverpool – 1878* (Liverpool, London & Edinburgh, W.H. Smith, Chatto & Windus and Thos. Gray, 1878), p. viii.

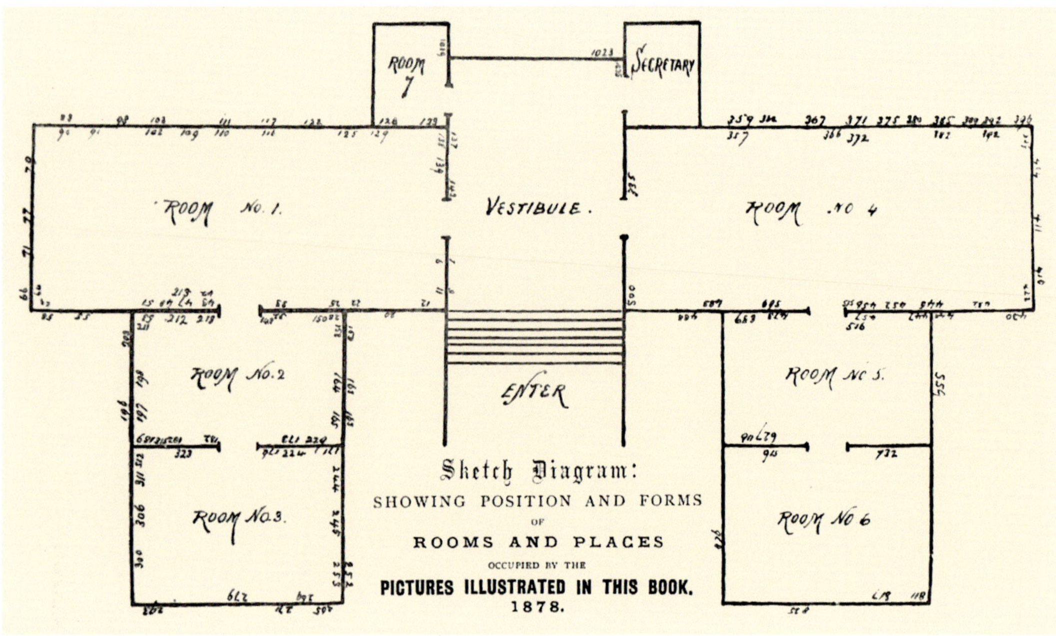

FIG. 14
Plan of the upper floor of the
Walker Art Gallery, from George
R. Halkett: *The Walker Art Gallery
Notes Liverpool* – 1878. The numbering
of the rooms was changed in 1878
from the previous year.

582 to 652, that of the watercolours from 574 to 637 – the Committee's 'prioritisation' of the oils in both the big galleries and 'relegation' of the watercolours represented an important statement of intent about the exhibition's perceived future.

Some sense of what all this meant in terms of the exhibition experience may be gained from the illustration commissioned by the *Graphic* at the time of the opening from the local artist John R. Brown (fig. 15).[5] Siting the spectator at the far end of Room No. 4, with the doorway to Room No. 5 on the right and the door from the vestibule in the centre background (the tall picture next to it on the right is identifiable as Gustave Doré's *Lorraine*),[6] Brown's view gives an idea of a much more generous and homogenous hang of medium and large-sized paintings than would have been possible in the Free Library, where it is clear that the smaller pictures had to be mixed with large ones much more abruptly and, 'skied' and 'floored', were often invisible. And even if only two of the rooms in the new gallery were large, the new building did away with the hanging of pictures in corridors and poorly lit recesses, a feature of the Free Library experience.

Psychologically, however, any feelings of change were offset by a strong element of continuity. The exhibition had not gone to a different part of the city; it had only moved next door from where it always had been. And the men who had run the exhibition for the previous six years continued to do so: there was no increase in the number of the Committee, and only one change of personnel: Andrew Barclay Walker (who became Mayor for the second time in 1877) stepping down and being replaced by Stewart H. Brown, who as a member of the parent Library Committee was fully conversant with the Exhibition Committee's activities. There was no move to mark the 1877 exhibition with purchasing on a large scale; indeed the Committee confined themselves to buying just one oil painting and one watercolour (though both were expensive).[7] They may have known, or predicted, that the opening of the gallery would yield more private gifts than before; in the first year these numbered seven works of sculpture, a Berlin China vase, three oils and one water-colour. Not all these items appeared in the 1877 Autumn Exhibition, but one that did was

5. Brown was one of the 83 ever-presents in the exhibitions of 1871–6 (see Appendix 1); from 1871 to 1874 his address was listed as the Liverpool Deaf and Dumb Institution. He was represented in the 1877 exhibition by his watercolour *Old Cottage, Capel Curig*. The illustration, published in the *Graphic*, 15 September 1877, was reproduced in Macleod 2013 [as at 'Introduction', note 3], p. 63; also in Giles Waterfield, *The People's Galleries: Art Museums and Exhibitions in Britain, 1800–1914* (New Haven and London, Yale University Press, 2015), p. 149.
6. This and its pendant *Alsace* were among 12 works lent by three local collectors, Peter Stuart, Holbrook Gaskell and Philip Eberle, 'who desired to do honor to His Worship the Mayor, A.B. WALKER, Esq.' (1877 Liverpool Autumn Exhibition catalogue, p. 72). The Dorés were owned by Peter Stuart.
7. The oil was Charles Napier Hemy's *A Nautical Argument*; the watercolour H.C. Whaite's *The Castle Rock of the Bridal of Triermain – Cumberland*.

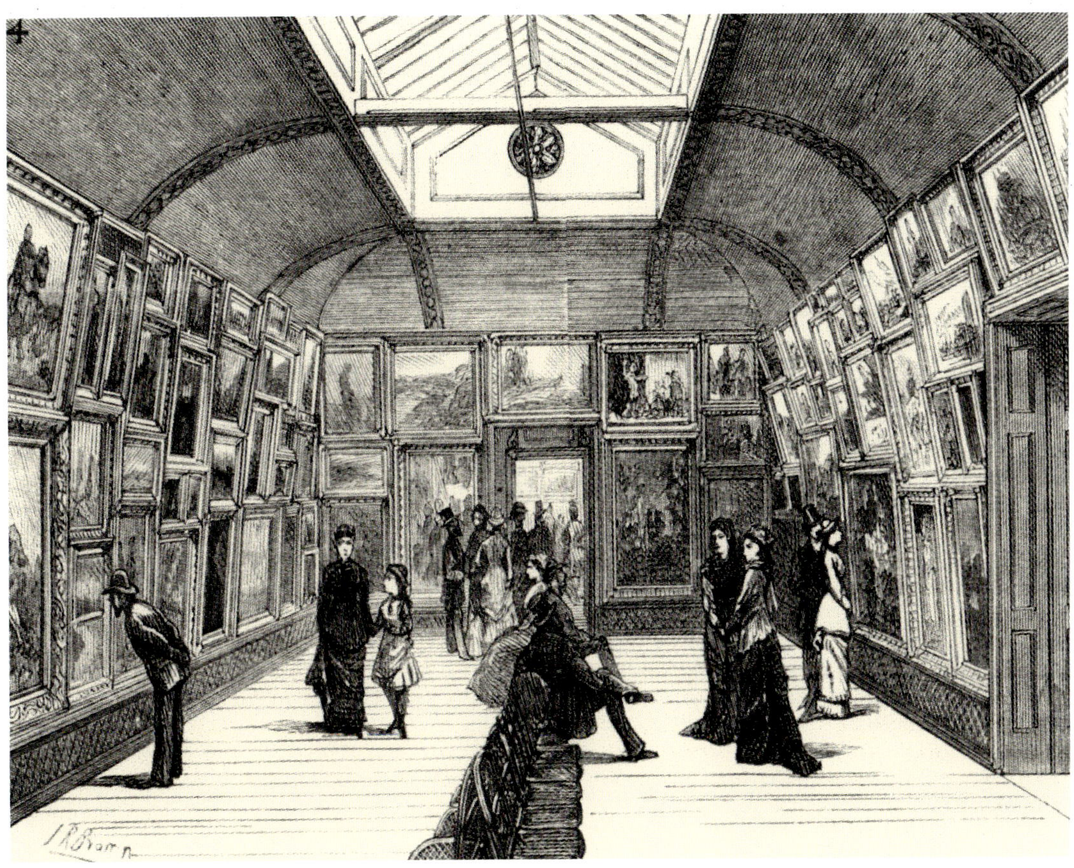

FIG. 15
Opening of the New Walker Art Gallery at Liverpool: View in One of the Galleries by John R. Brown, from the *Graphic*, 15 September 1877.

Armitage's large painting *Serf Emancipation* – purchased and given immediately to the gallery by Alderman Bennett, in a powerful gesture of continuity with his donation of the same artist's *Julian the Apostate* in 1875.

Although a tone of quiet pride is detectable in the Library Committee's report for the year signed by Picton,[8] and the report itself does lead off with a pen picture of the new gallery's opening day, the information given about the Autumn Exhibition – figures up healthily in all categories[9] – is brief and matter-of-fact, with no purple passages about its benefits to local artists or the education of the working classes. By this time such matters were taken as read. The report's closing remark, that the gallery in its first year had been visited (astoundingly) by over 300,000 people, is tossed away almost as an afterthought.[10] Such understatement sums up a seven-year process of learning and receptivity on the part of a small group of dedicated and disinterested idealists who, quietly and tactfully, had identified and addressed the pressure points and problems of successive exhibitions and had learnt how to tinker. Above all, this process had been gradual. The Committee had confined experiments to limited and specific goals, had embraced a principle of continuity over change, and had been content with small year-on-year gains. If those of 1877 did not exceed precedent in every category, they were larger than most, and the upward trend was reassuringly familiar.

8. *Twenty-Fifth Annual Report of the Committee of the Free Public Library, Museum and Walker Art Gallery of the Borough of Liverpool* (Liverpool, Henry Greenwood, 1878).
9. The numbers of pictures sold rose from 255 to 302 (1875: 345) and income from commissions on sales from £440 15s to £537 11s 2d (1875: £616 1s 3d). Attendances rose from 44,409 to 72,105. Income from attendances rose from £1,436 17s to £2,313 15s 3d; and from season ticket sales from £221 to £443; income from catalogue sales rose from £301 to £454 [*Ibid.* p. 21].
10. *Ibid.*

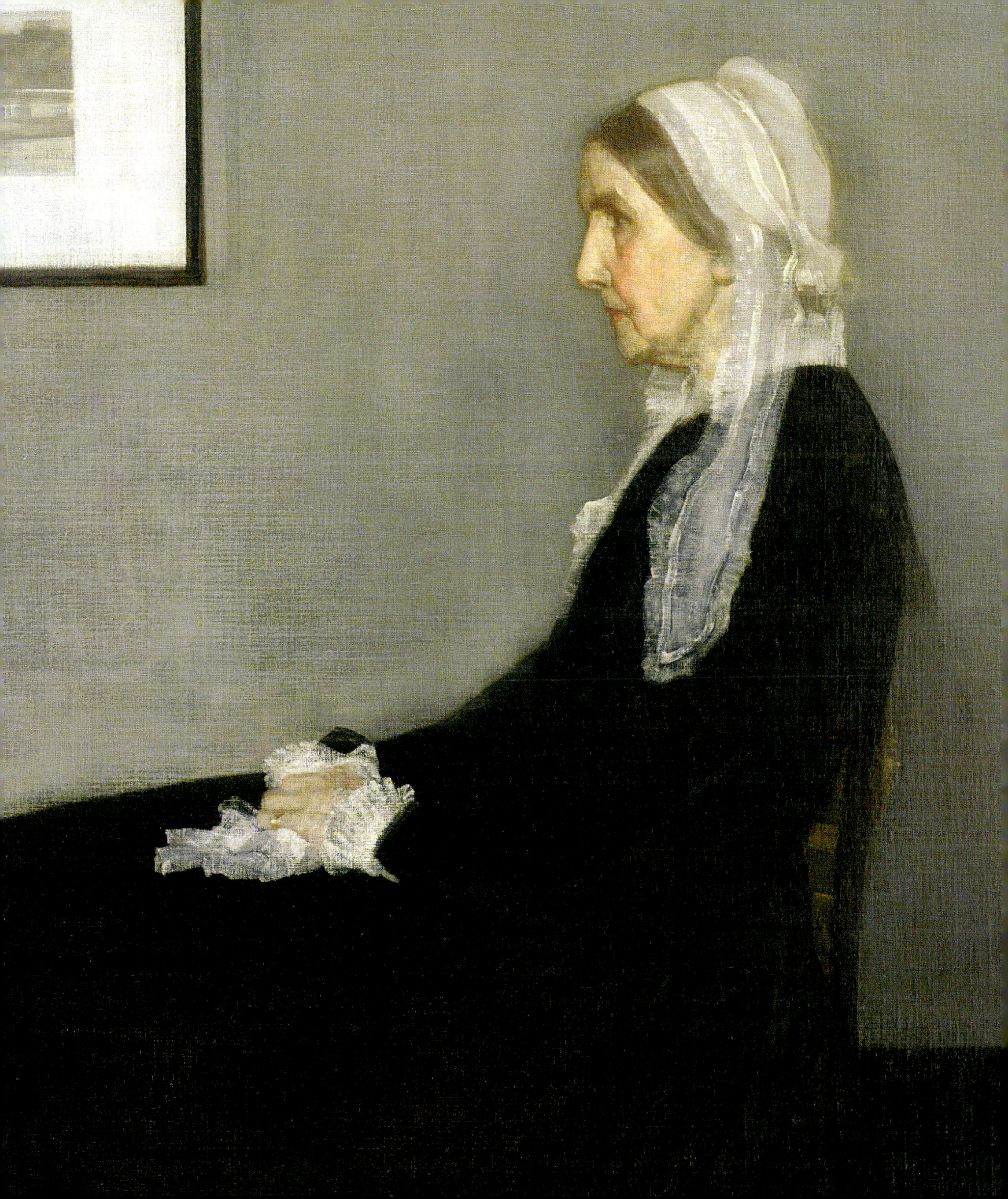

1871

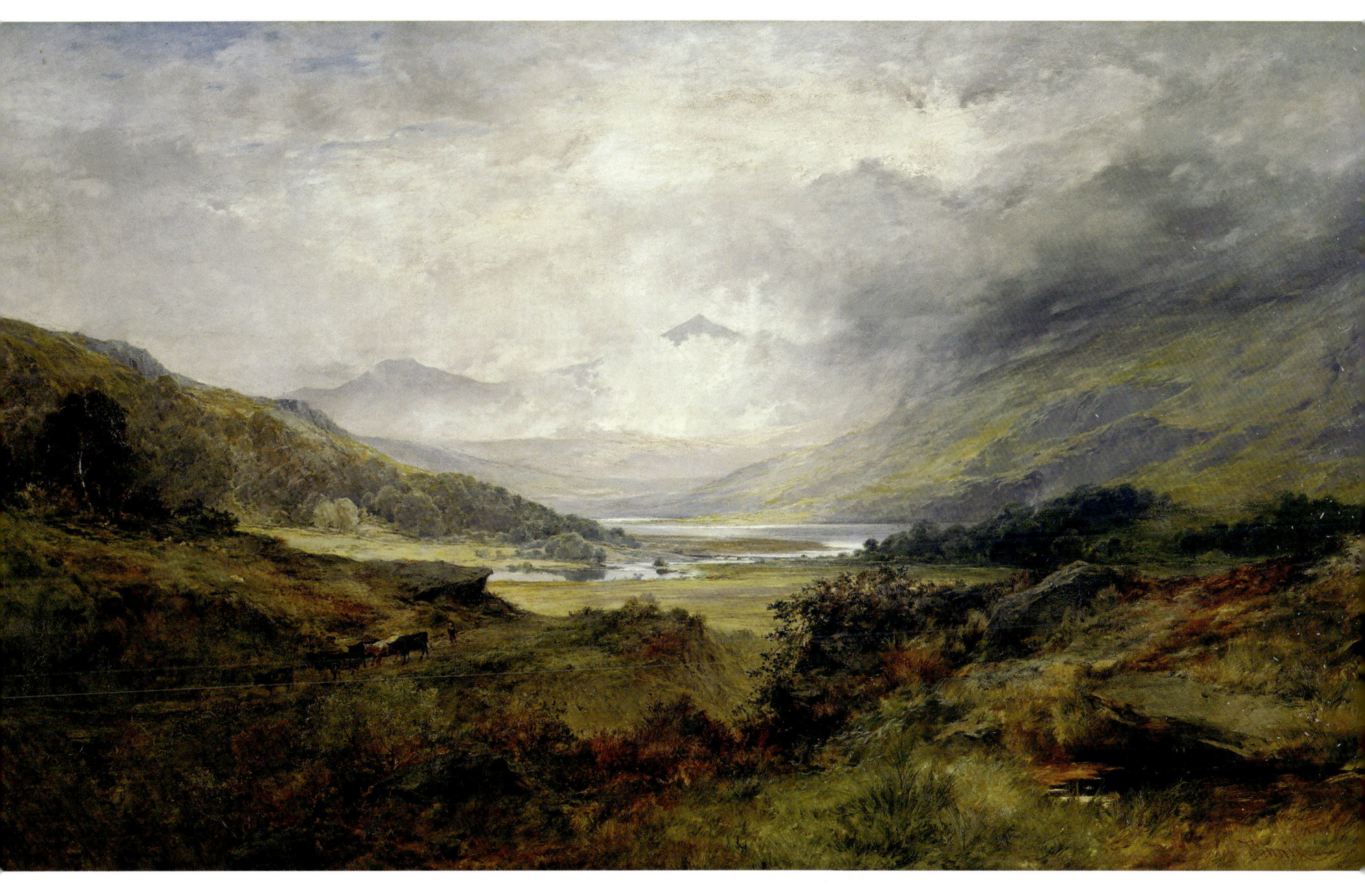

PLATE 1 · *Snowdon* · **John Finnie**
oil on canvas · 91.5 x 152.5 cm · 1871 Autumn Exhibition no. 235
National Museums Liverpool (Walker Art Gallery)

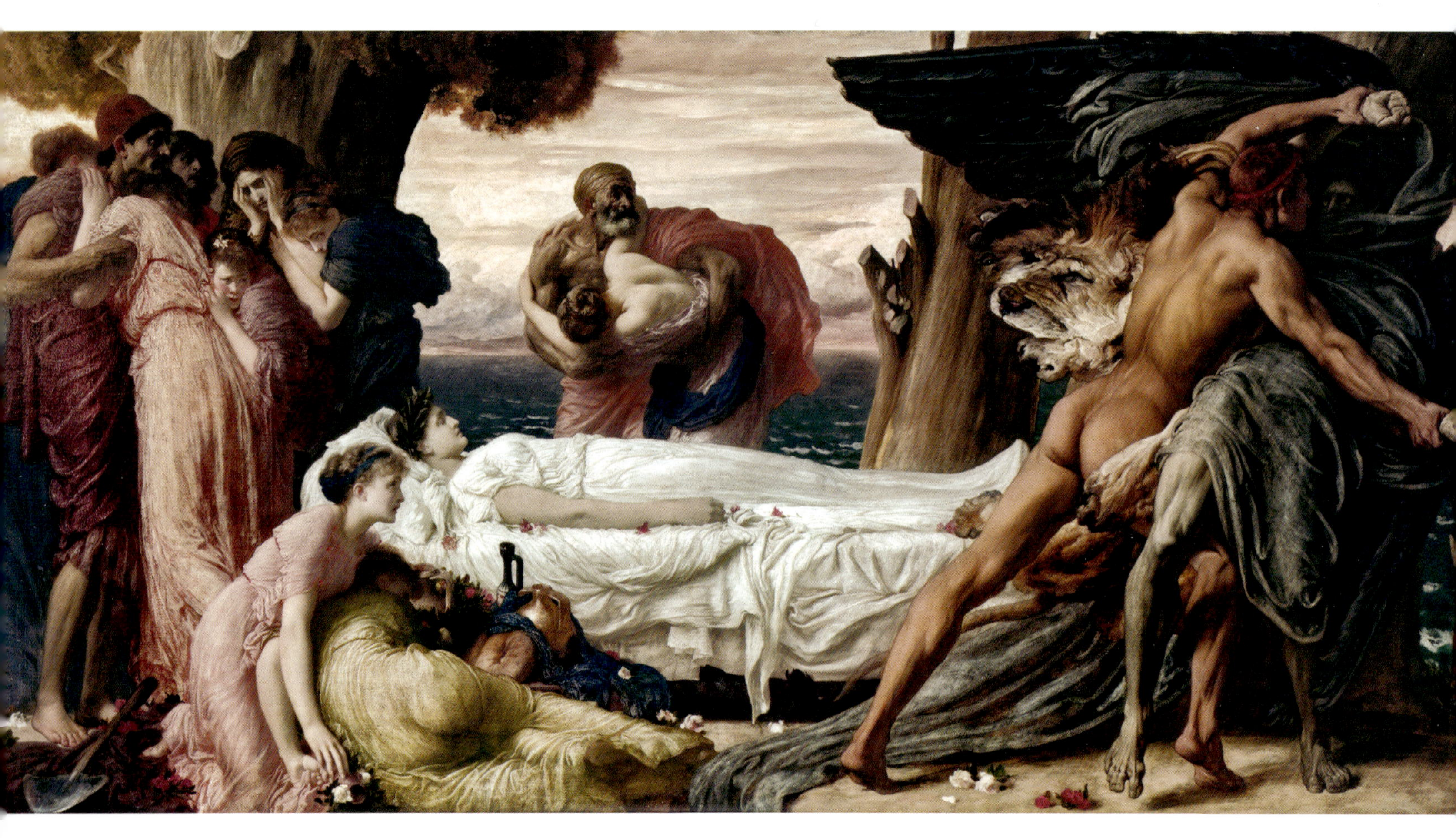

PLATE 2 · *Hercules Wrestling with Death for the Body of Alcestis* · Frederic Leighton
oil on canvas · 153 x 269 cm · 1871 Autumn Exhibition no. 192
Wadsworth Atheneum Museum of Art, Hartford, CT, The Ella Gallup Sumner and Mary Caitlin Sumner Collection Fund

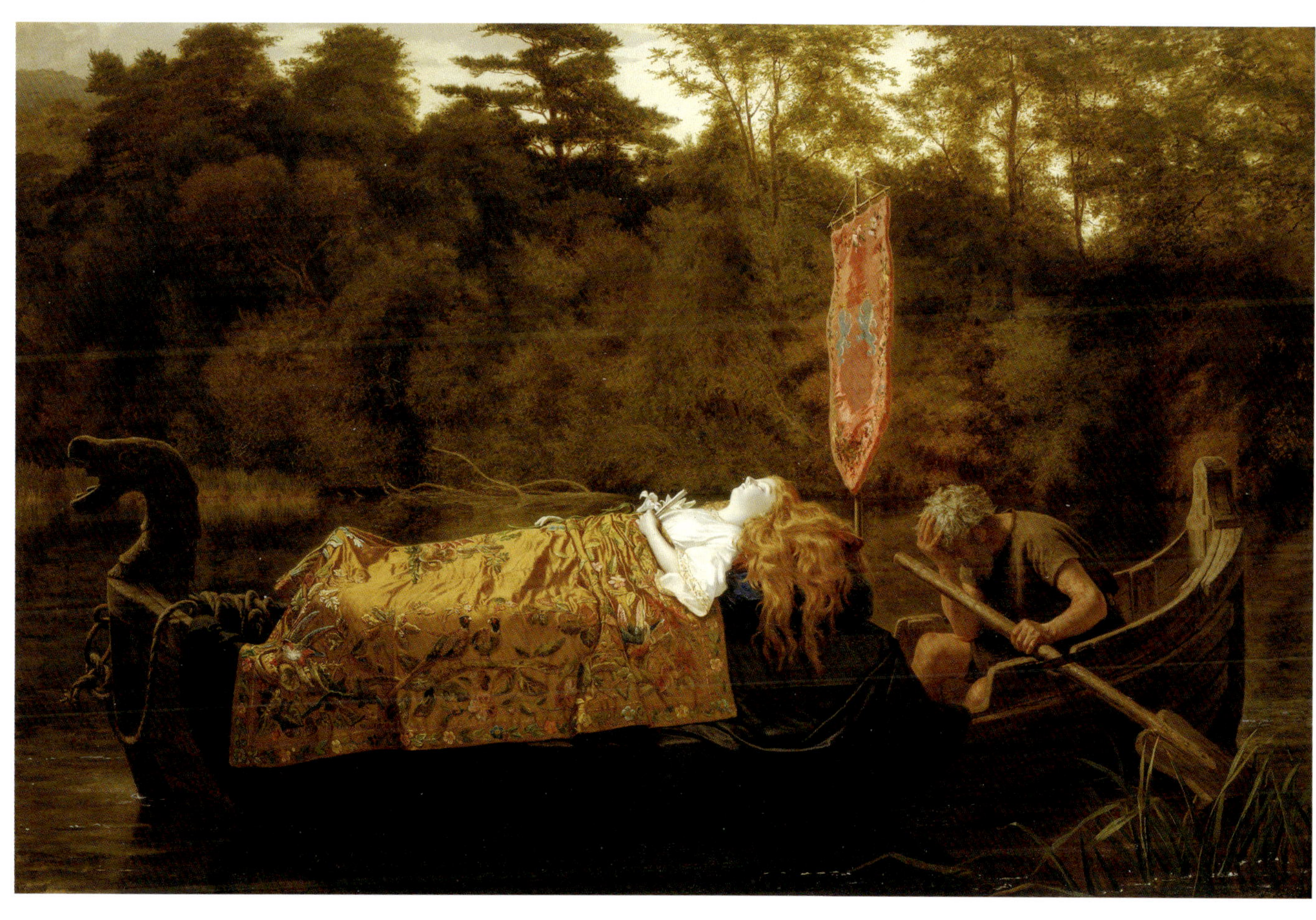

PLATE 3 · *Elaine* · Sophie Anderson
oil on canvas · 158.5 x 240.5 cm · 1871 Autumn Exhibition no. 323
National Museums Liverpool (Walker Art Gallery)

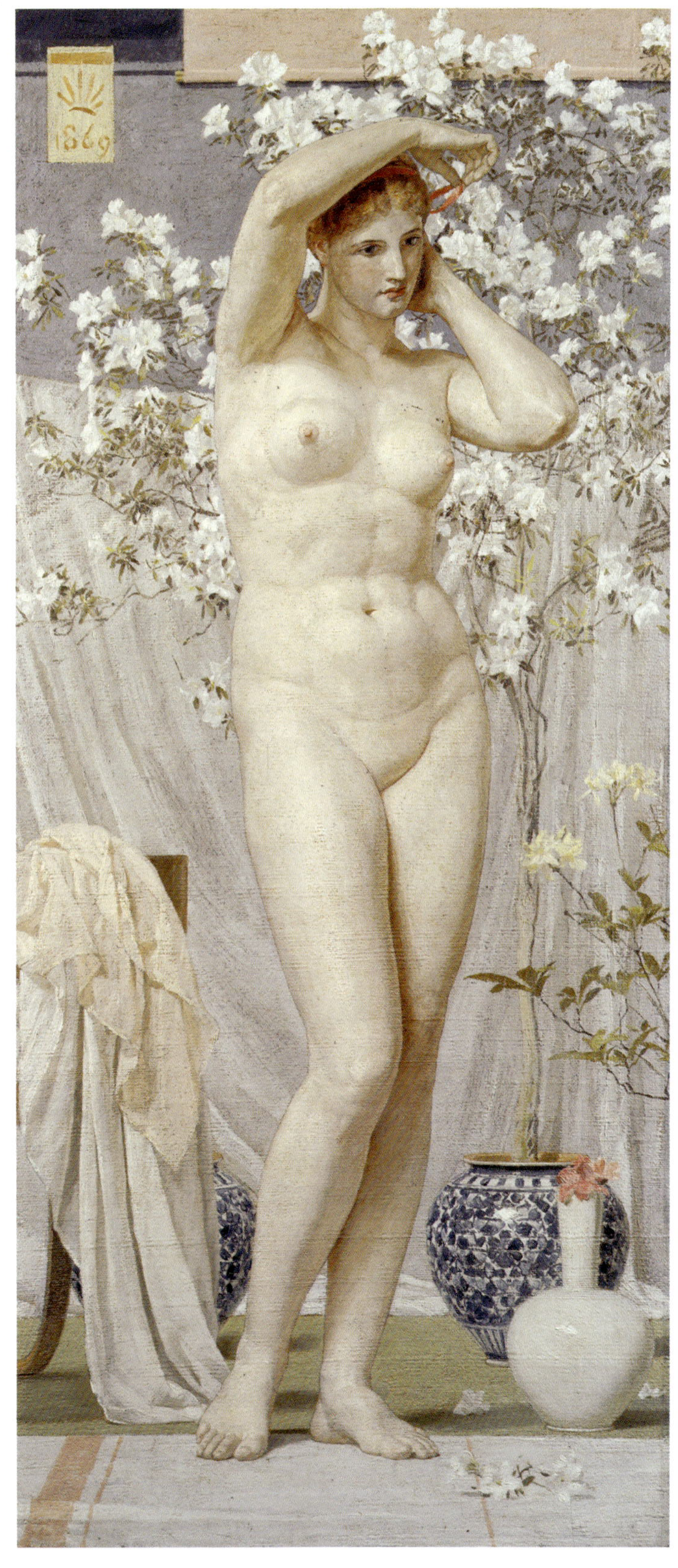

PLATE 4 · *A Venus* · Albert Moore
oil on canvas · 160 x 76 cm · 1871 Autumn Exhibition no. 30
courtesy York Museums Trust (York Art Gallery)

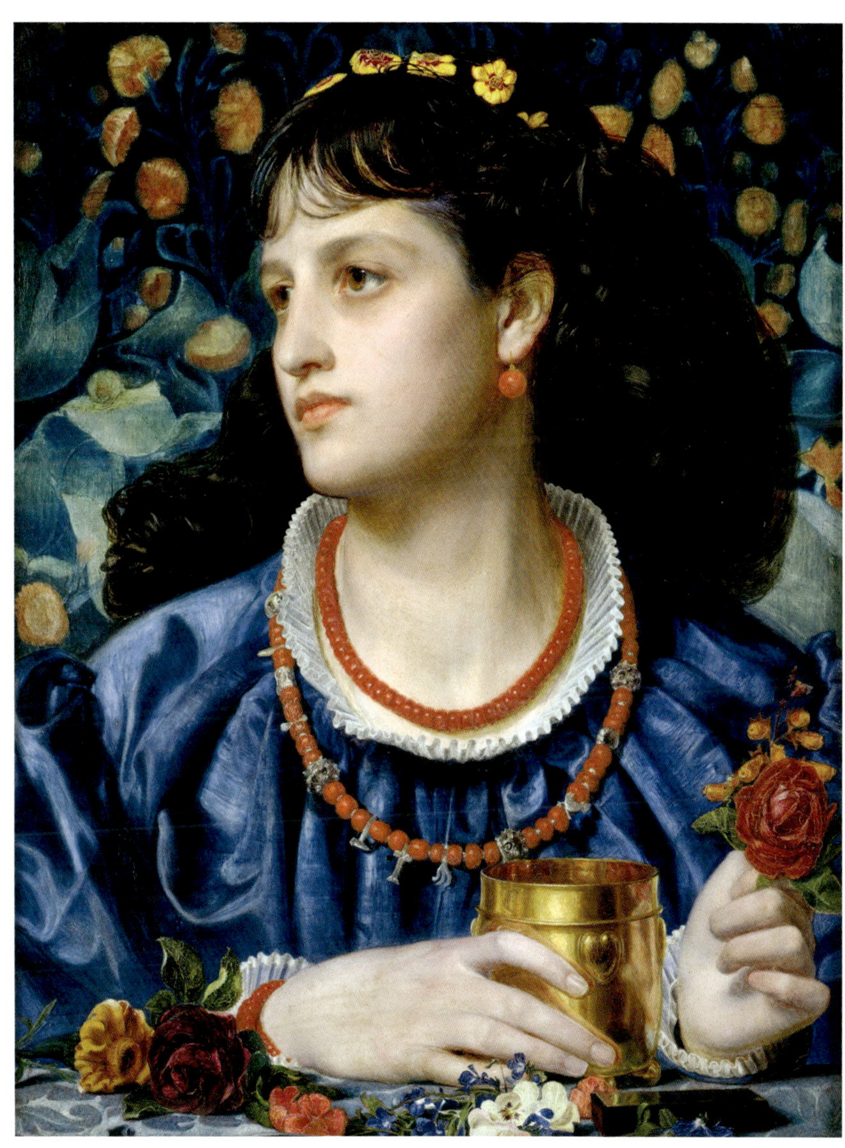

PLATE 5 · *Ysulte* · Frederick Sandys
oil on panel · 45 x 35 cm · 1871 Autumn Exhibition no. 339
Museo de Ponce, Puerto Rico

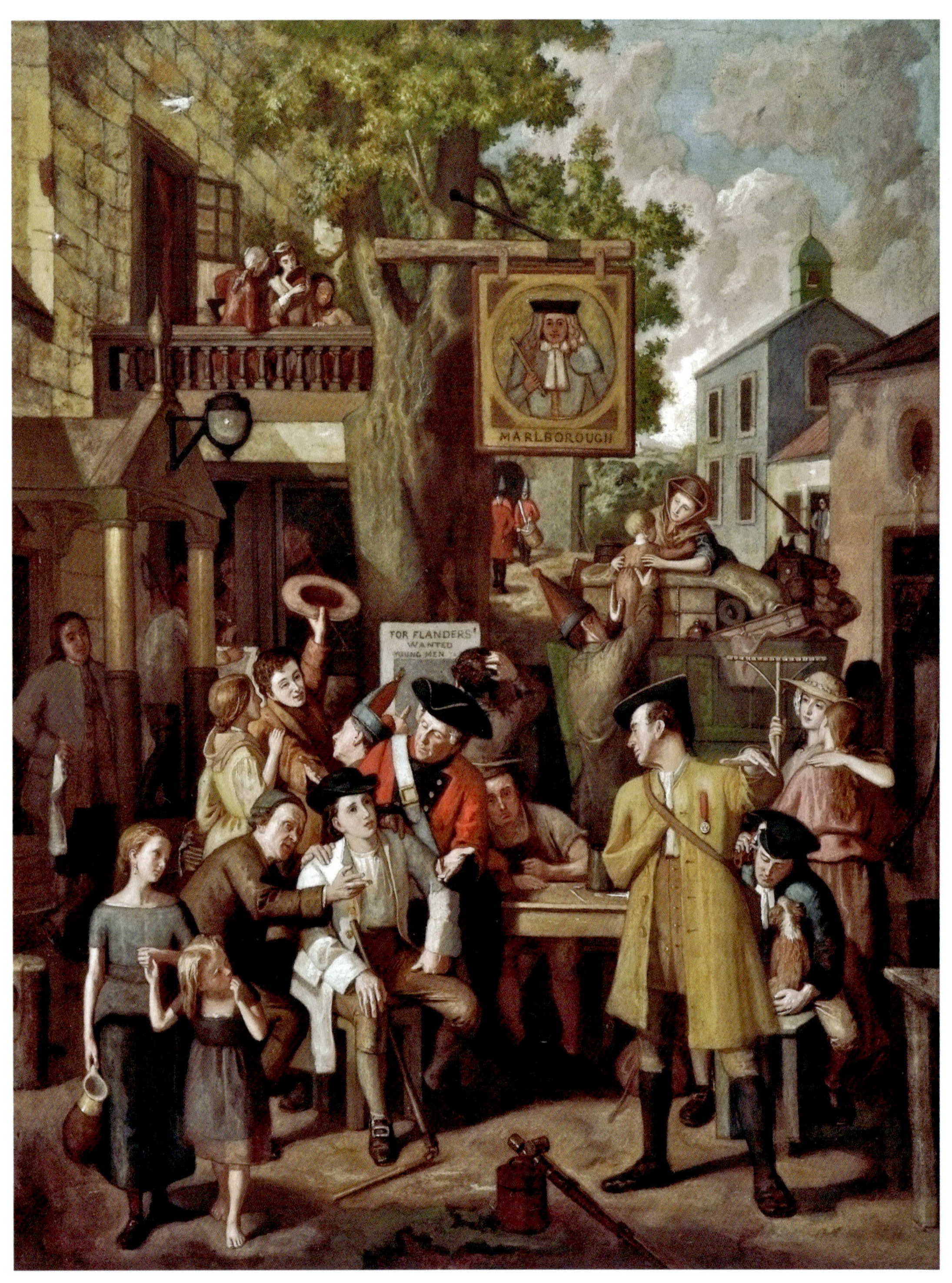

PLATE 6 · *The King's Shilling* · **James Campbell**
oil on canvas · 92 x 71.5 cm · 1871 Autumn Exhibition no. 378
National Museums Liverpool (Walker Art Gallery)

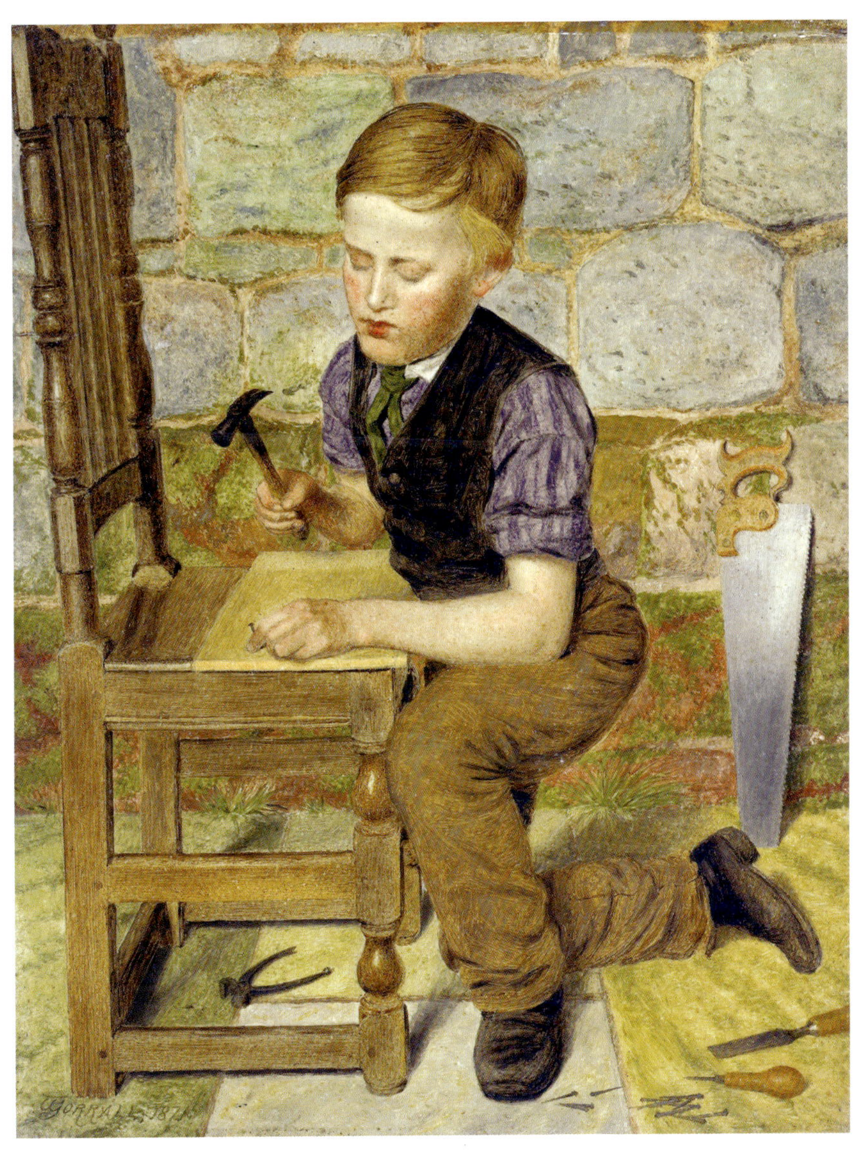

PLATE 7 · *Cobbling* · **Joseph E. Worrall**
oil on board · 25.5 x 20 cm · 1871 Autumn Exhibition no. 276
National Museums Liverpool (Walker Art Gallery)

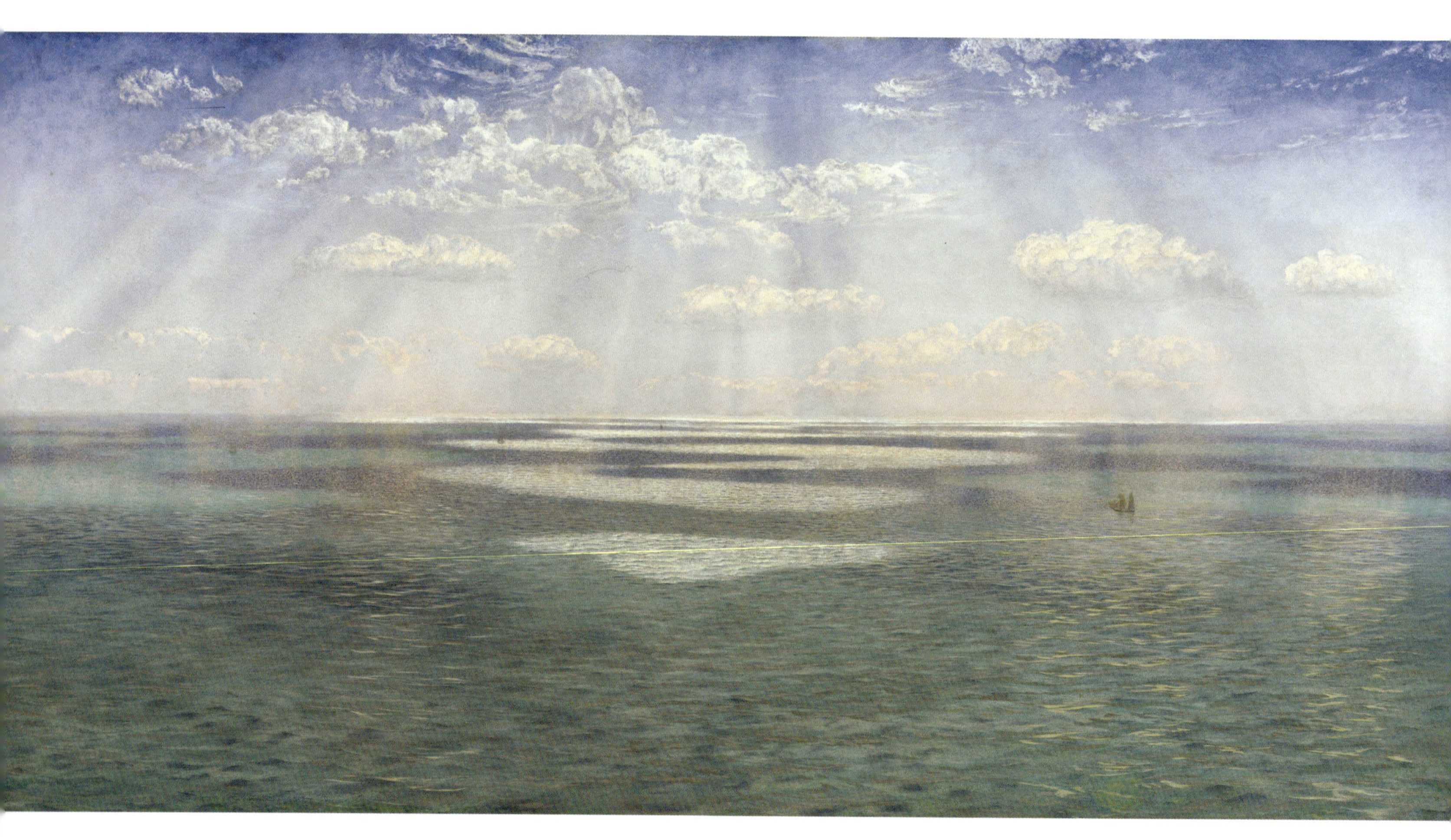

PLATE 8 · *The British Channel seen from the Dorsetshire Cliffs* · John Brett
oil on canvas · 106 x 212.5 cm · 1871 Autumn Exhibition no. 113
Tate · © Tate, London 2019

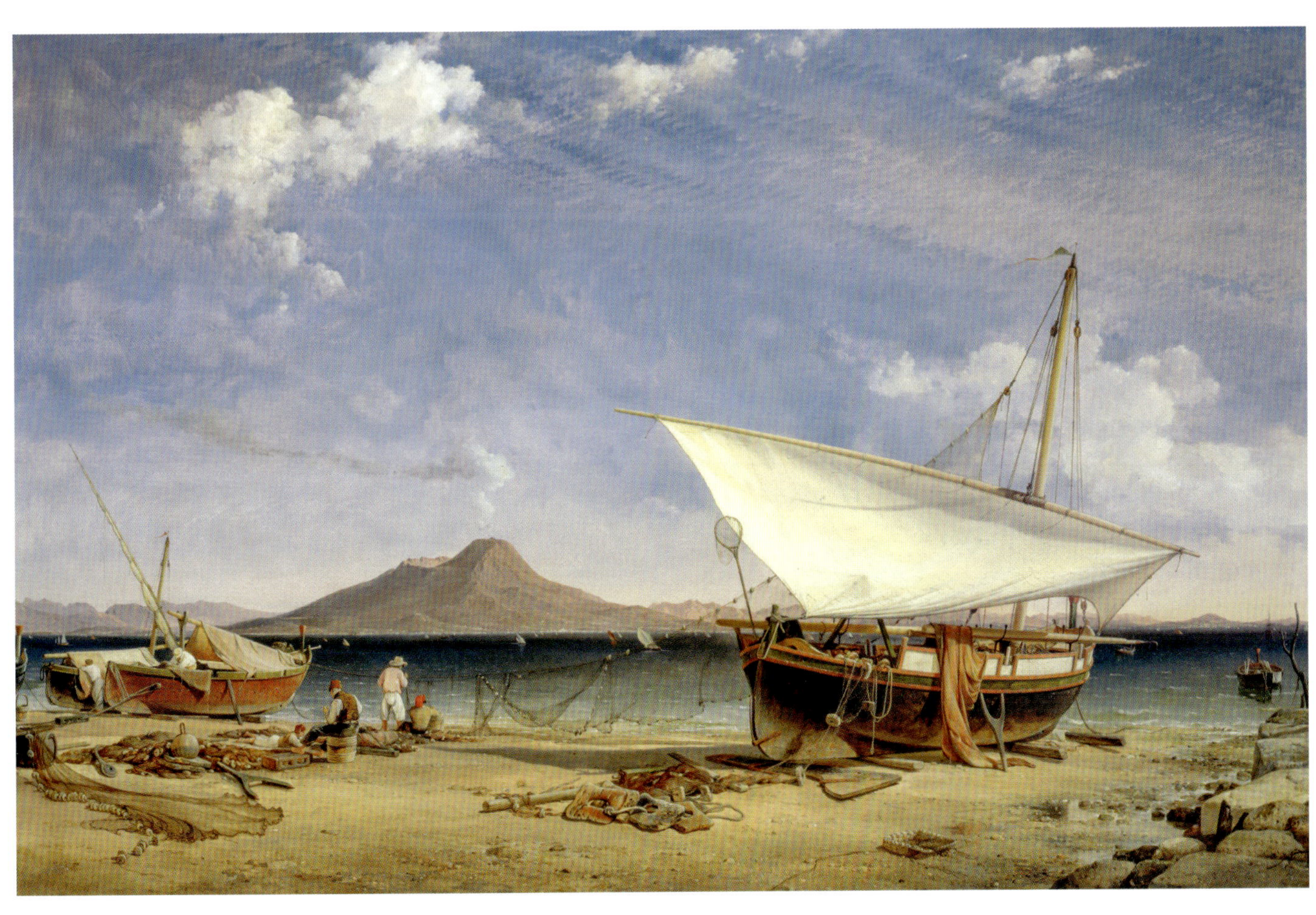

PLATE 9 · *Mending Nets, Bay of Naples* · E.W. Cooke
oil on canvas · 89.5 x 136.5 cm · 1871 Autumn Exhibition no. 336
private collection · photograph courtesy Richard Green Gallery, London

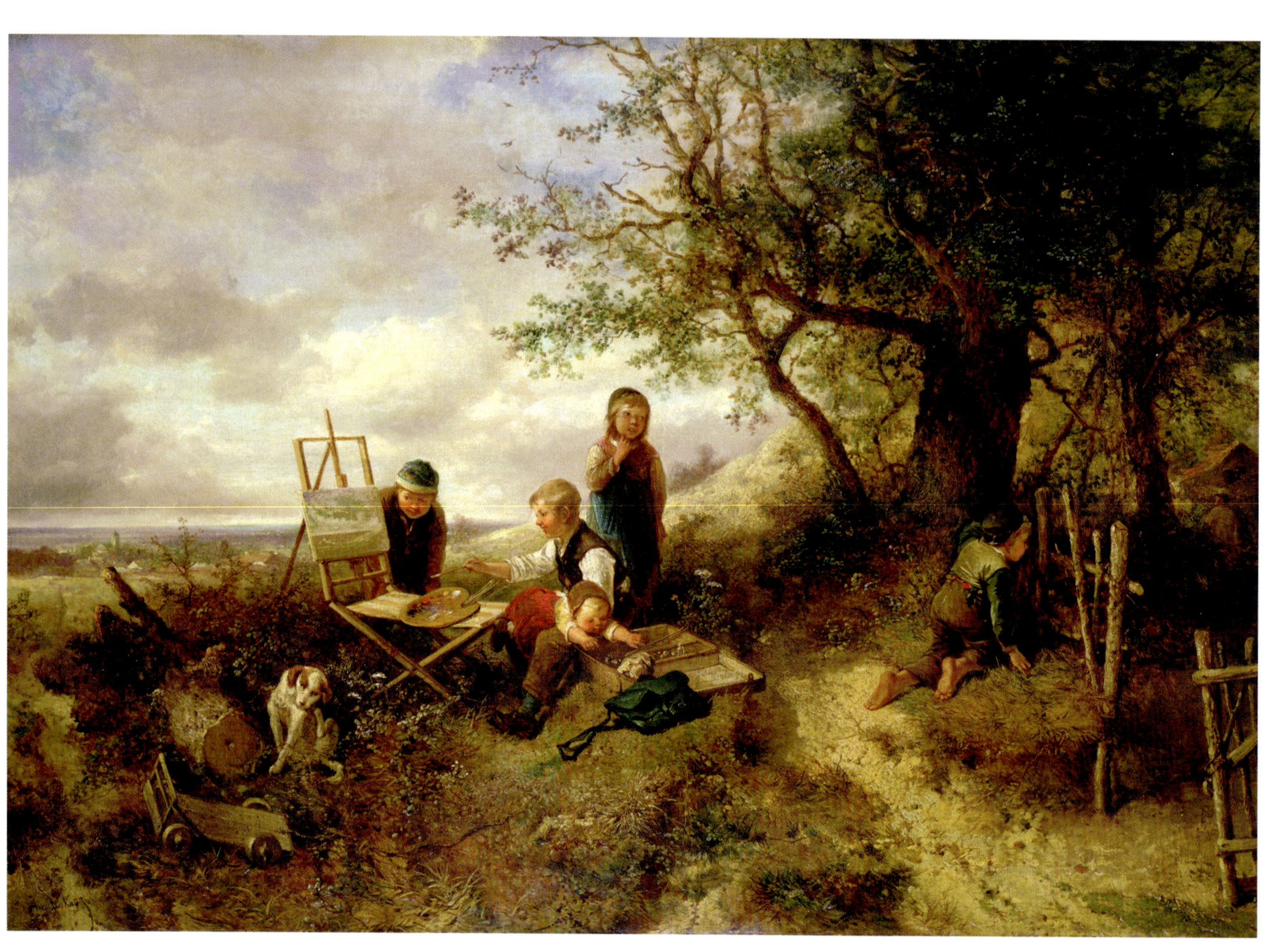

PLATE 10 · *The Absence of the Painter* · Mari Ten Kate
oil on canvas · 64.5 x 94 cm · 1871 Autumn Exhibition no. 115
private collection · photograph © Christie's Images/Bridgeman Images

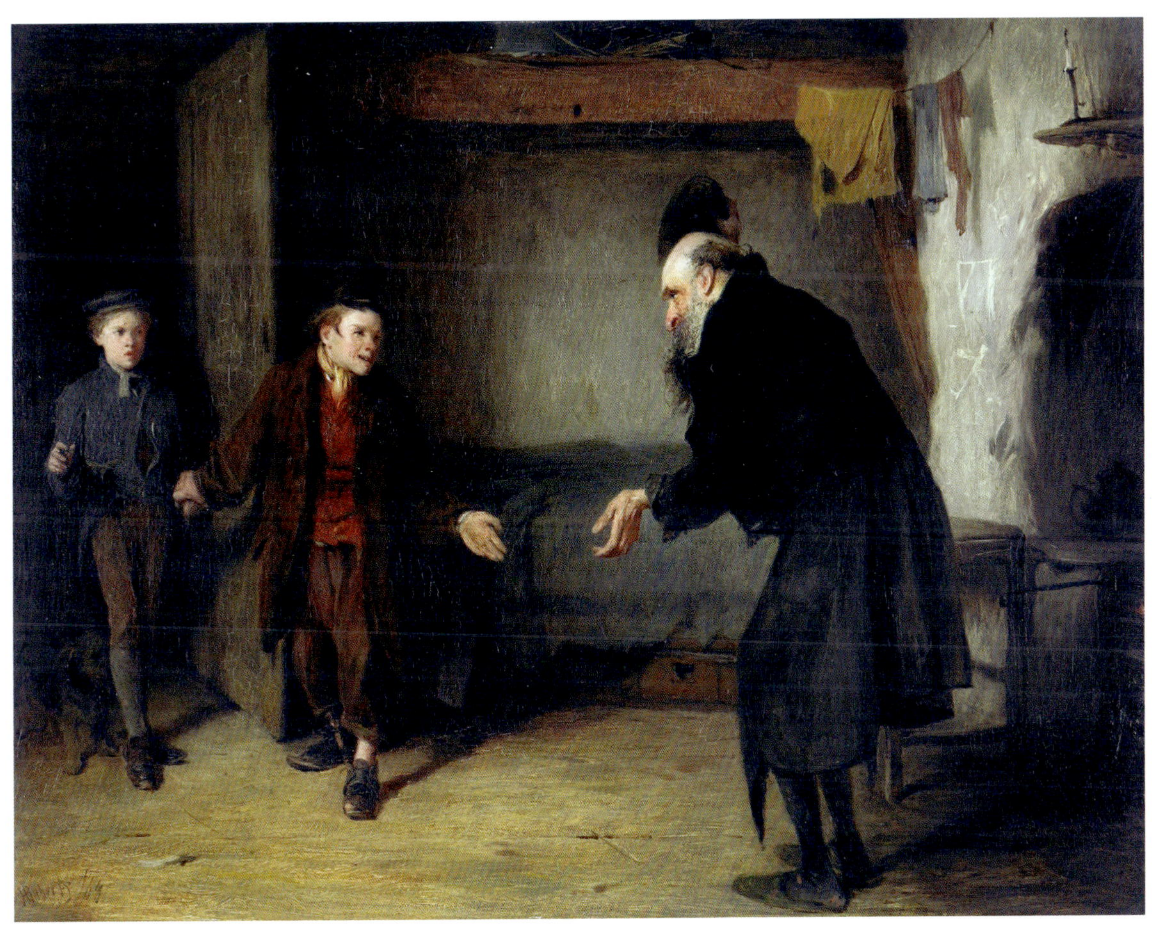

PLATE 11 · *Oliver Twist – First Introduction to Fagin* · Henry Benjamin Roberts
oil on board · 35.5 x 45.5 cm · 1871 Autumn Exhibition no. 280
National Museums Liverpool (Walker Art Gallery)

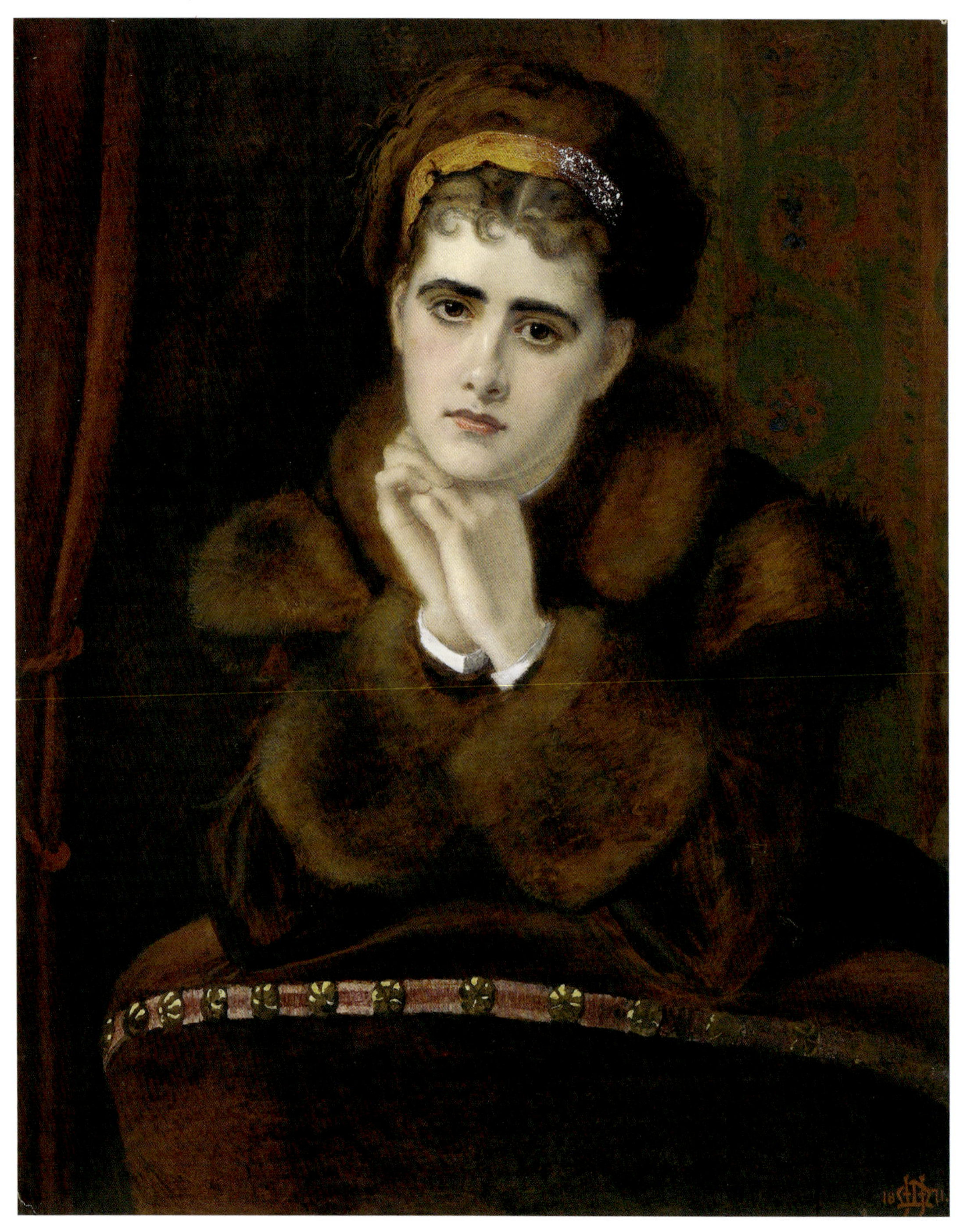

PLATE 12 · *"Sweet eyes of starry tenderness"* · **J.M. Jopling**
watercolour on paper · 73.5 x 58.5 cm · 1871 Autumn Exhibition no. 638
National Museums Liverpool (Walker Art Gallery)

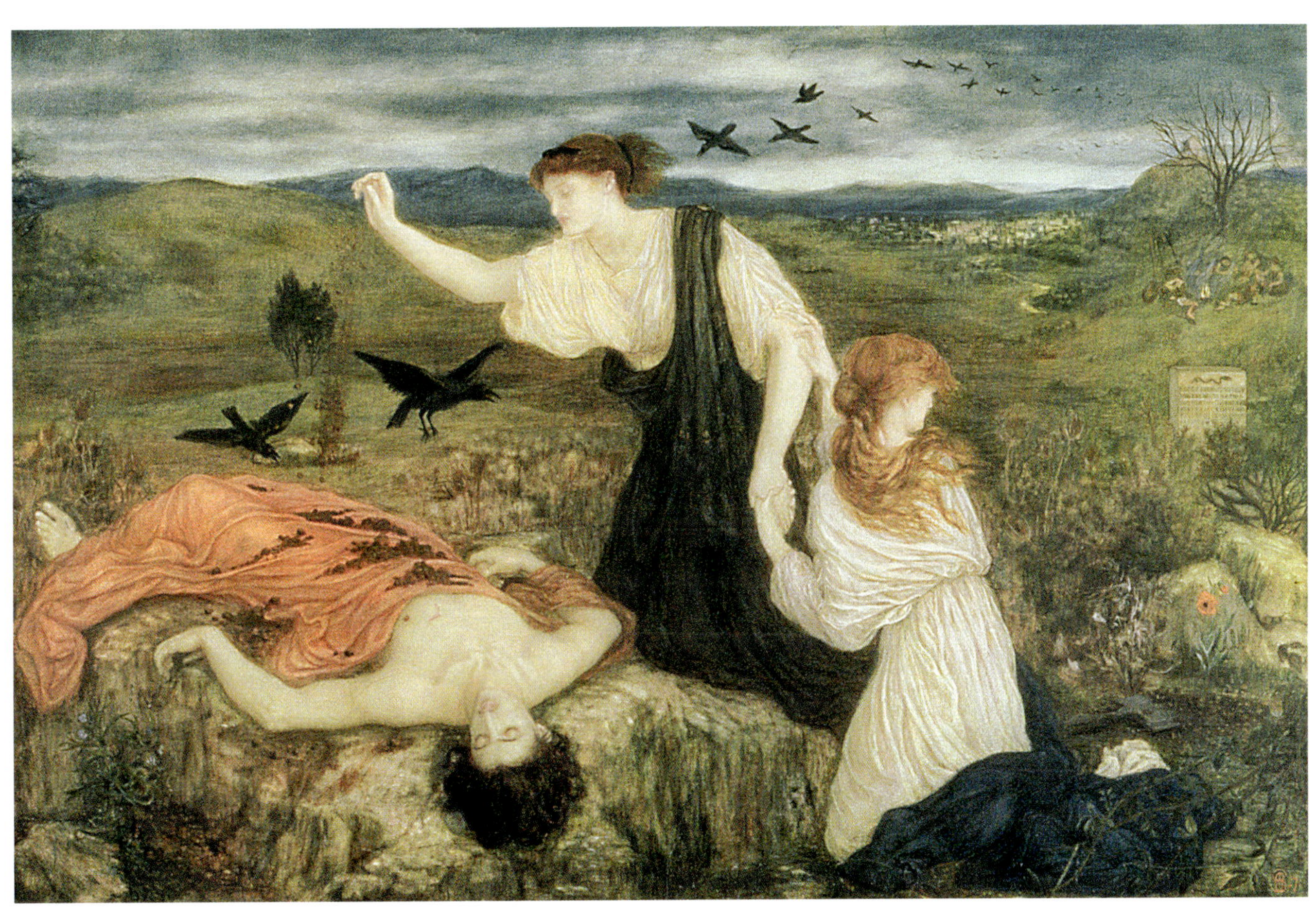

PLATE 13 · *Antigone* · Marie Spartali Stillman
gouache and watercolour[?] on paper · dimensions unrecorded · 1871 Autumn Exhibition no. 658
Simon Carter Gallery, Woodbridge, Suffolk, UK / Bridgeman Images

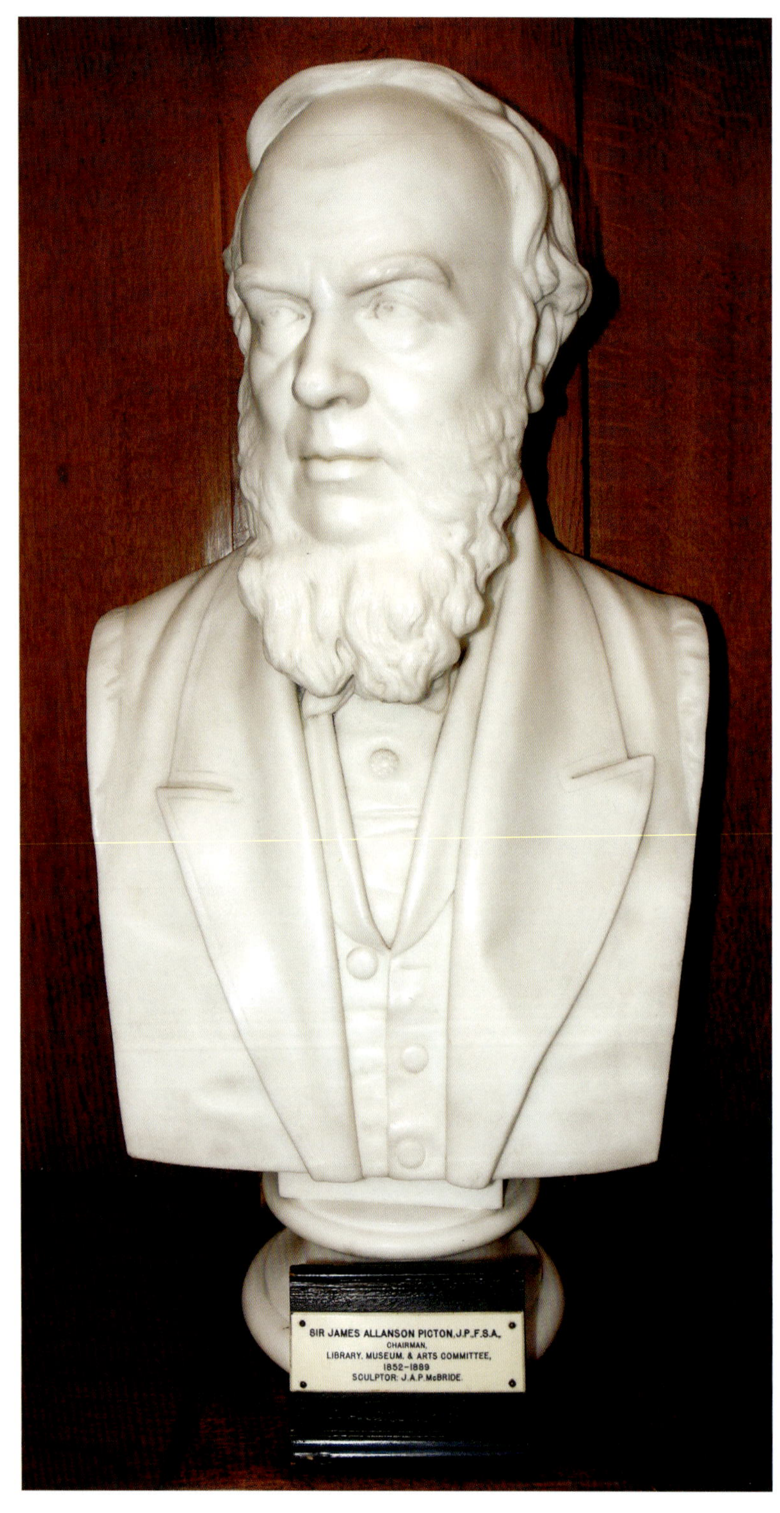

PLATE 14 · *James Allanson Picton* · J.A.P. Macbride
marble · 69.5 cm high (including socle) · 1871 Autumn Exhibition no. 901
Liverpool City Council (Liverpool Central Library)

		No. of artists	Oils	Works on paper	Sculpture	Total no. of works
Liverpool	Men	30	38	42	5	85
	Women	4	4	5	–	9
	Not known	27	19	24	3	46
	Total	61	61	71	8	140
Birkenhead	Men	3	2	4	–	6
	Women	2	4	2	–	6
	Not known	1	–	1	–	1
	Total	6	6	7	–	13
Chester	Men	2	3	6	–	9
	Women	1	–	2	–	2
	Not known	3	2	4	–	6
	Total	6	5	12	–	17
Wirral excluding Birkenhead	Men	–	–	–	–	–
	Women	–	–	–	–	–
	Not known	1	1	–	–	1
	Total	1	1	–	–	1
Manchester	Men	–	–	–	–	–
	Women	2	2	1	–	3
	Not known	4	2	4	–	6
	Total	6	4	5	–	9
Lancashire excluding Manchester	Men	7	9	11	–	20
	Women	2	–	5	–	5
	Not known	3	1	3	–	4
	Total	12	10	19	–	29
N.W. England excluding Lancashire and Wirral	Men	–	–	–	–	–
	Women	–	–	–	–	–
	Not known	–	–	–	–	–
	Total	–	–	–	–	–
North Wales	Men	1	1	3	–	4
	Women	1	–	1	–	1
	Not known	2	1	3	–	4
	Total	4	2	7	–	9
Edinburgh	Men	9	6	8	1	15
	Women	2	2	1	–	3
	Not known	–	–	–	–	–
	Total	11	8	9	1	18
The rest of Scotland and Ireland	Men	–	–	–	–	–
	Women	–	–	–	–	–
	Not known	1	–	2	–	2
	Total	1	–	2	–	2
Birmingham	Men	4	12	2	–	14
	Women	–	–	–	–	–
	Not known	8	16	7	–	23
	Total	12	28	9	–	37
South of England	Men	12	10	15	–	25
	Women	6	3	7	–	10
	Not known	5	4	4	–	8
	Total	23	17	26	–	43
West of England	Men	3	4	3	–	7
	Women	3	2	5	–	7
	Not known	3	4	–	–	4
	Total	9	10	8	–	18

		No. of artists	Oils	Works on paper	Sculpture	Total no. of works
East Anglia and The Midlands	Men	2	–	4	–	4
	Women	7	1	12	–	13
	Not known	3	6	–	–	6
	Total	12	7	16	–	23
N.E. England	Men	–	–	–	–	–
	Women	–	–	–	–	–
	Not known	4	2	4	–	6
	Total	4	2	4	–	6
Foreign addresses	Men	4	5	–	–	5
	Women	–	–	–	–	–
	Not known	–	–	–	–	–
	Total	4	5	–	–	5
No address	Men	14	9	10	–	19
	Women	4	2	4	–	6
	Not known	11	5	9	–	14
	Total	29	16	23	–	39
London: Hampstead	Men	6	6	4	–	10
	Women	1	–	5	–	5
	Not known	6	5	5	–	10
	Total	13	11	14	–	25
London: Haverstock Hill	Men	12	13	23	–	36
	Women	–	–	–	–	–
	Not known	2	–	4	–	4
	Total	14	13	27	–	40
London: St John's Wood	Men	16	12	22	–	34
	Women	2	–	4	–	4
	Not known	5	6	3	–	9
	Total	23	18	29	–	47
London: Kensington	Men	15	26	1	–	27
	Women	4	2	4	–	6
	Not known	12	12	7	–	19
	Total	31	40	12	–	52
London: Regent's Park	Men	4	7	4	–	11
	Women	2	–	3	–	3
	Not known	7	14	1	–	15
	Total	13	21	8	–	29
London: Fitzroy Square	Men	3	5	3	–	8
	Women	2	–	2	–	2
	Not known	4	6	4	–	10
	Total	9	11	9	–	20
The rest of inner London	Men	60	56	56	12	124
	Women	15	9	22	–	31
	Not known	59	62	44	–	106
	Total	134	127	122	12	261
London: suburbs	Men	3	3	6	–	9
	Women	3	–	4	–	4
	Not known	7	7	5	–	12
	Total	13	10	15	–	25
Grand totals	Men	211	227	227	18	472
	Women	63	31	89	–	120
	Not known	178	175	138	3	316
	Total	**451**	**433**	**454**	**21**	**908**

1872

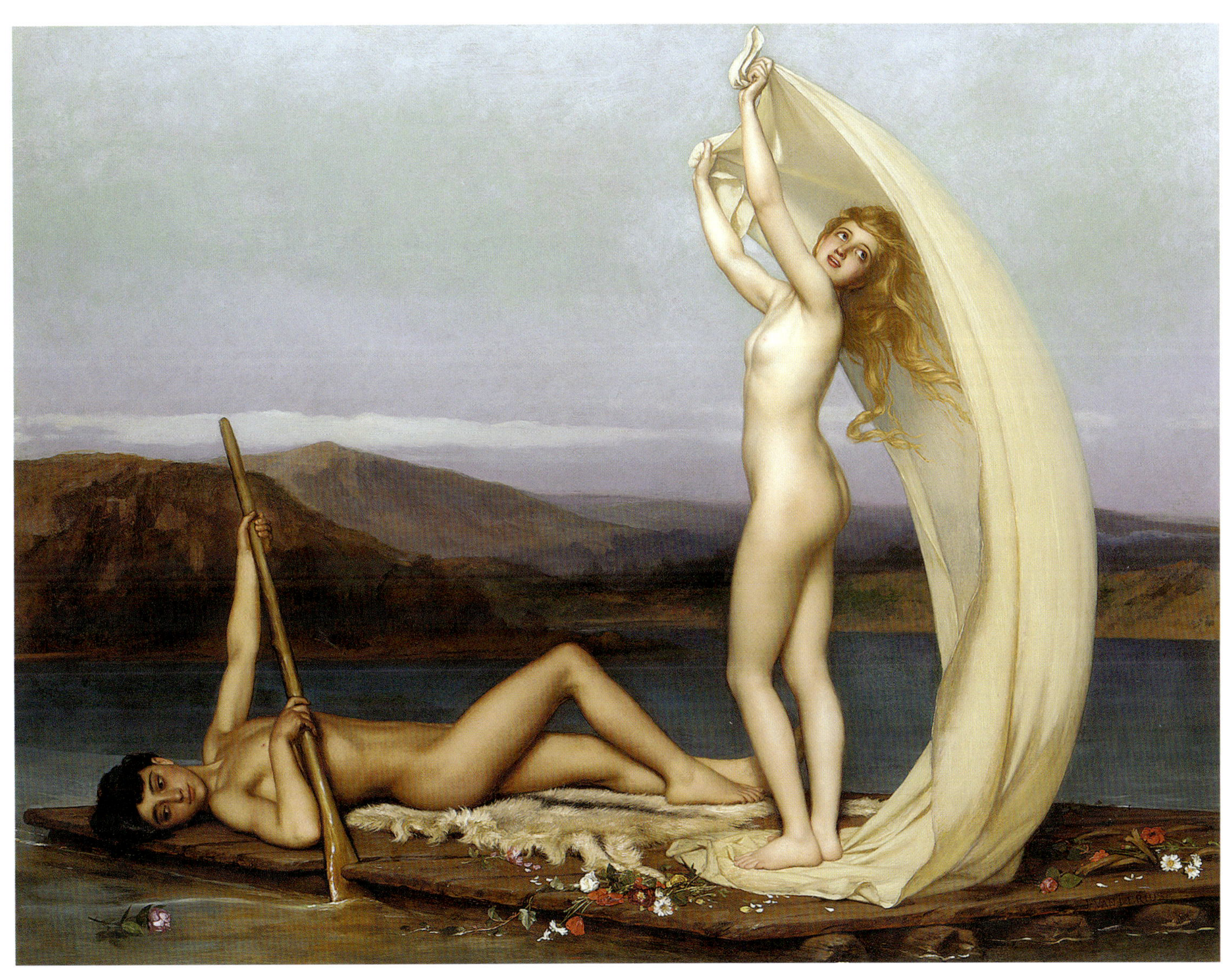

PLATE 15 · *The First Sail* · Josef Van Lerius

oil on panel · 120.5 x 159 cm · 1872 Autumn Exhibition no. 349

Christie's East, 30 October 2001 (lot 194) · © 2001 Christie's Images

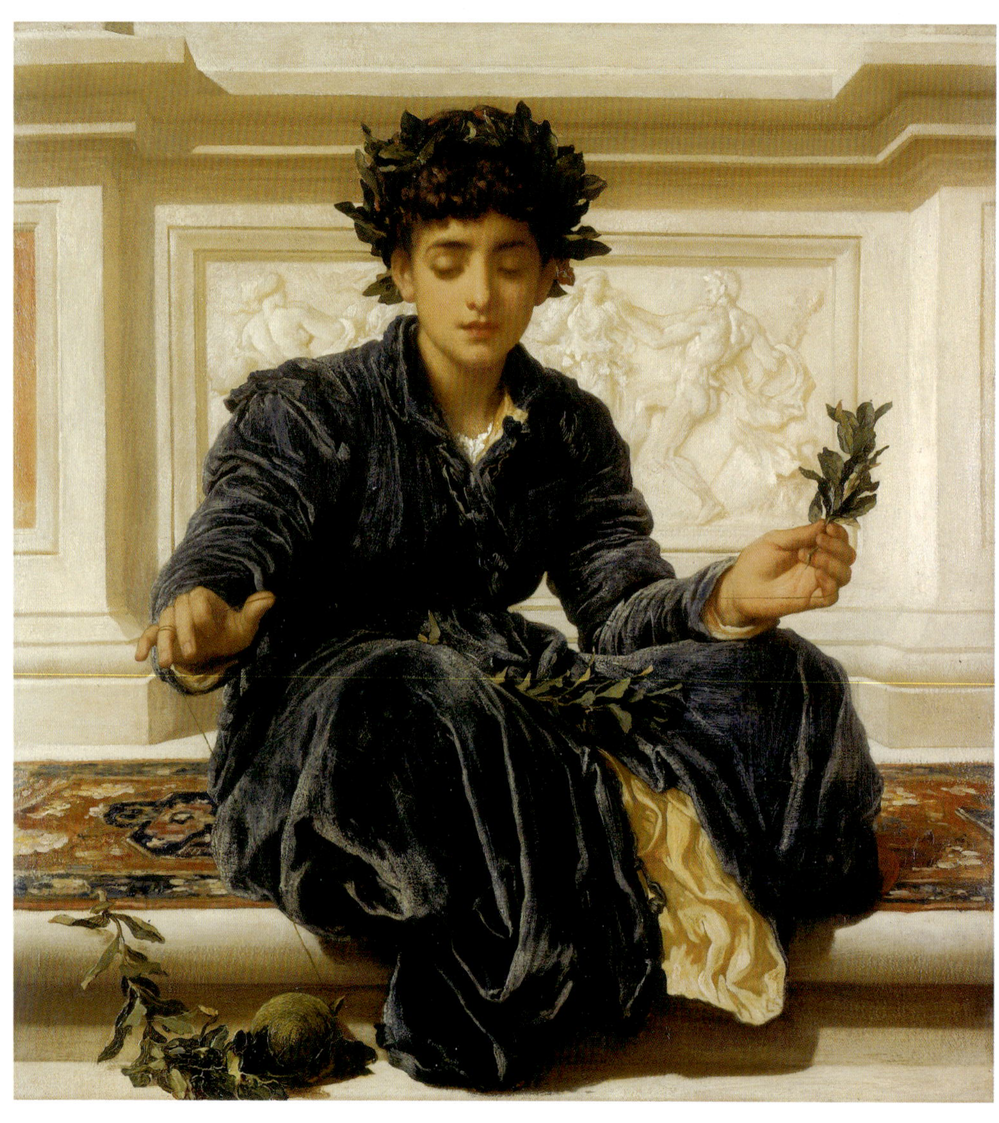

PLATE 16 · *Weaving the Wreath* · **Frederic Leighton**
oil on canvas · 63.5 x 60 cm · 1872 Autumn Exhibition no. 256
National Museums Liverpool (Sudley House)

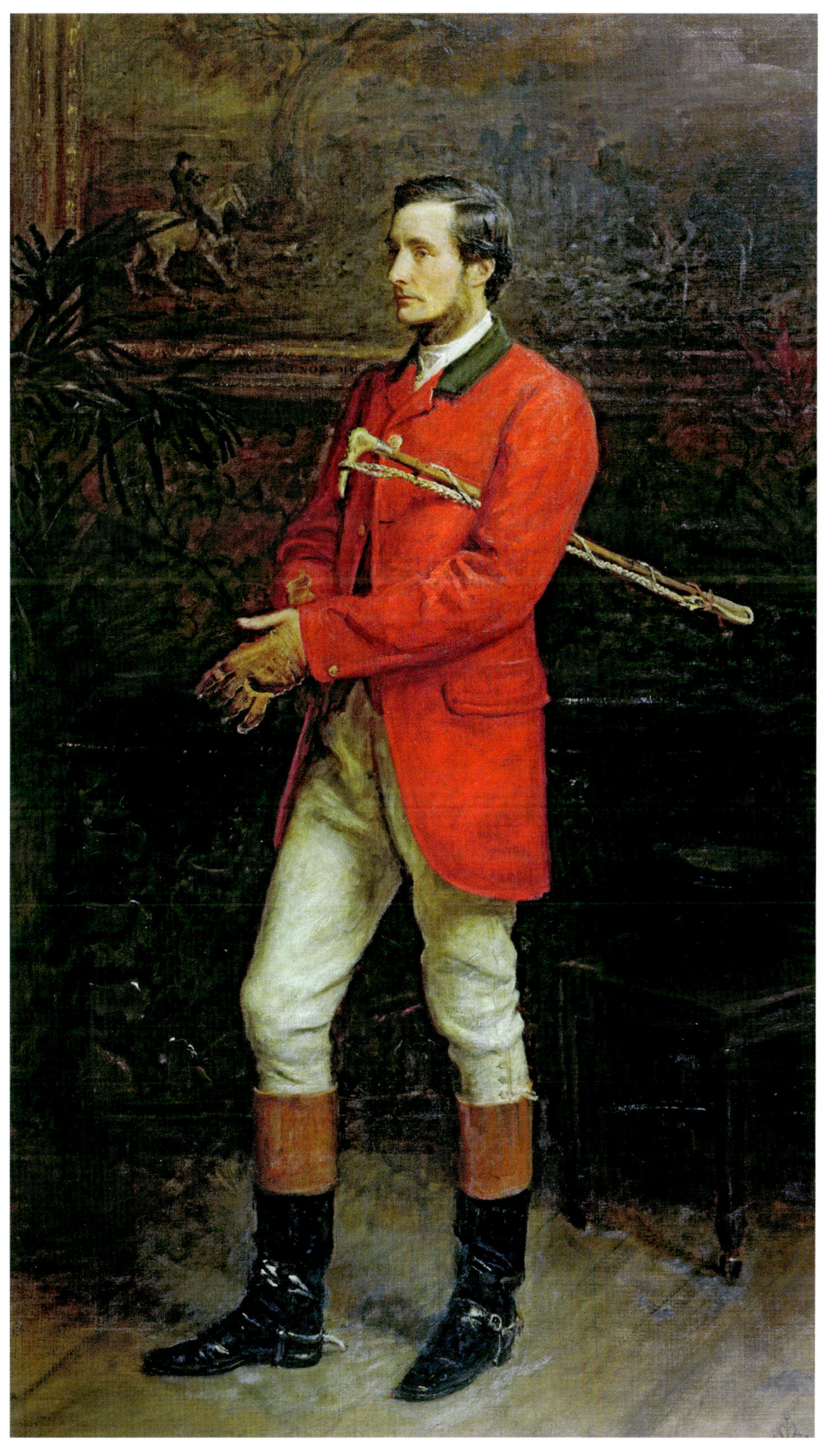

PLATE 17 · *Hugh Lupus Grosvenor, Marquis of Westminster, K.G.* · J.E. Millais
oil on canvas · 223.5 x 137 cm · 1872 Autumn Exhibition no. 290
private collection/Bridgeman Images

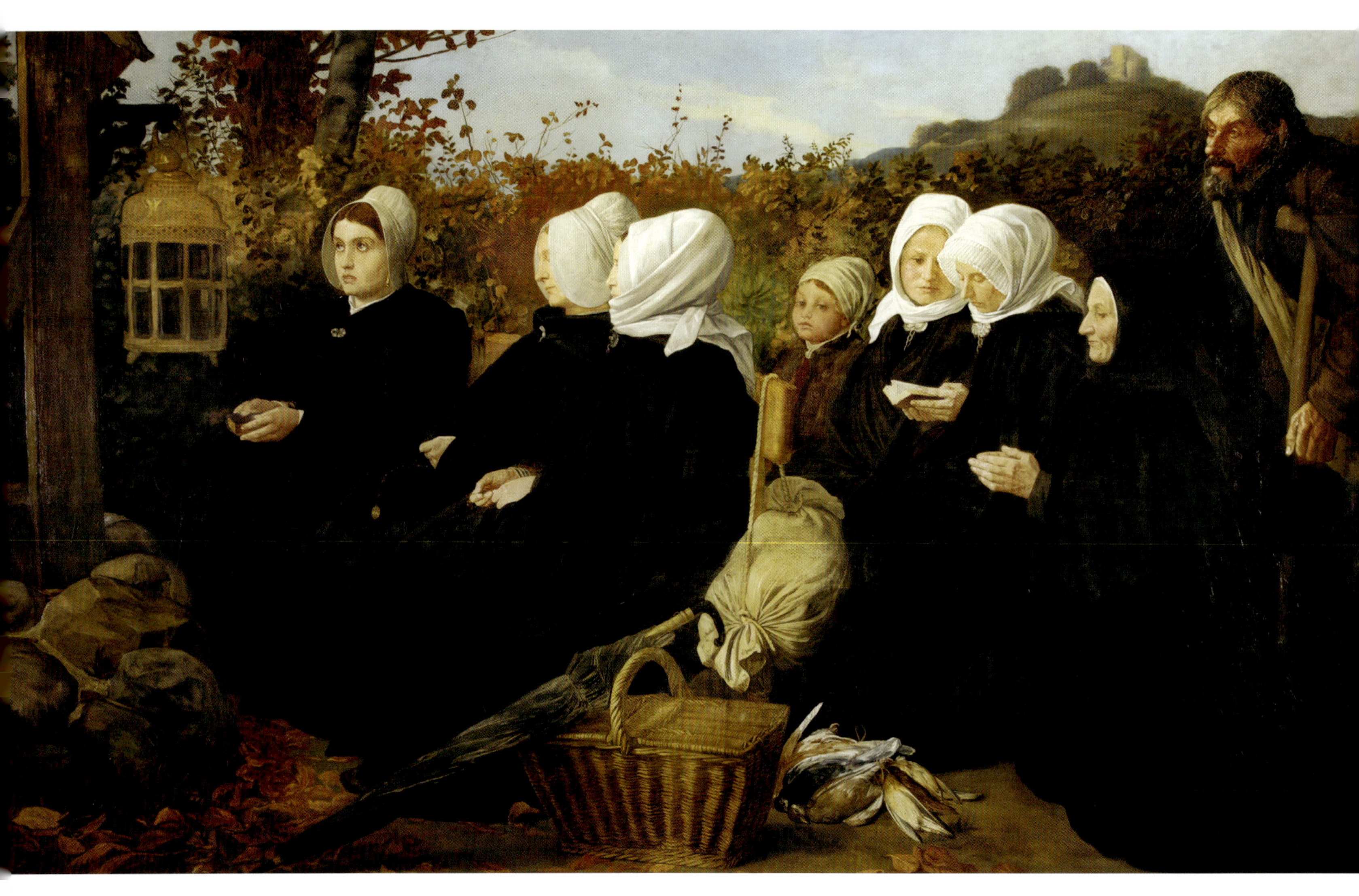

PLATE 18 · *The Pilgrimage* · **Alphonse Legros**
oil on canvas · 137.5 x 226 cm · 1872 Autumn Exhibition no. 54
National Museums Liverpool (Walker Art Gallery)

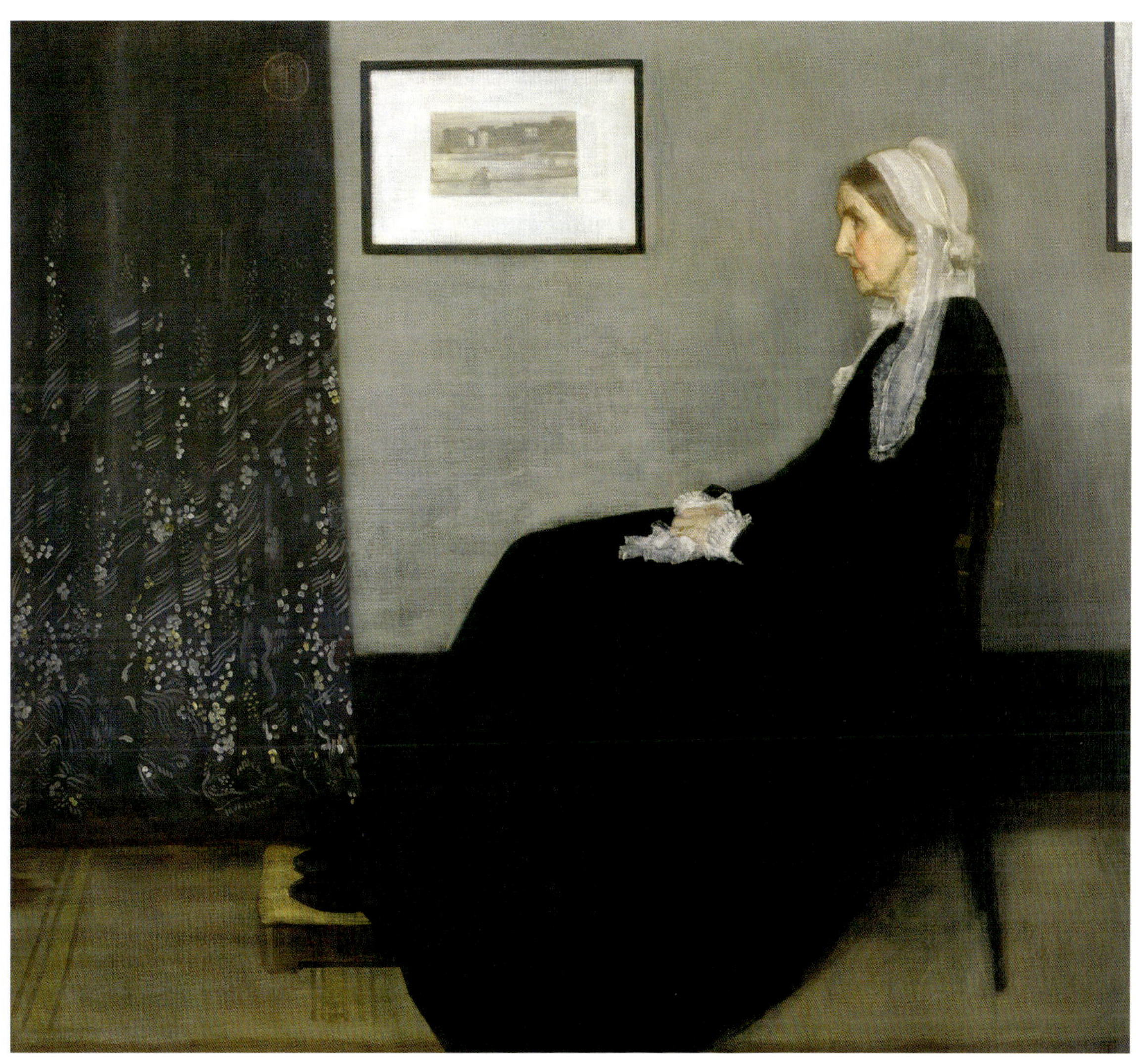

PLATE 19 · *Arrangement in Grey and Black – Portrait of the Painter's Mother* · J.A.M. Whistler
oil on canvas · 144.5 x 162.5 cm · 1872 Autumn Exhibition no. 221
Musée d'Orsay, Paris, France/Bridgeman Images

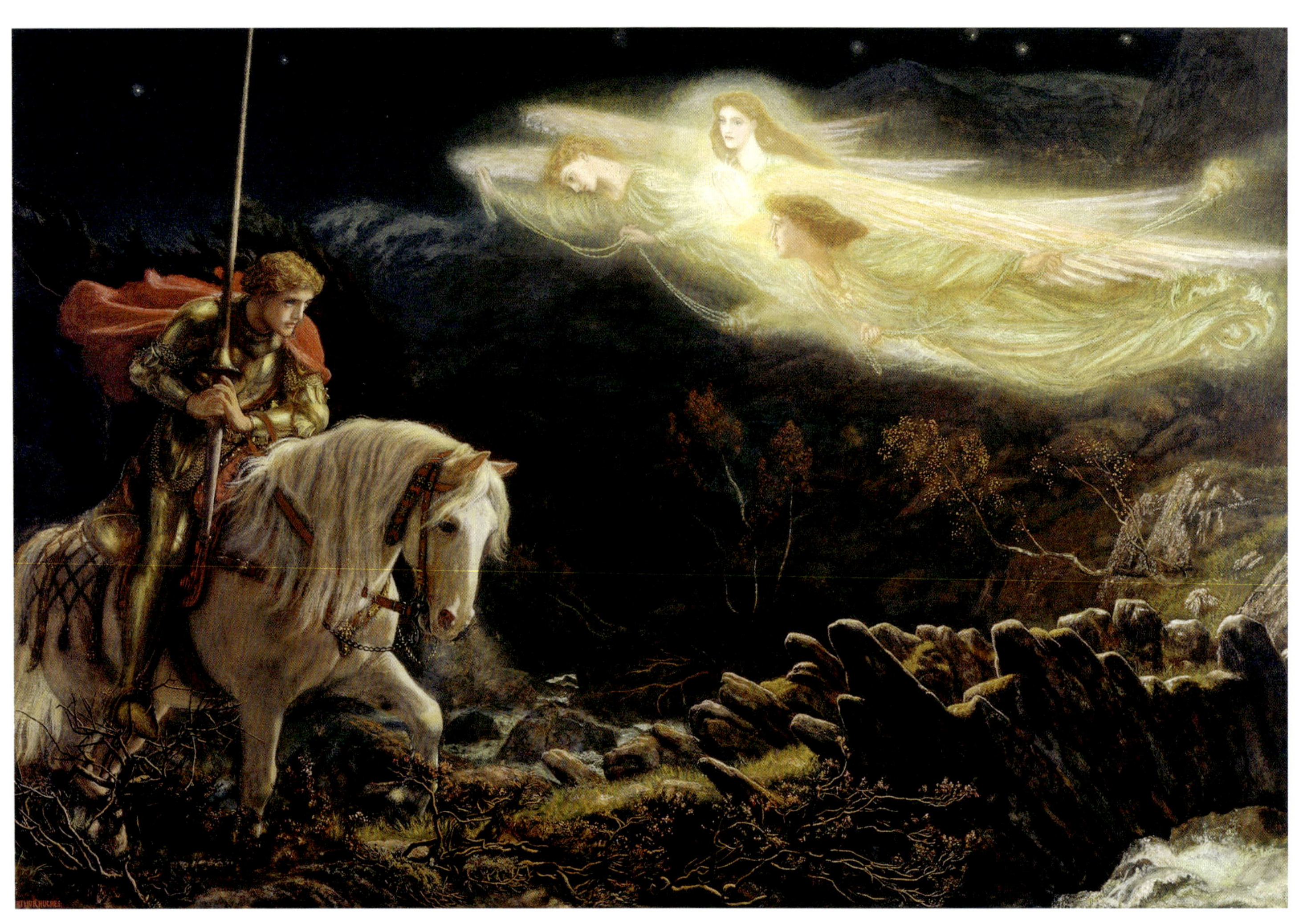

PLATE 20 · *Sir Galahad* · Arthur Hughes
oil on canvas · 113 x 167.5 cm · 1872 Autumn Exhibition no. 136
National Museums Liverpool (Walker Art Gallery)

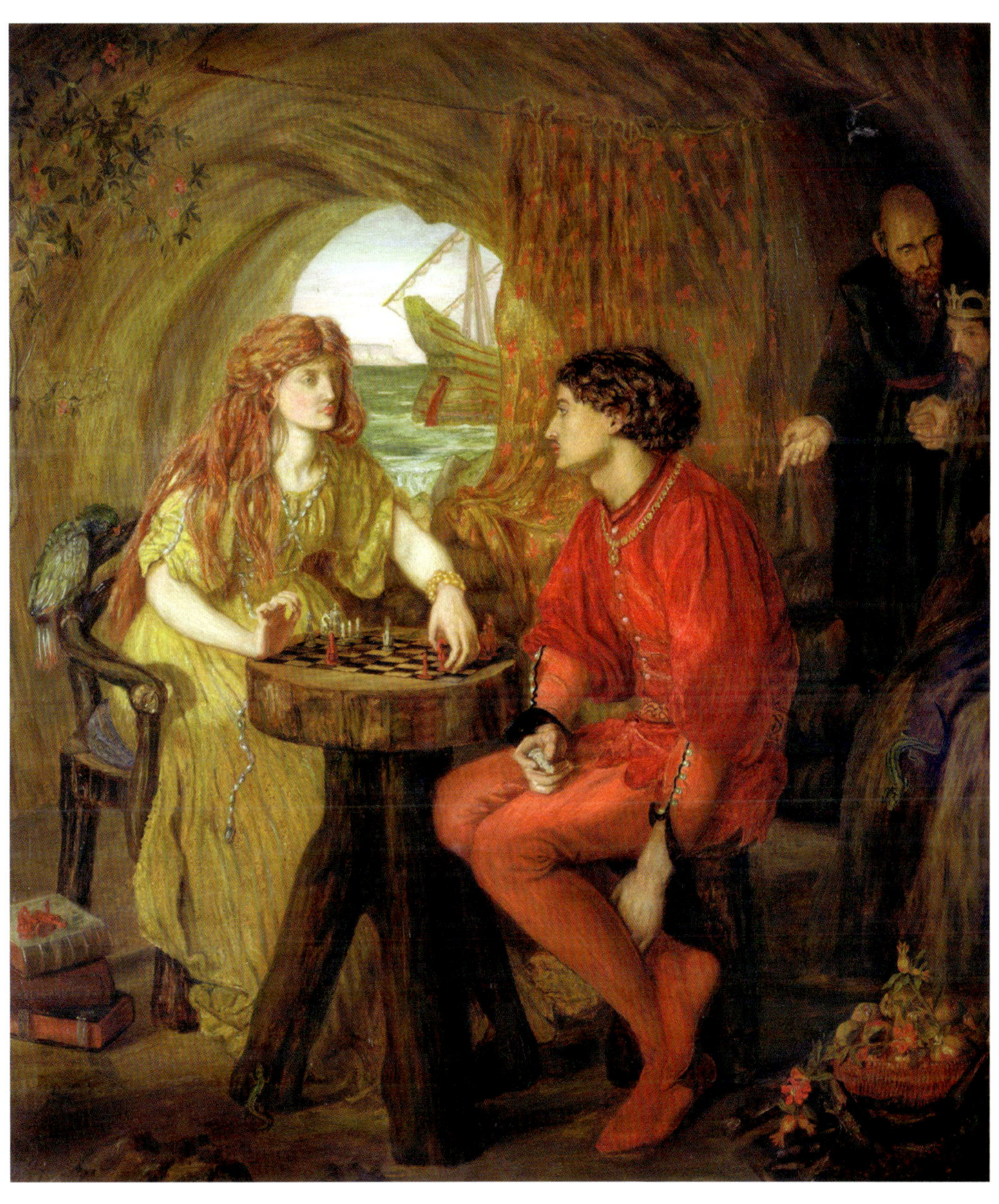

PLATE 21 · *Ferdinand and Miranda* · Lucy Madox Brown
oil on canvas · 68 x 61 cm · 1872 Autumn Exhibition no. 329
private collection/Bridgeman Images

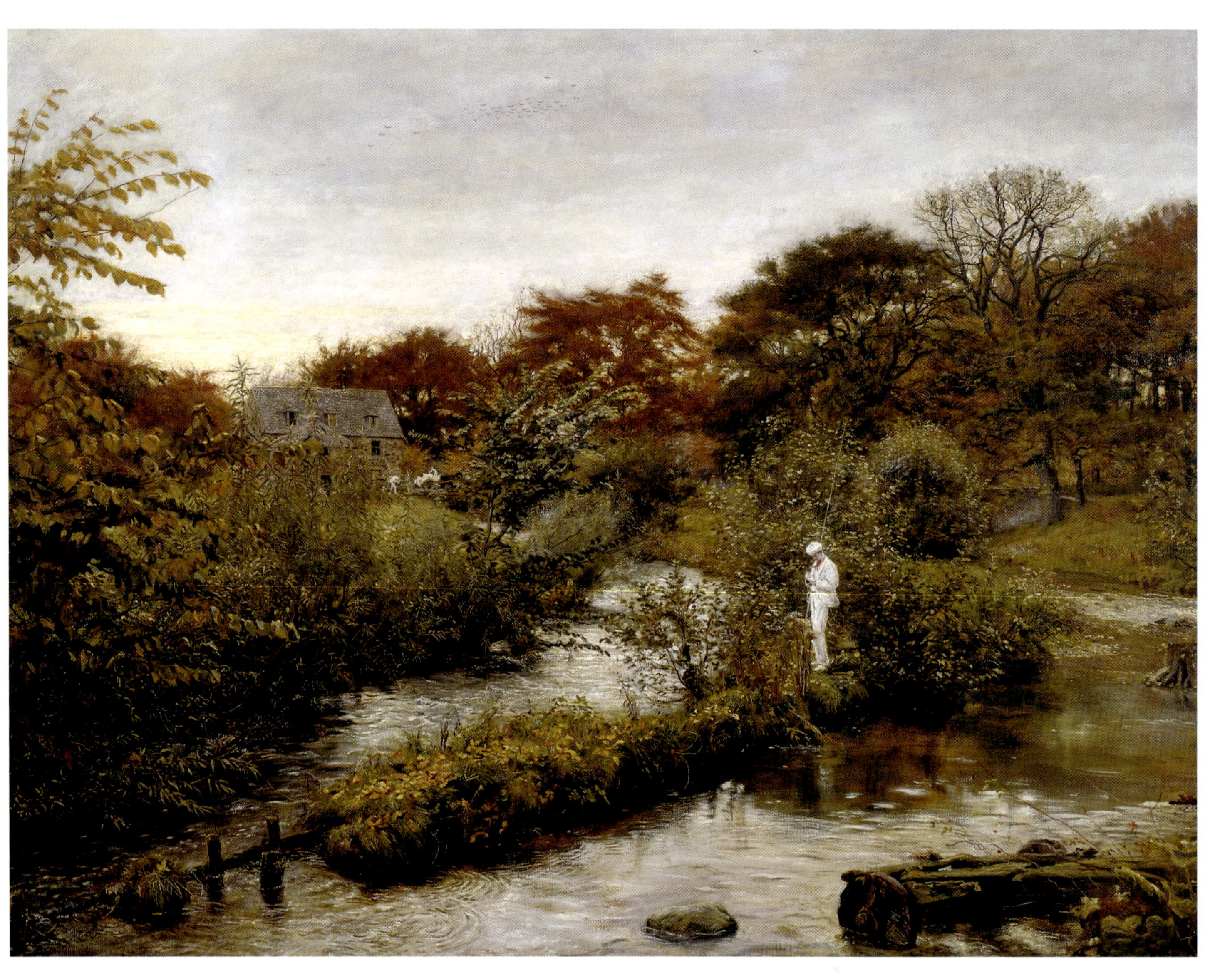

PLATE 22 · *Flowing to the River* · J.E. Millais
oil on canvas · 139.5 x 188 cm · 1872 Autumn Exhibition no. 206
private collection, on loan to Tate · © Tate, London 2019

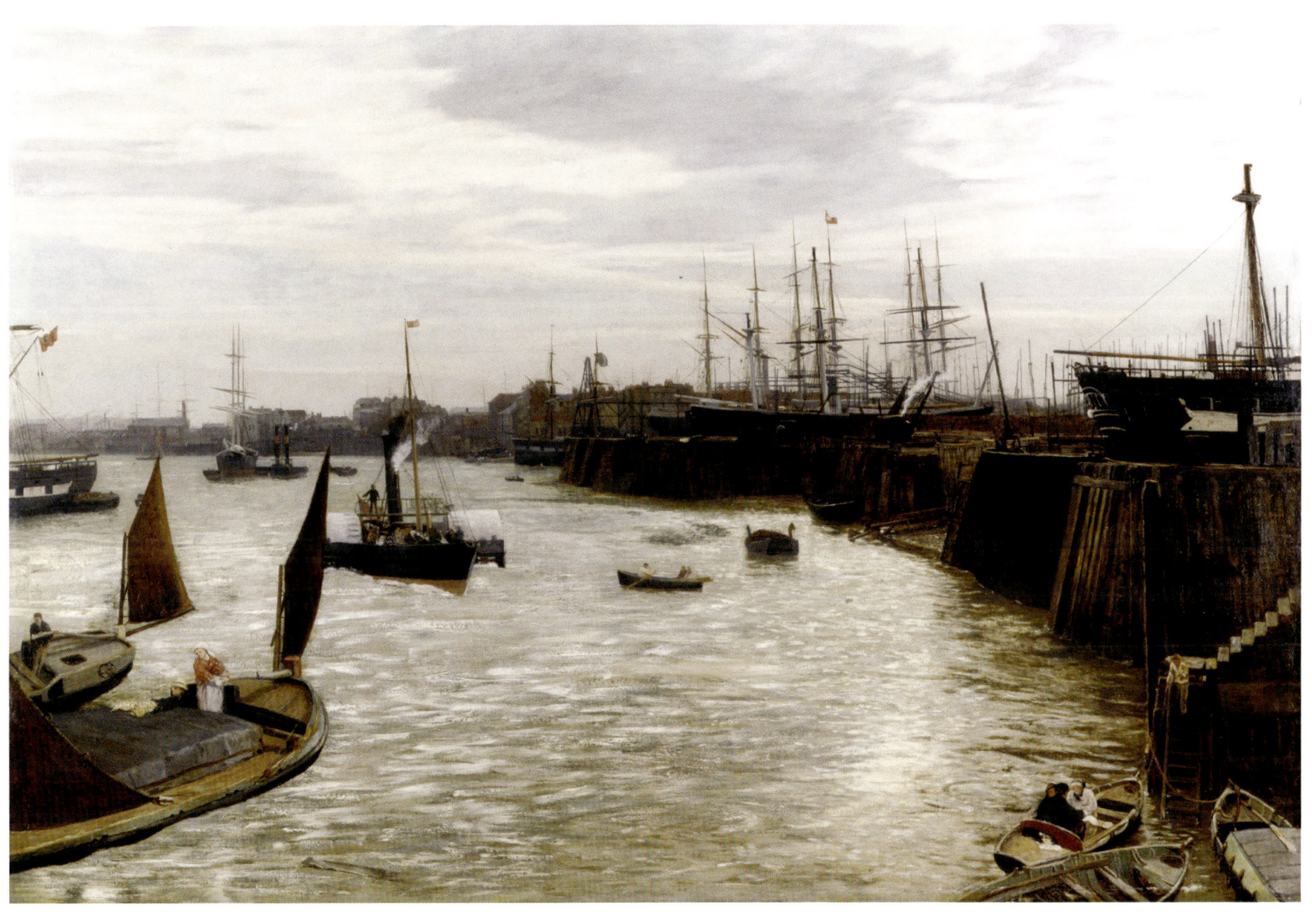

PLATE 23 · ***Blackwall*** · **Charles Napier Hemy**
oil on canvas · 106.5 x 183 cm · 1872 Autumn Exhibition no. 235
© Museum of London

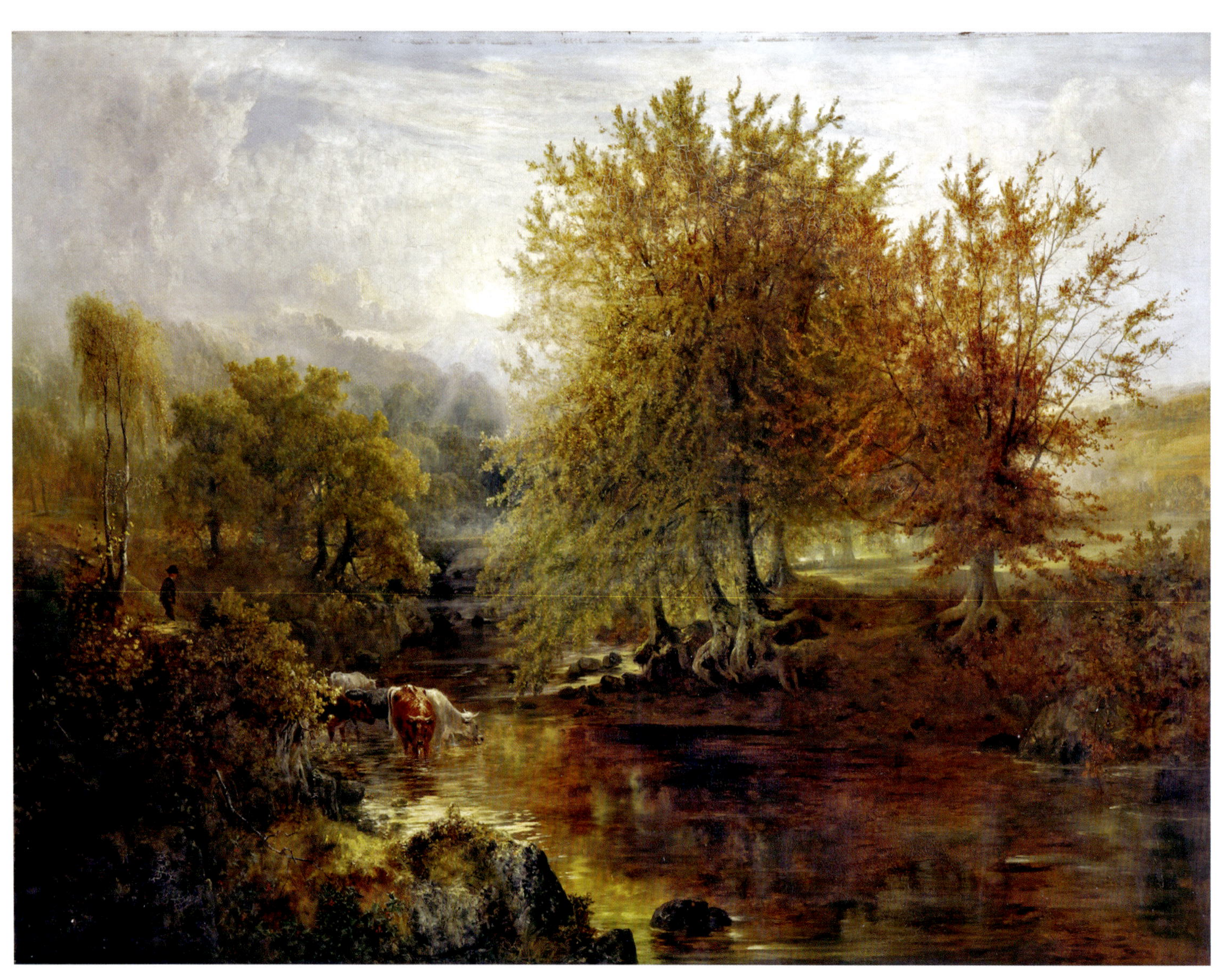

PLATE 24 · *A North Devon Glen – Autumn* · J.W. Oakes
oil on canvas · 124 x 167 cm · 1872 Autumn Exhibition no. 31
National Museums Liverpool (Walker Art Gallery)

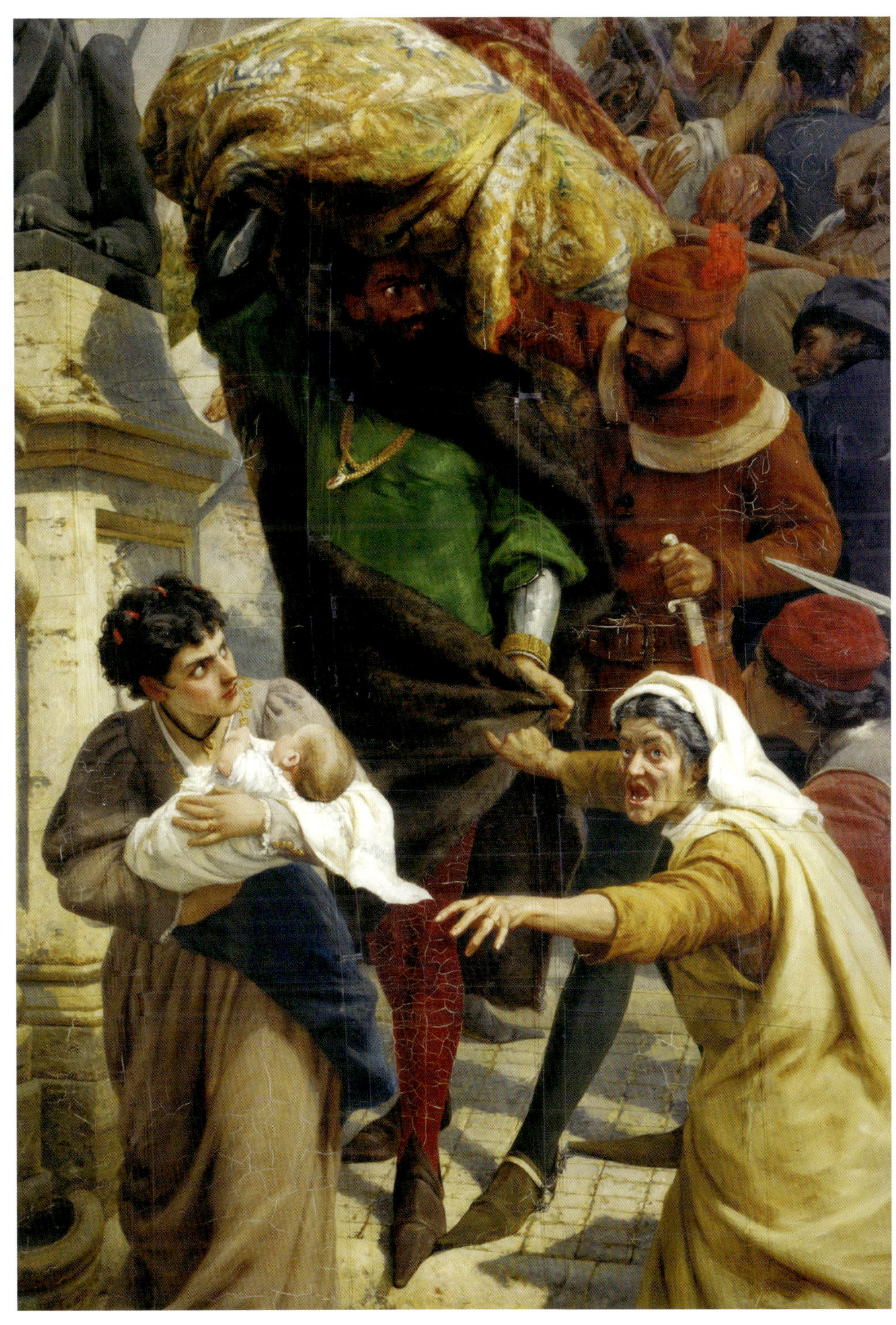

PLATE 25 · *The Fall of Rienzi, the Last Roman Tribune* · F.W.W. Topham
oil on canvas · 152.5 x 107.5 cm · 1872 Autumn Exhibition no. 188
National Museums Liverpool (Walker Art Gallery)

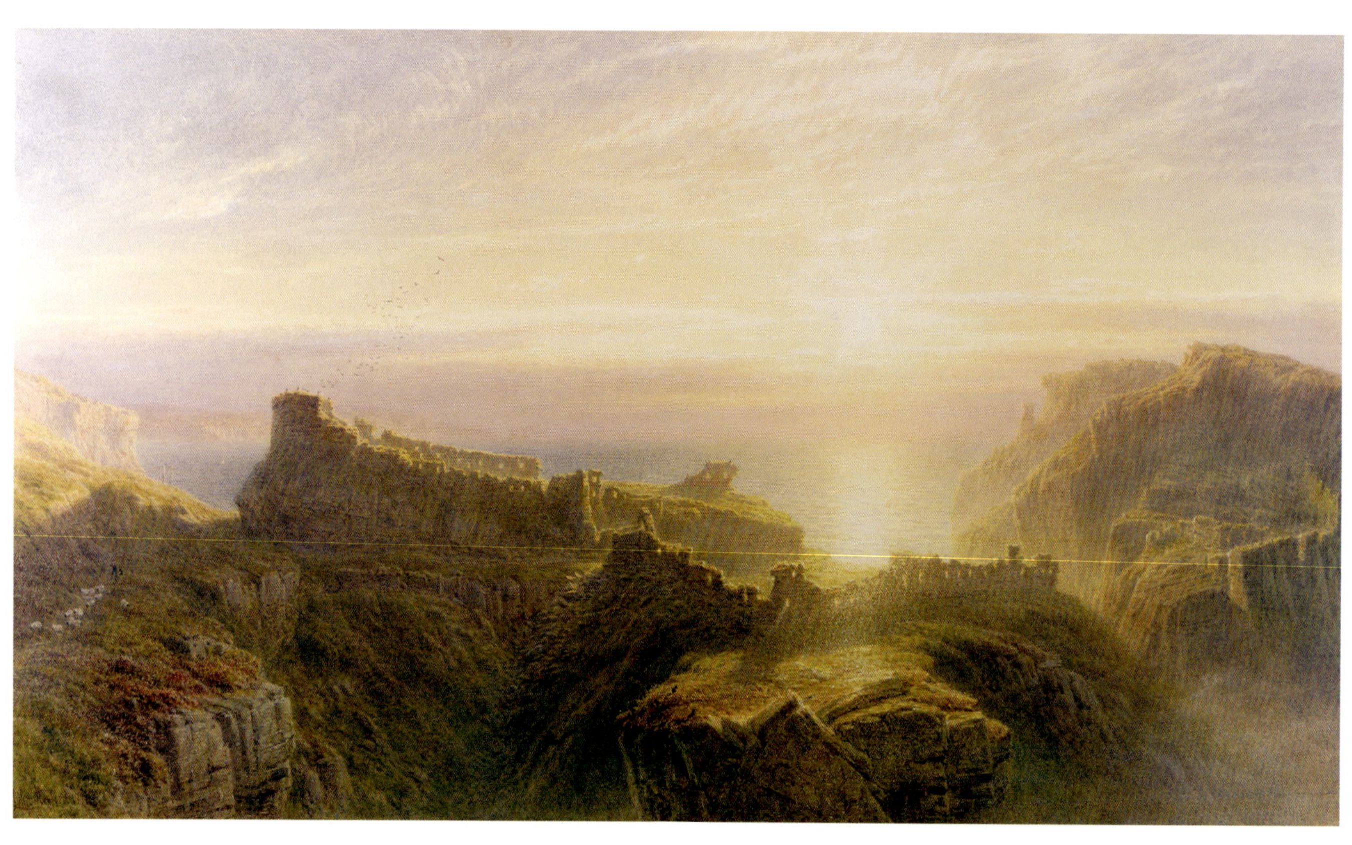

PLATE 26 · *King Arthur's Castle* · John Mogford
watercolour on paper · 44 x 75.5 cm · 1872 Autumn Exhibition no. 441
Croydon Art Collection, Museum of Croydon, UK/Bridgeman Images

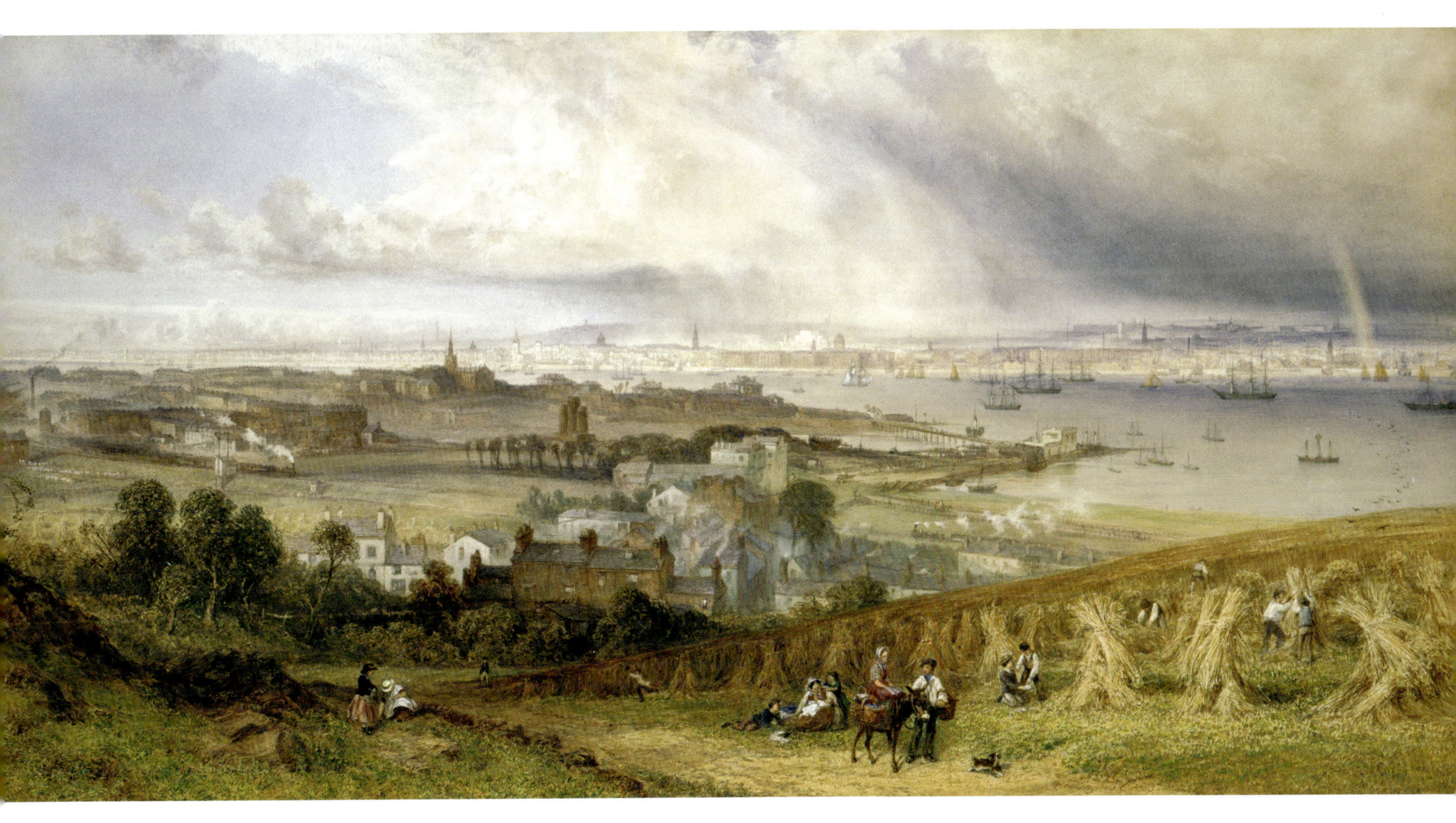

PLATE 27 · *Liverpool* · William Collingwood
watercolour on paper · 59.5 x 120 cm · 1872 Autumn Exhibition no. 635
National Museums Liverpool (Walker Art Gallery)

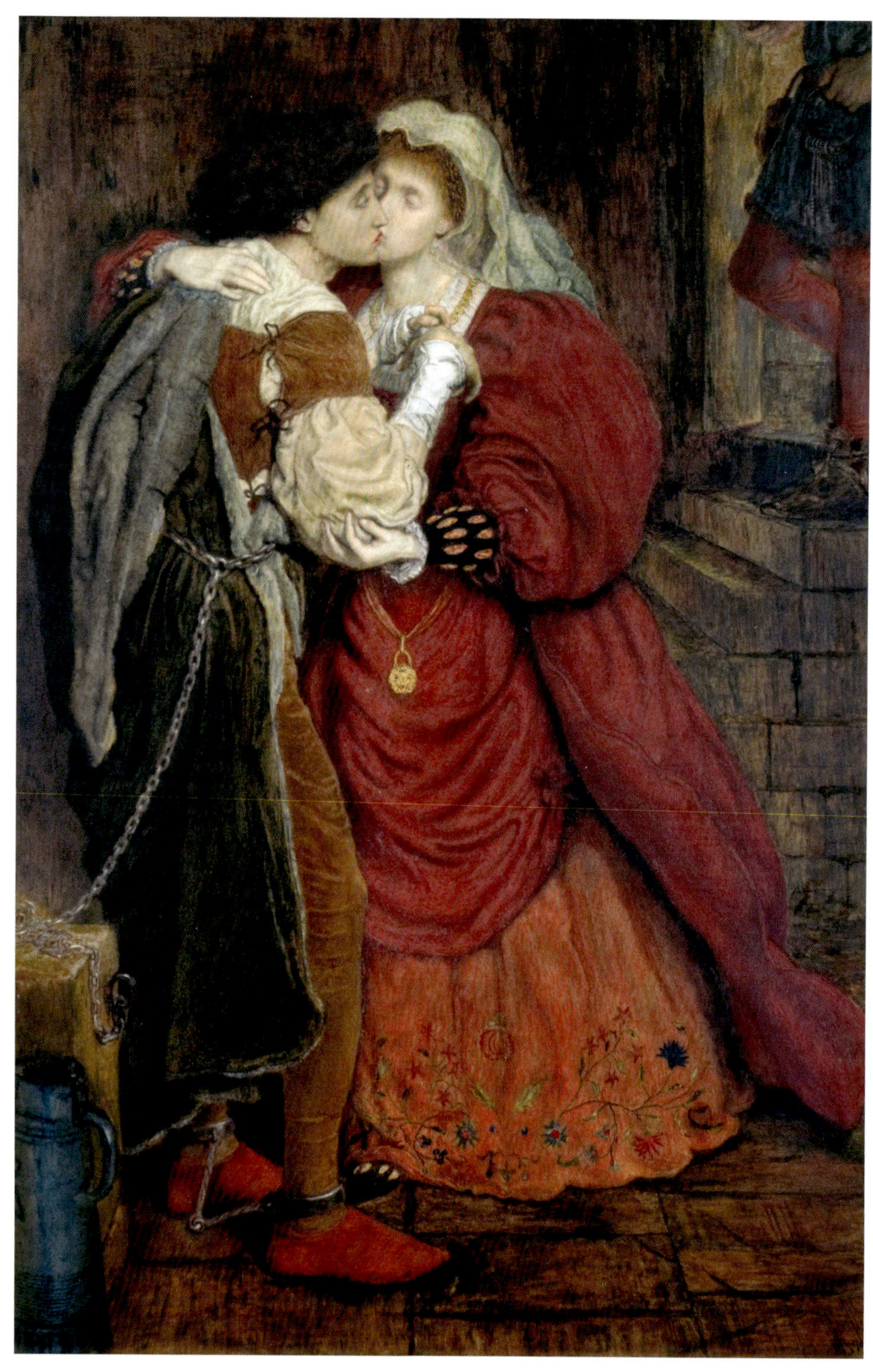

PLATE 28 · *Jacobo Foscari* · Ford Madox Brown
watercolour on paper · 94 x 61 cm · 1872 Autumn Exhibition no. 639
William Morris Gallery, London Borough of Waltham Forest

Paintings by numbers 1872

		No. of artists	Oils	Works on paper	Sculpture	Total no. of works
Liverpool	Men	31	27	64	6	97
	Women	8	5	11	–	16
	Not known	25	13	27	1	41
	Total	64	45	102	7	154
Birkenhead	Men	3	3	2	–	5
	Women	1	4	–	–	4
	Not known	3	2	3	–	5
	Total	7	9	5	–	14
Chester	Men	3	–	8	–	8
	Women	2	1	4	–	5
	Not known	1	–	2	–	2
	Total	6	1	14	–	15
Wirral excluding Birkenhead	Men	–	–	–	–	–
	Women	2	–	6	–	6
	Not known	1	1	1	–	2
	Total	3	1	7	–	8
Manchester	Men	4	2	2	–	4
	Women	2	2	–	–	2
	Not known	3	1	2	–	3
	Total	9	5	4	–	9
Lancashire excluding Manchester	Men	5	1	9	–	10
	Women	2	–	6	–	6
	Not known	3	1	3	–	4
	Total	10	2	18	–	20
N.W. England excluding Lancashire and Wirral	Men	2	2	–	–	2
	Women	–	–	–	–	–
	Not known	3	3	3	–	6
	Total	5	5	3	–	8
North Wales	Men	–	–	–	–	–
	Women	–	–	–	–	–
	Not known	5	1	8	–	9
	Total	5	1	8	–	9
Edinburgh	Men	12	16	7	–	23
	Women	1	2	–	–	2
	Not known	5	4	2	–	6
	Total	18	22	9	–	31
The rest of Scotland and Ireland	Men	2	5	–	–	5
	Women	–	–	–	–	–
	Not known	1	1	–	–	1
	Total	3	6	–	–	6
Birmingham	Men	6	9	9	–	18
	Women	1	–	2	–	2
	Not known	7	9	4	–	13
	Total	14	18	15	–	33
South of England	Men	12	19	10	–	29
	Women	2	1	4	–	5
	Not known	6	6	3	–	9
	Total	20	26	17	–	43
West of England	Men	2	4	–	–	4
	Women	2	–	6	–	6
	Not known	6	7	3	–	10
	Total	10	11	9	–	20
East Anglia and The Midlands	Men	3	2	1	–	3
	Women	2	1	7	–	8
	Not known	4	3	1	–	4
	Total	9	6	9	–	15
N.E. England	Men	3	4	–	–	4
	Women	2	1	1	–	2
	Not known	4	2	10	–	12
	Total	9	7	11	–	18
Foreign addresses	Men	6	9	–	–	9
	Women	–	–	–	–	–
	Not known	1	1	–	–	1
	Total	7	10	–	–	10
No address	Men	21	14	7	2	23
	Women	6	6	3	–	9
	Not known	21	7	27	–	34
	Total	48	27	37	2	66
London: Hampstead	Men	7	5	6	–	11
	Women	2	–	2	–	2
	Not known	3	2	6	–	8
	Total	12	7	14	–	21
London: Haverstock Hill	Men	9	6	17	–	23
	Women	2	–	3	–	3
	Not known	3	1	4	–	5
	Total	14	7	24	–	31
London: St John's Wood	Men	7	7	4	–	11
	Women	–	–	–	–	–
	Not known	9	9	10	–	19
	Total	16	16	14	–	30
London: Kensington	Men	17	26	6	–	32
	Women	6	3	6	–	9
	Not known	7	8	5	–	13
	Total	30	37	17	–	54
London: Regent's Park	Men	6	7	3	–	10
	Women	2	–	6	–	6
	Not known	4	6	1	–	7
	Total	12	13	10	–	23
London: Fitzroy Square	Men	6	1	9	–	10
	Women	2	1	4	–	5
	Not known	3	1	10	–	11
	Total	11	3	23	–	26
The rest of inner London	Men	73	79	68	6	153
	Women	17	10	25	–	35
	Not known	48	51	41	–	92
	Total	138	140	134	6	280
London: suburbs	Men	2	4	–	–	4
	Women	2	–	8	–	8
	Not known	2	1	2	–	3
	Total	6	5	10	–	15
Grand totals	Men	242	252	232	14	498
	Women	66	37	104	–	141
	Not known	178	141	178	1	320
	Total	**486**	**430**	**514**	**15**	**959**

1873

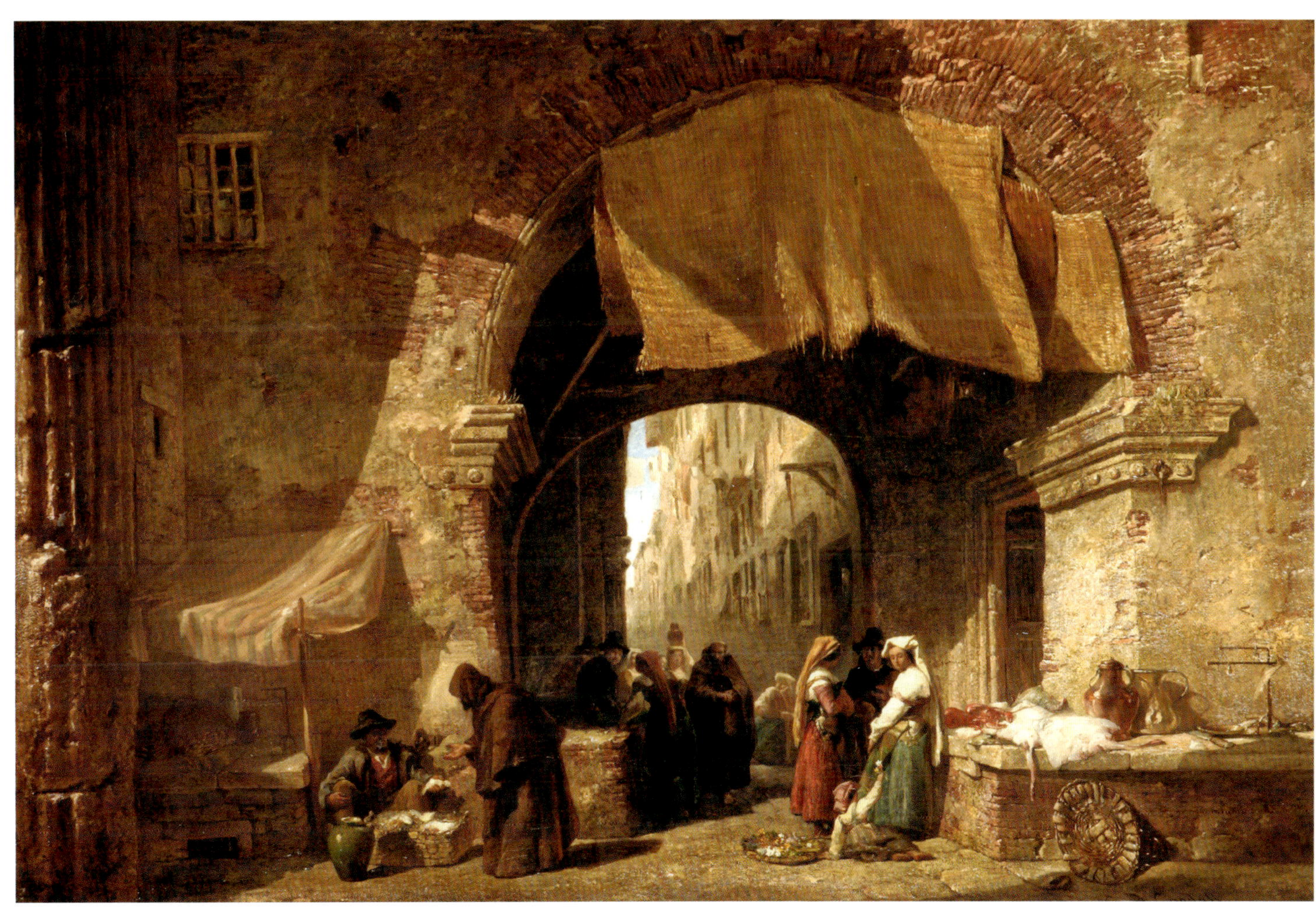

PLATE 29 · *The Pescheria in the Ghetto – Rome* · Edward A. Goodall
oil on canvas · 91.5 x 122.5 cm · 1873 Autumn Exhibition no. 36
National Museums Liverpool (Walker Art Gallery)

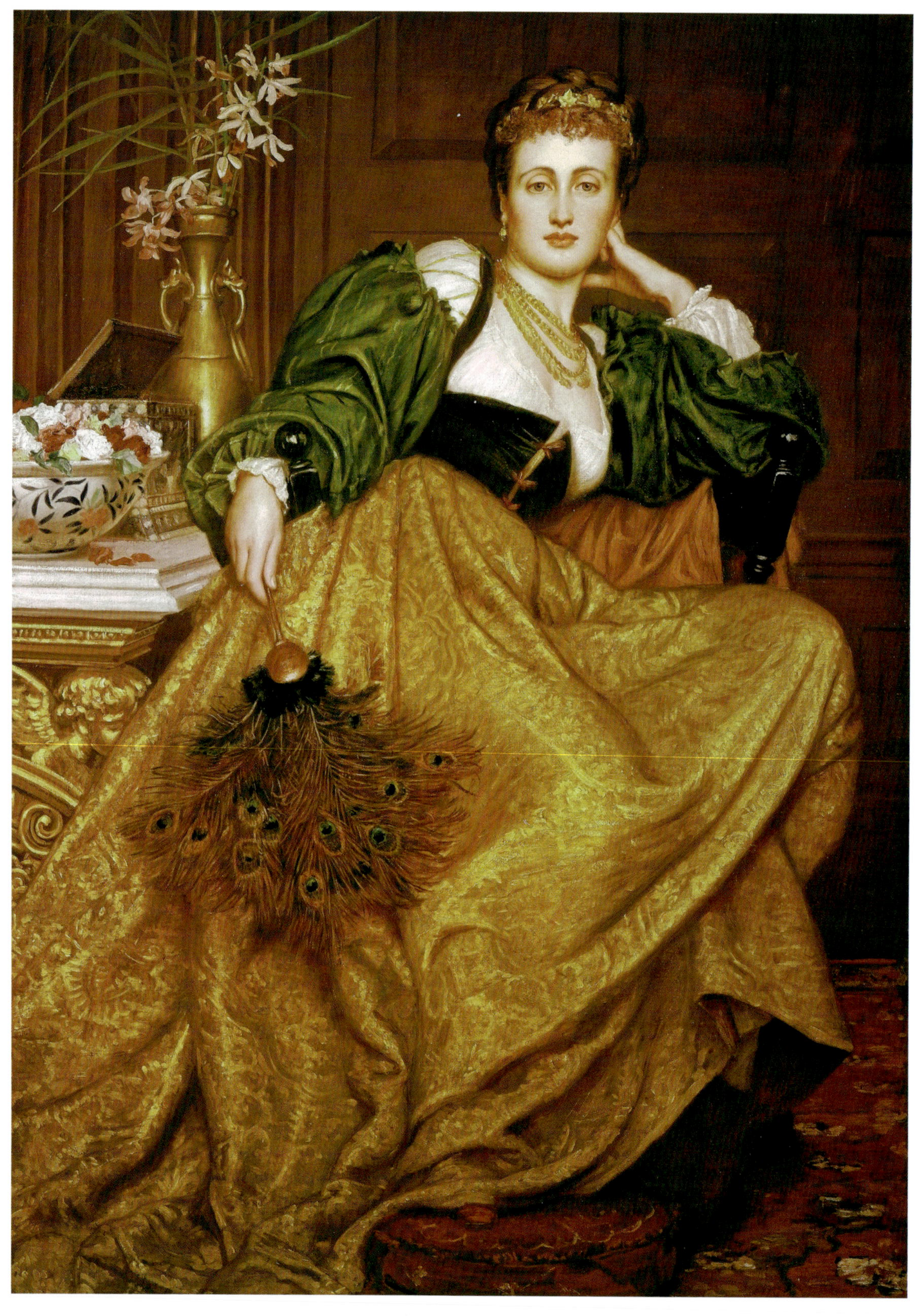

PLATE 30 · ***Leonora di Mantua*** · **Val Prinsep**

oil on canvas · 167.5 x 124 cm · 1873 Autumn Exhibition no. 188

National Museums Liverpool (Walker Art Gallery)

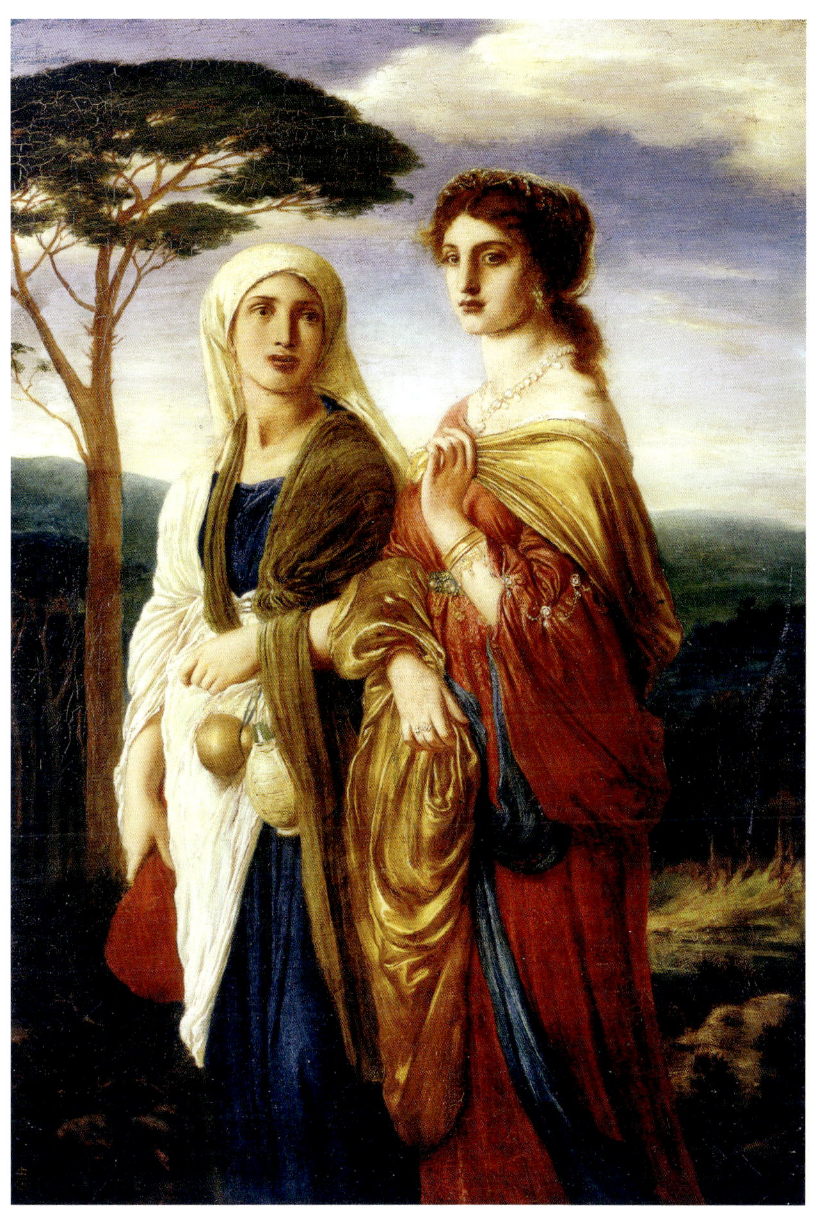

PLATE 31 · *Judith and Her Attendant Going to the Assyrian Camp* · Simeon Solomon
oil on canvas · 82 x 56.5 cm · 1873 Autumn Exhibition no. 214
private collection · photograph © Christie's Images/Bridgeman Images

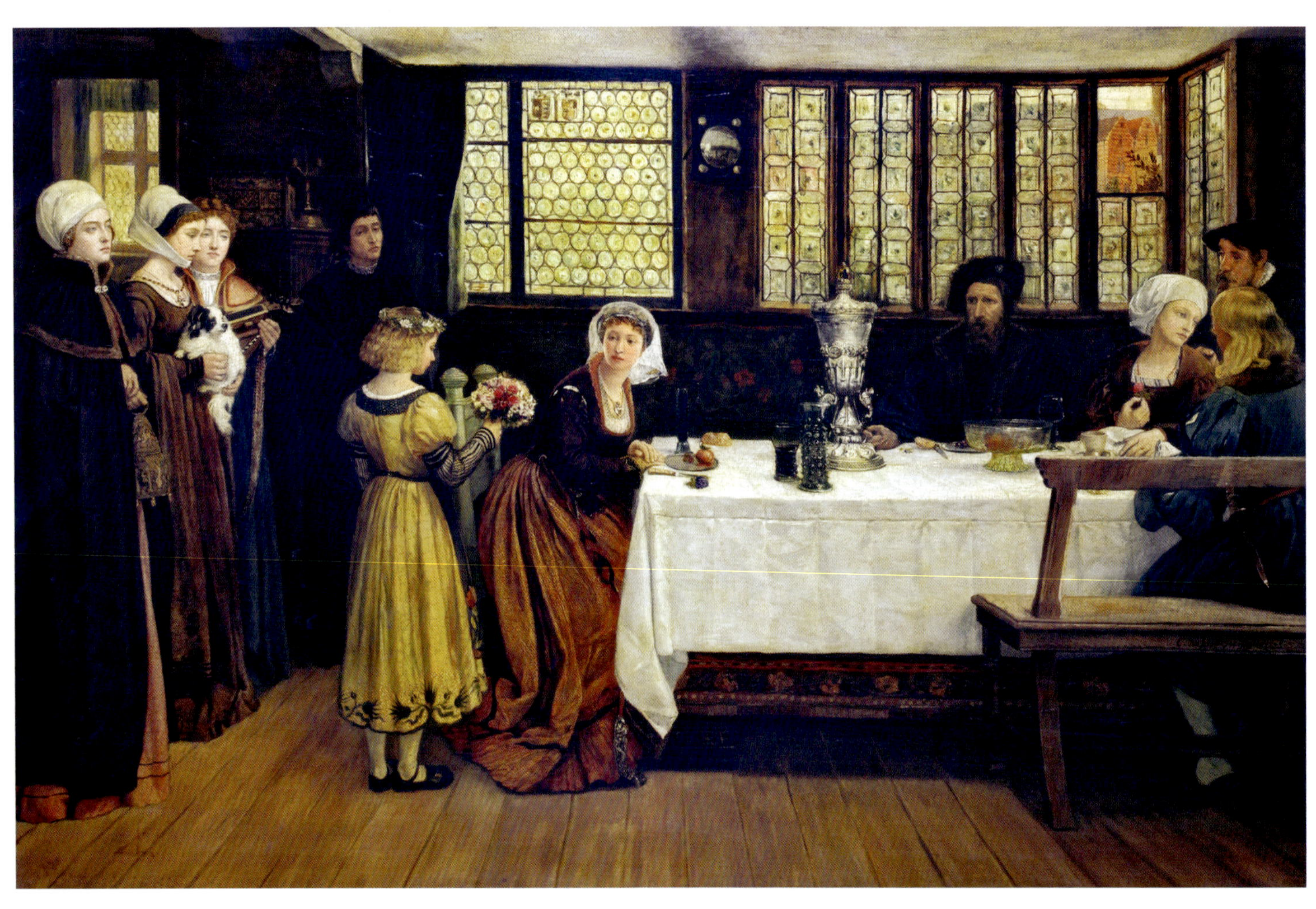

PLATE 32 · *A Birthday*, A.D. 1550 · Charles Napier Hemy
oil on canvas · 91.5 x 136.5 cm · 1873 Autumn Exhibition no. 349
National Museums Liverpool (Walker Art Gallery)

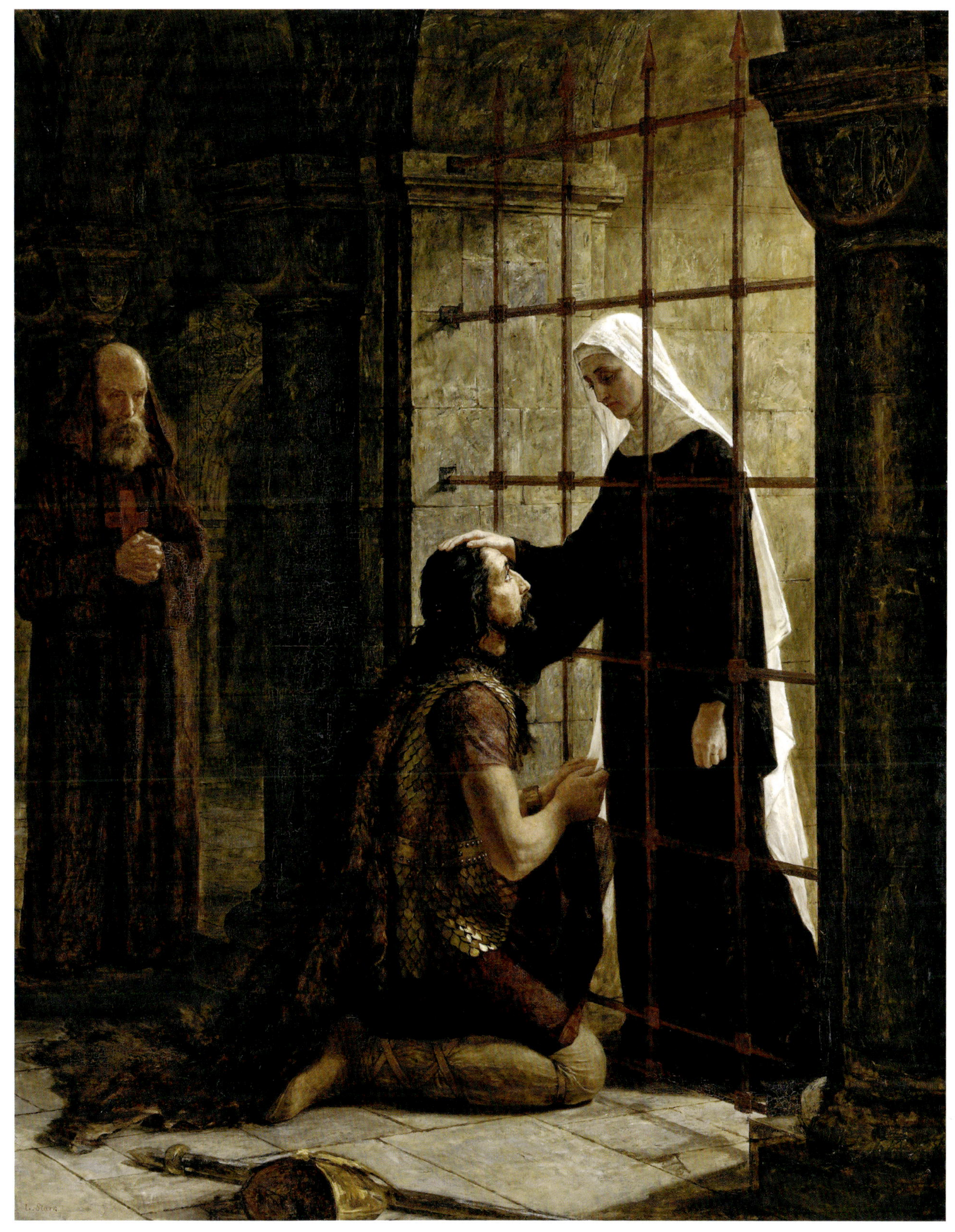

PLATE 33 · *Sintram* · Louisa Starr
oil on canvas · 153.5 x 123 cm · 1873 Autumn Exhibition no. 162
National Museums Liverpool (Walker Art Gallery)

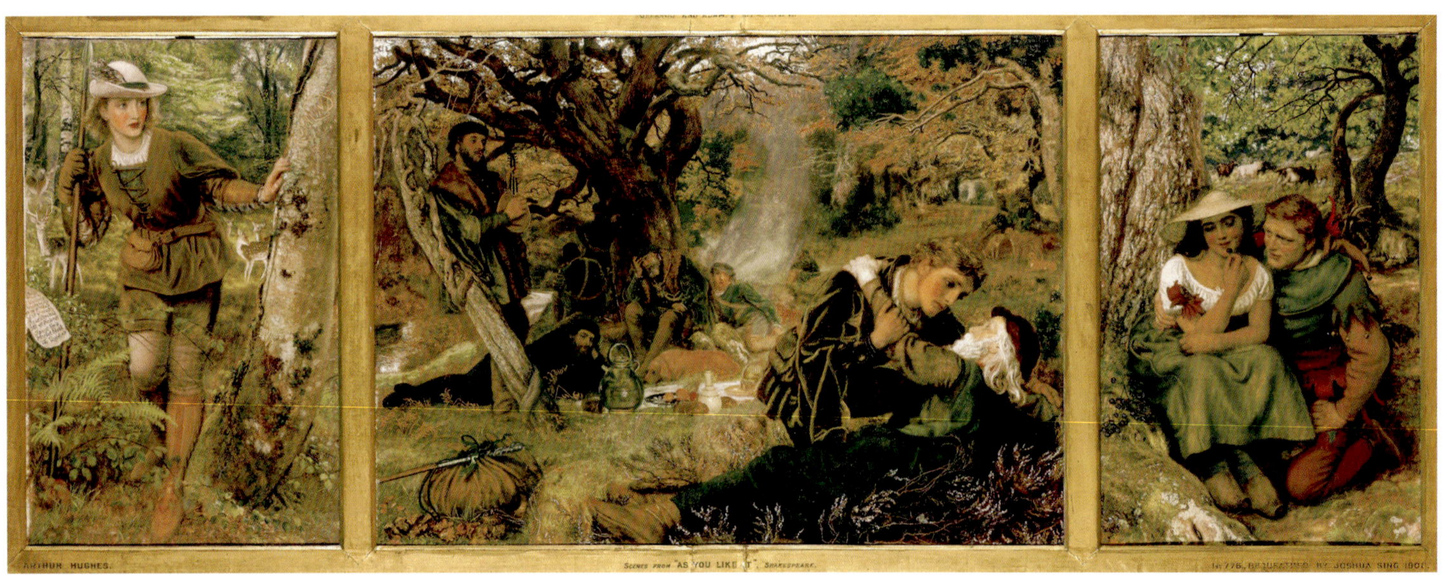

PLATE 34 · *The Love Makings of Orlando and Touchstone – "As You Like It"* · Arthur Hughes
oil on canvas (triptych) · centre 71 x 99 cm; wings each 71 x 46 cm · 1873 Autumn Exhibition no. 223
National Museums Liverpool (Walker Art Gallery)

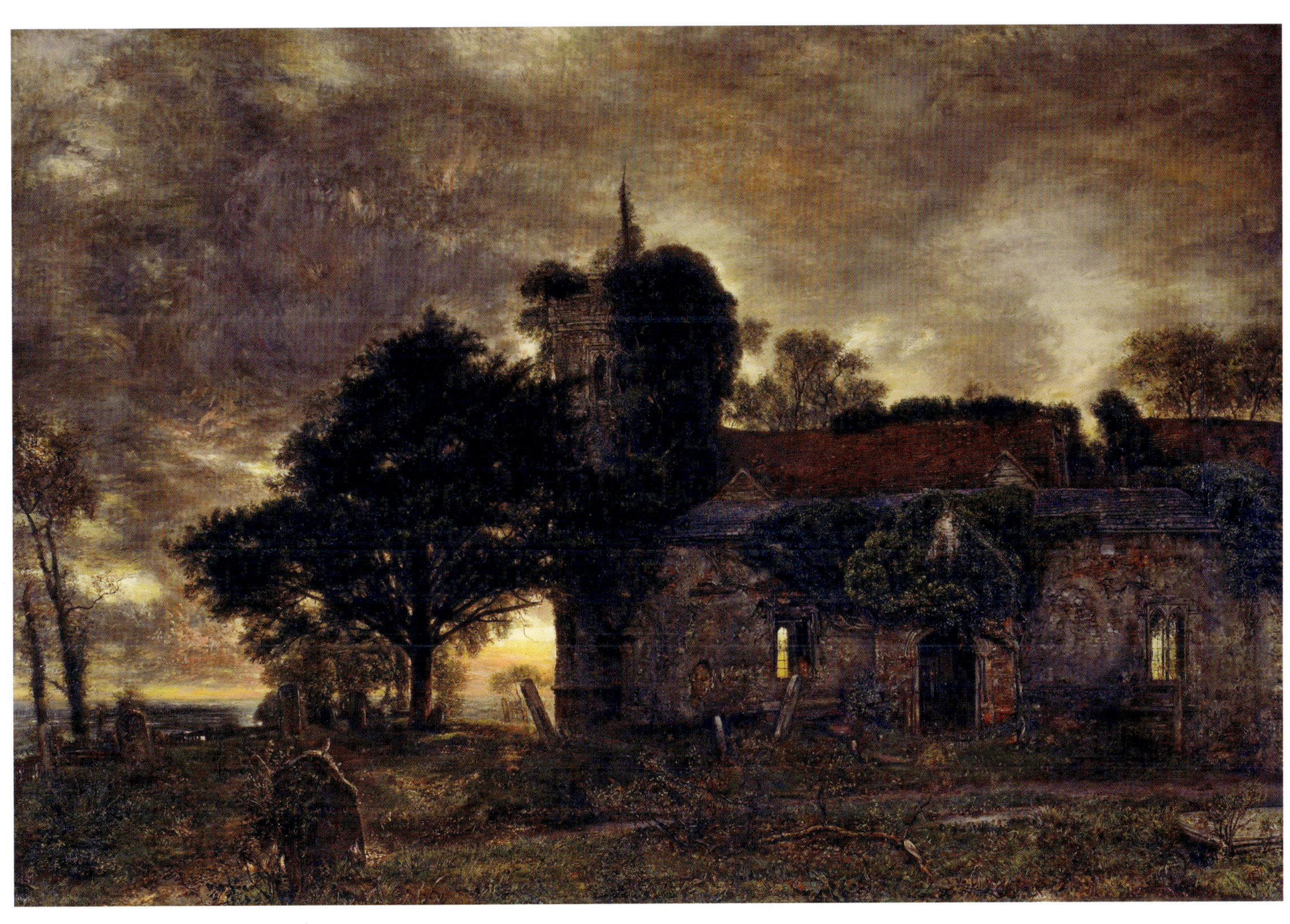

PLATE 35 · *Evensong* · Mark Anthony
oil on canvas · 145.5 x 212.5 cm · 1873 Autumn Exhibition no. 152
National Museums Liverpool (Walker Art Gallery)

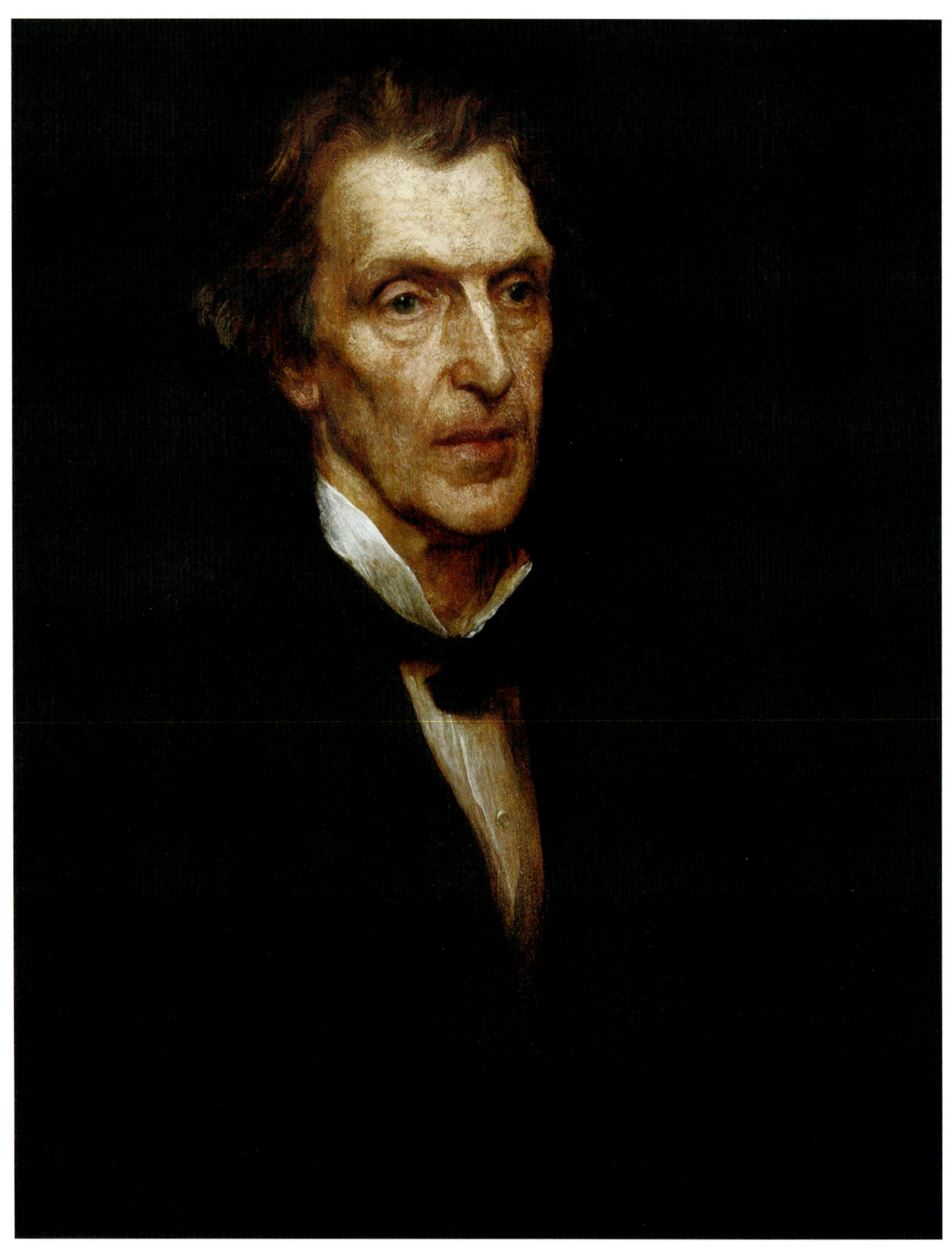

PLATE 36 · *James Martineau* · George Frederick Watts
oil on canvas · 68.5 x 53.5 cm · 1873 Autumn Exhibition no. 74
Harris Manchester College, University of Oxford

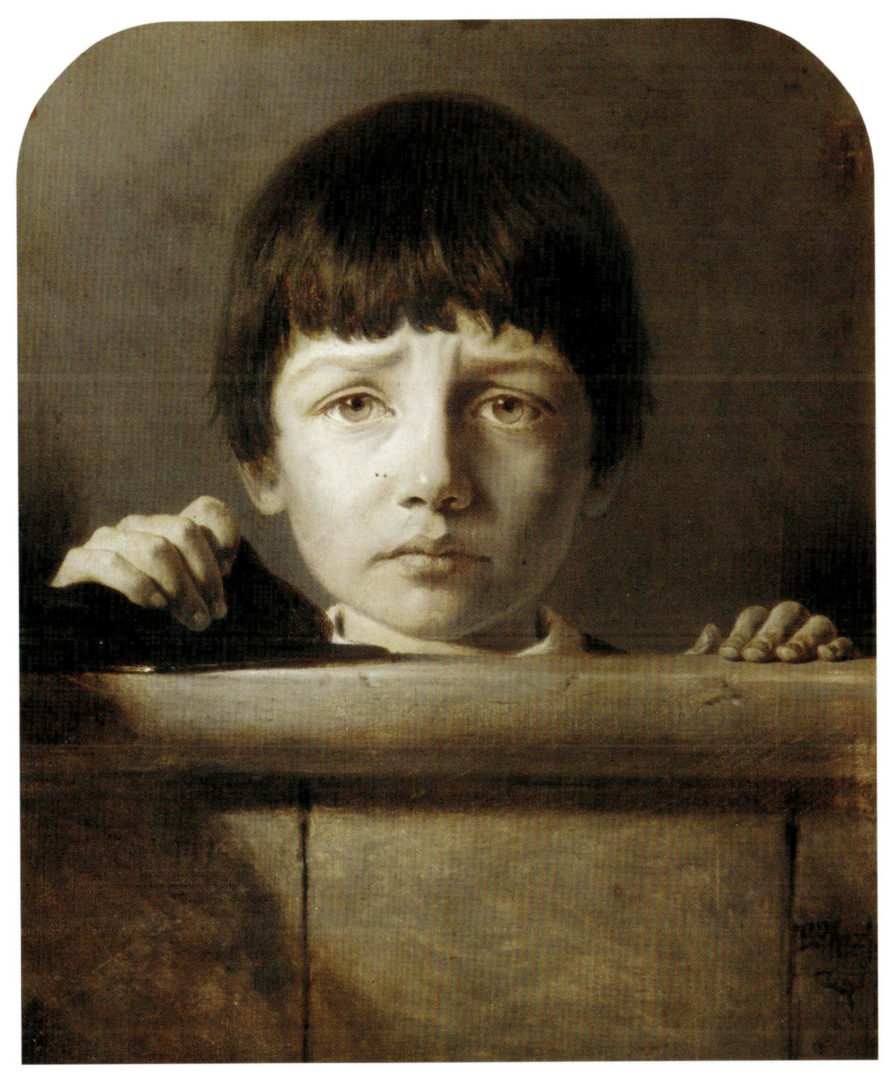

PLATE 37 · *The Dock* · Barnett Samuel Marks
oil on canvas · 35 x 31 cm · 1873 Autumn Exhibition no. 95
National Museums Liverpool (Walker Art Gallery)

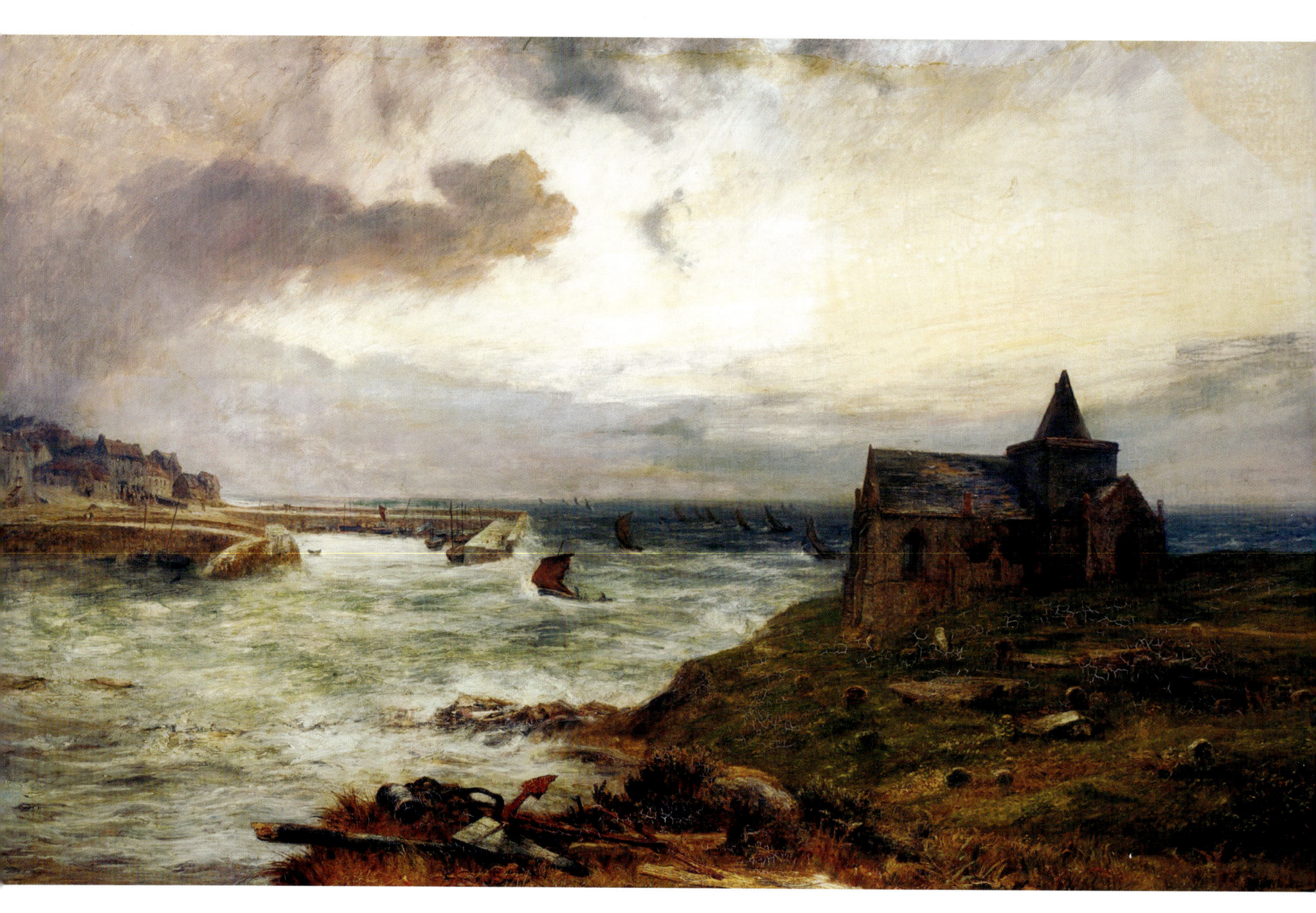

PLATE 38 · *The Fisherman's Haven* · John MacWhirter
oil on canvas · 120 x 188 cm · 1873 Autumn Exhibition no. 197
Touchstones, Rochdale (Rochdale Arts & Heritage Services)/Bridgeman Images

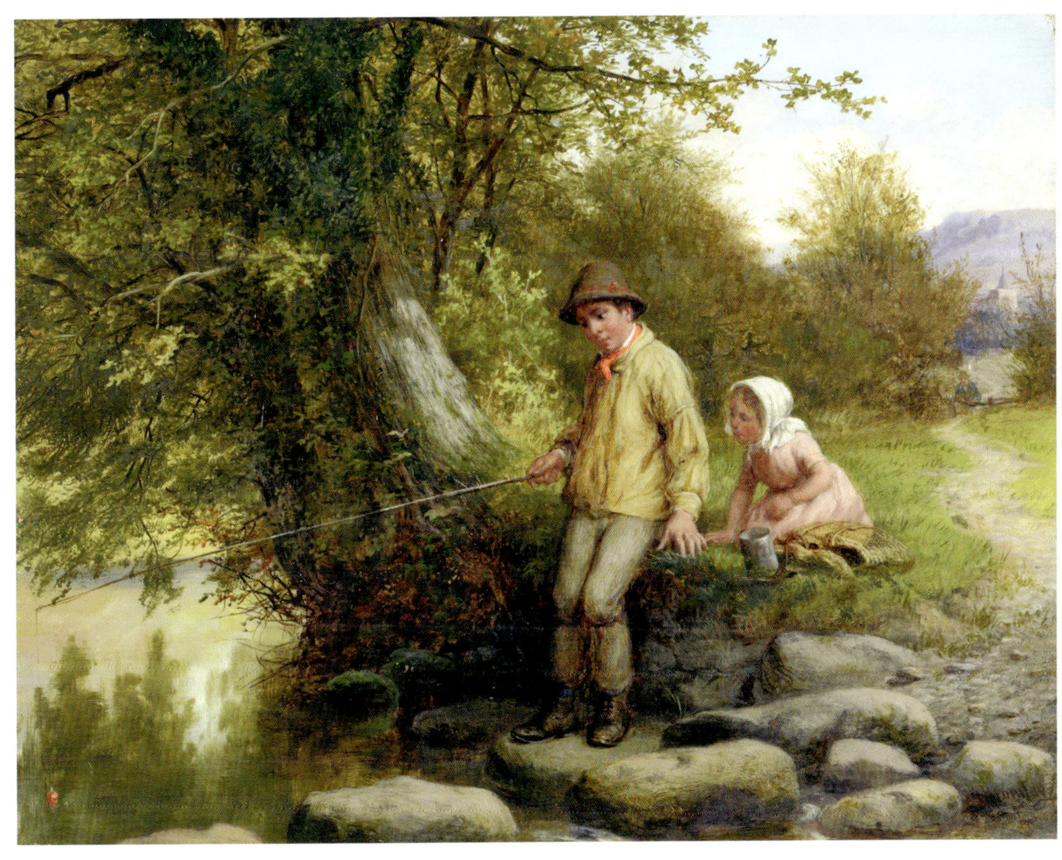

PLATE 39 · ***Waiting for a Nibble*** · **William Bromley**
oil on canvas · 34 x 44.5 cm · 1873 Autumn Exhibition no. 266
Williamson Art Gallery, Birkenhead

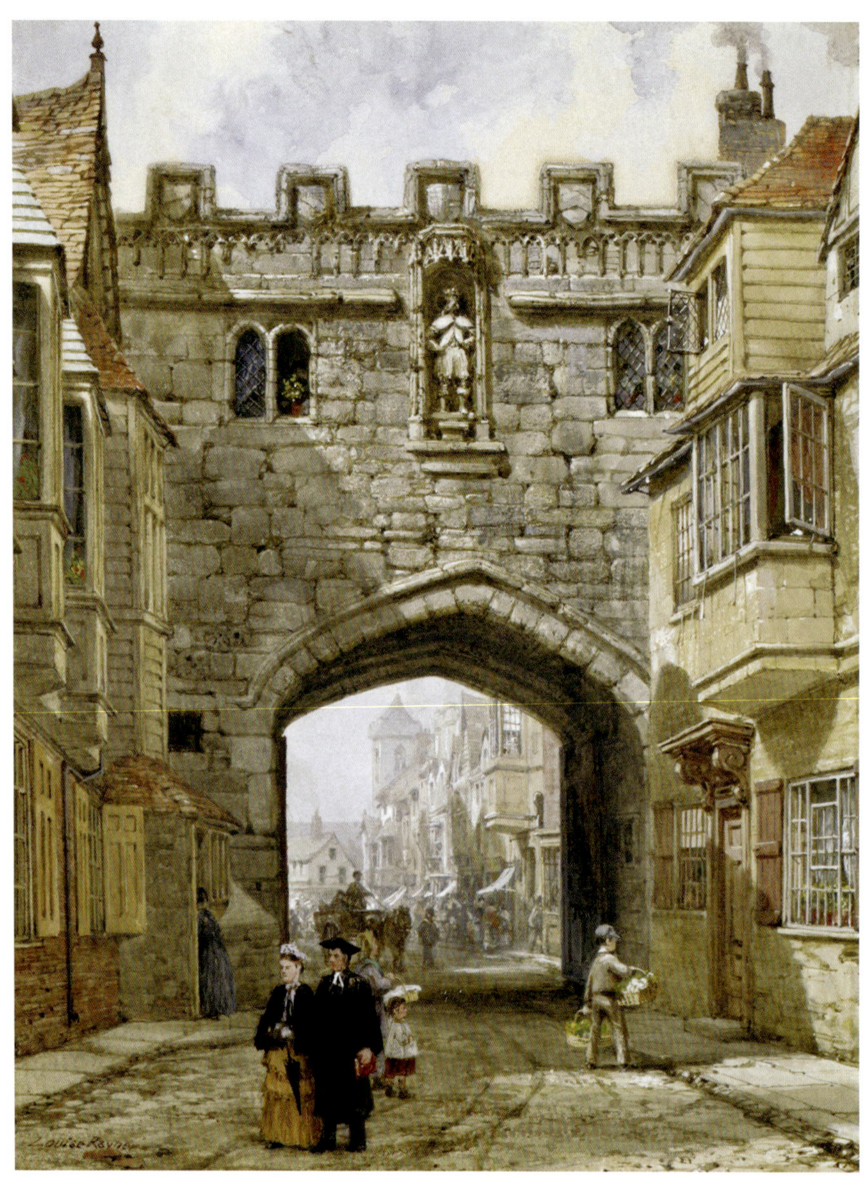

PLATE 40 · *St Stephen's Gateway, Salisbury* · **Louise Rayner**
watercolour and gouache on paper · 34 x 26 cm · 1873 Autumn Exhibition no. 910
Sotheby's, 5 June 1996 (lot 15) · © Sotheby's/akg-images

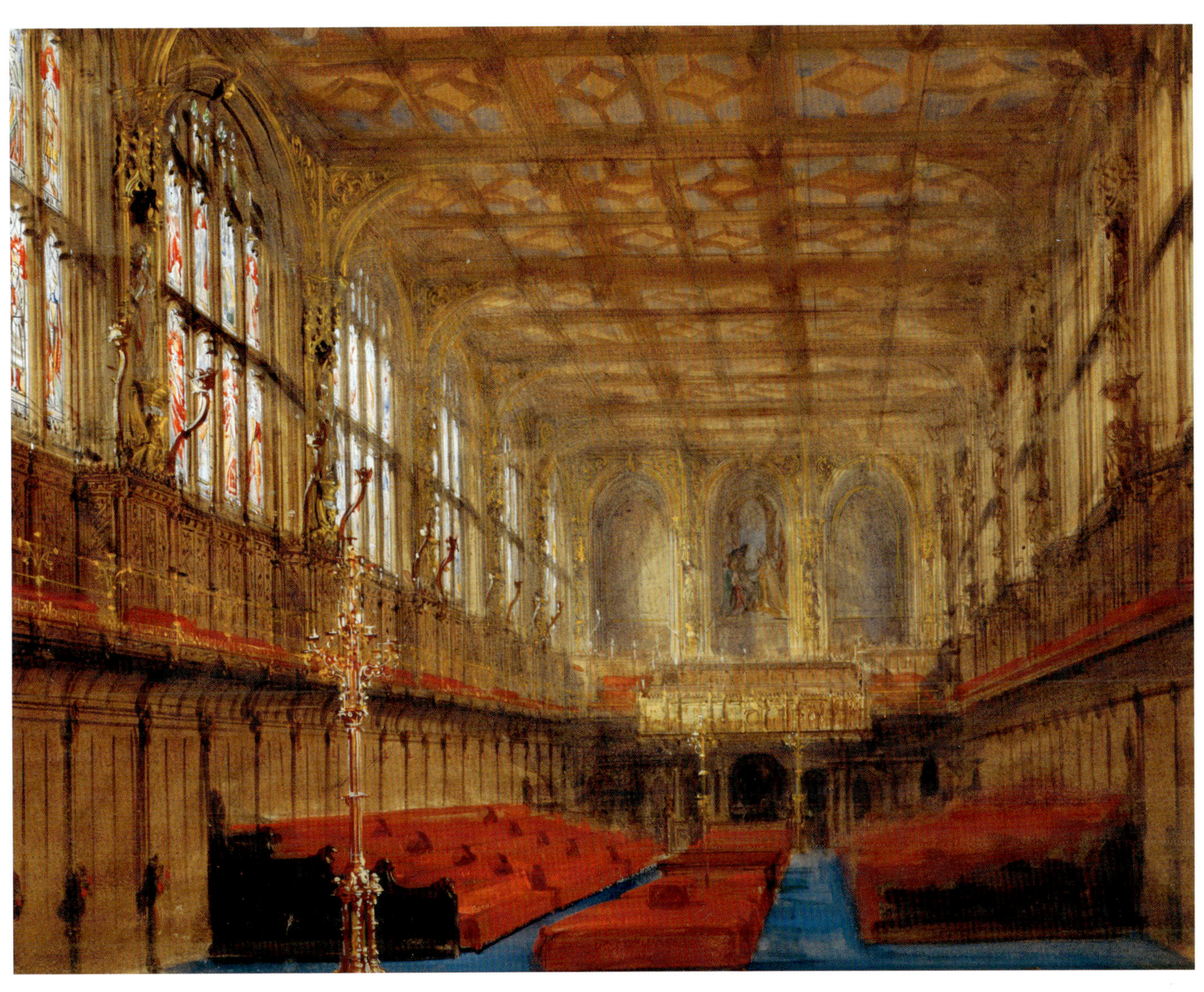

PLATE 41 · *House of Lords* · Joseph Nash
pencil, watercolour and bodycolour on paper on board · 39.5 x 49.5 cm · 1873 Autumn Exhibition no. 1005
Christie's New York, 29–30 March 2016 (lot 375) · © 2016 Christie's Images Limited

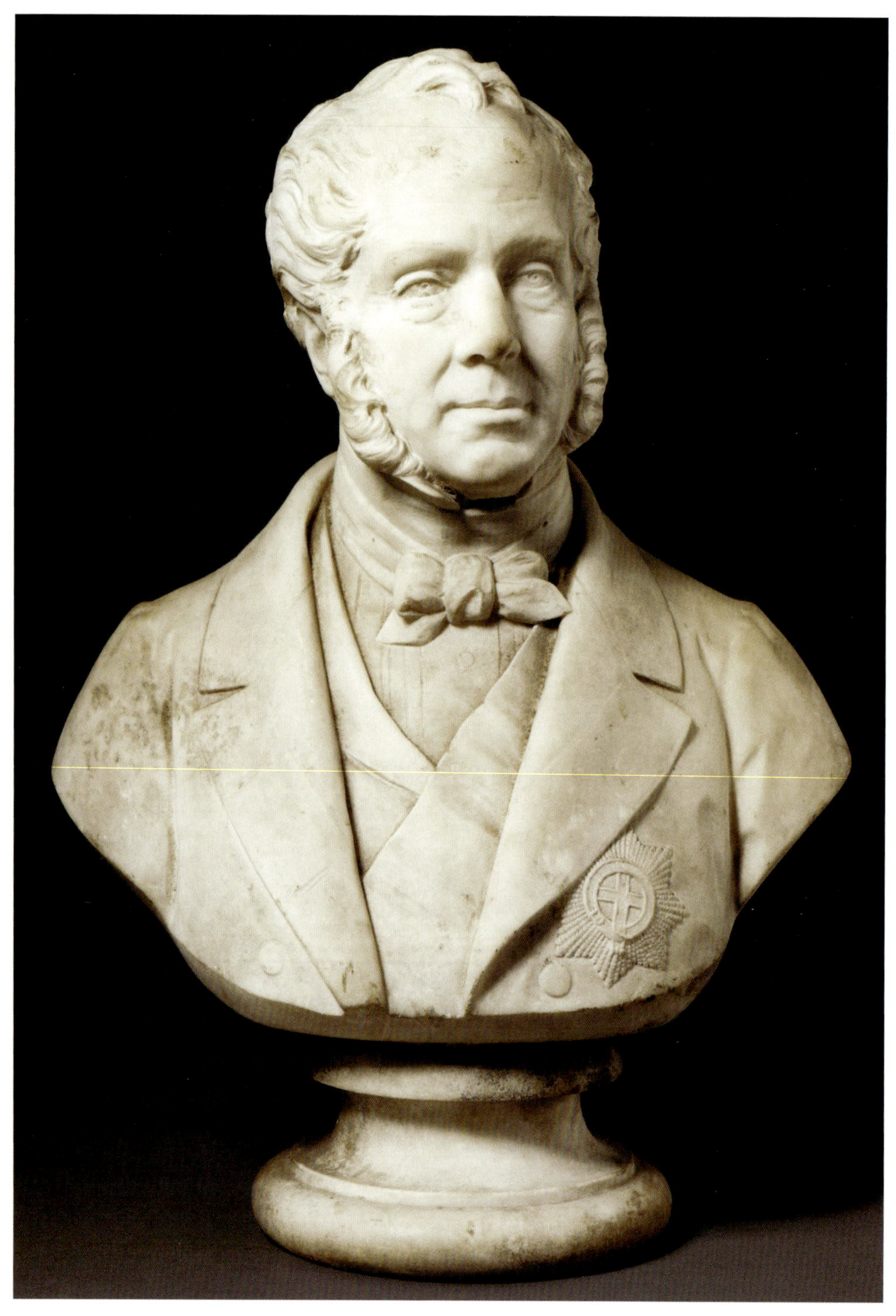

PLATE 42 · *The Late Viscount Palmerston* · George Gammon Adams
marble · 31 cm high · 1873 Autumn Exhibition no. 1047
Victoria & Albert Museum · given by Miss I.D. Adams

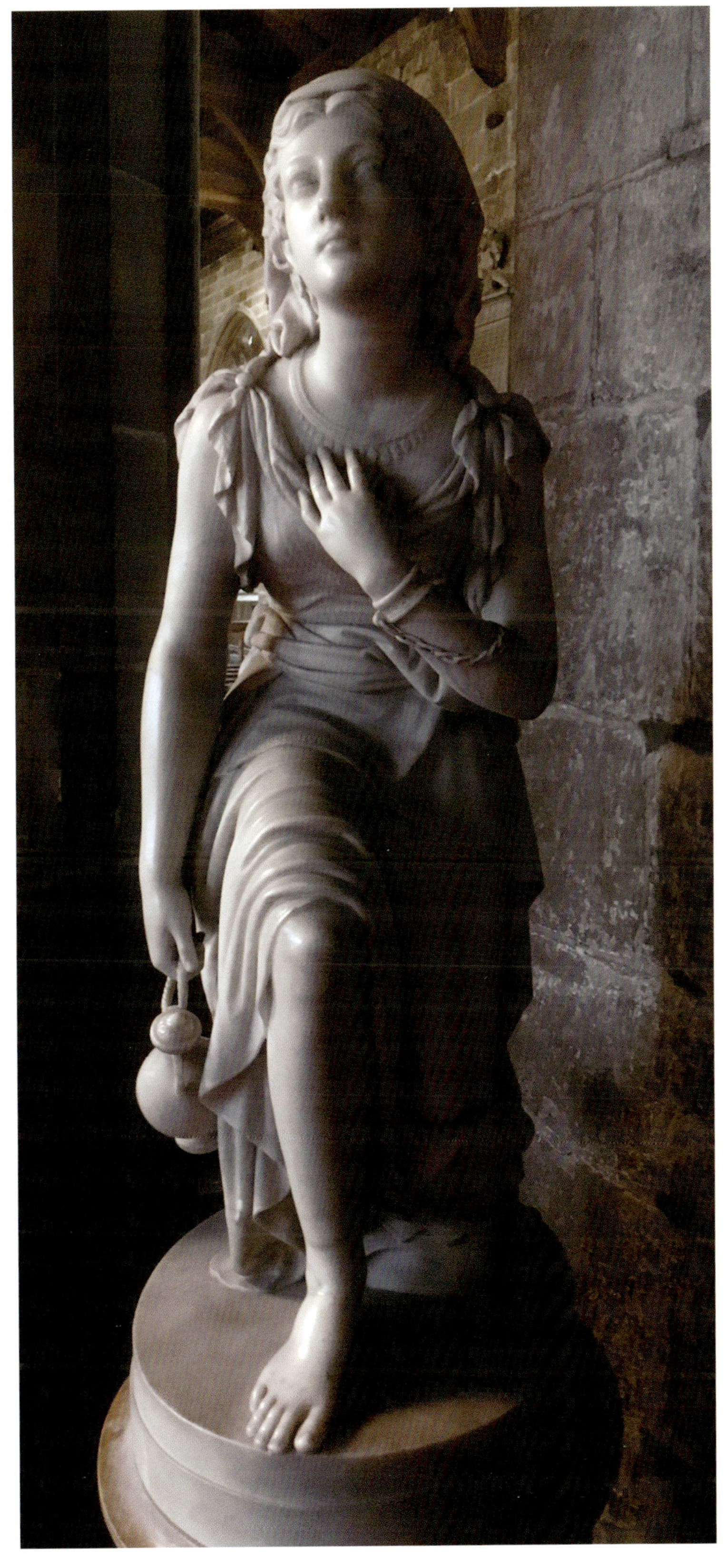

PLATE 43 · *The Israelitish Maid* · John Warrington Wood
marble · 119.5 cm high (including upper plinth) · 1873 Autumn Exhibition no. 1037
private collection

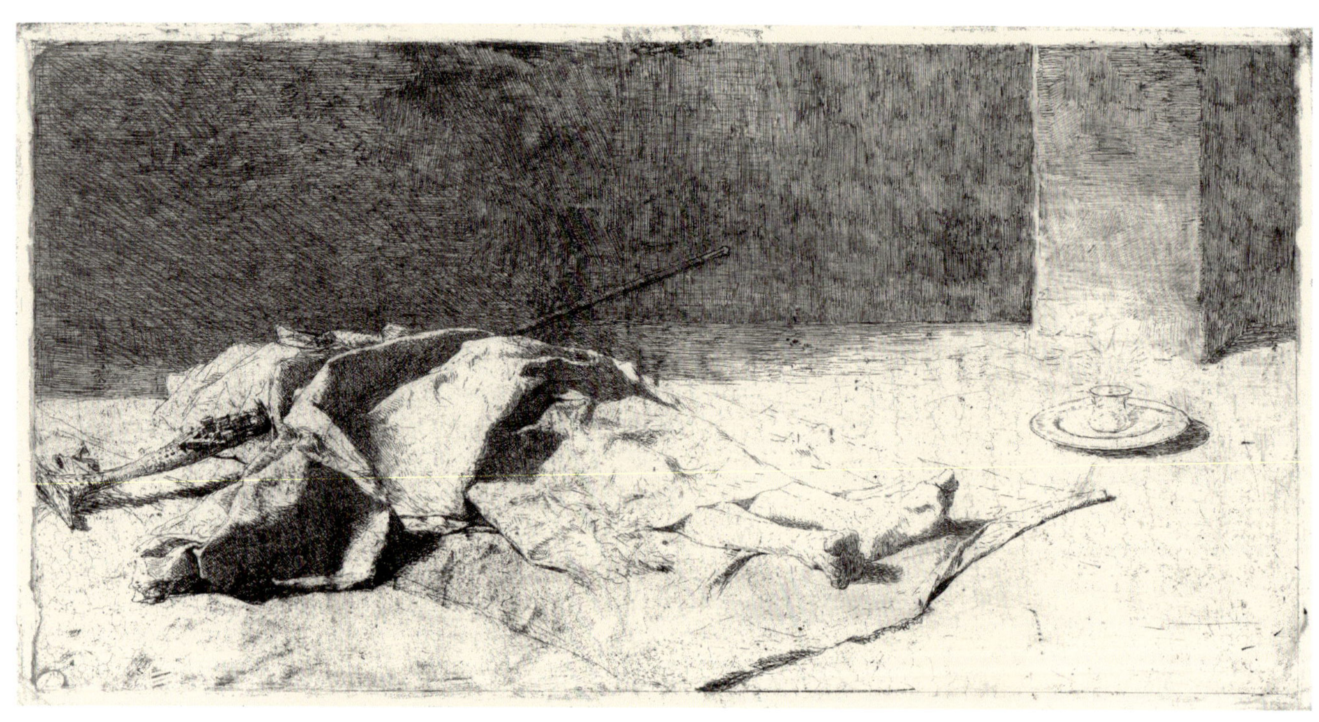

PLATE 44 · ***The Dead Kabyl*** · **Mariano Fortuny**
etching on paper · 22 x 41 cm · 1873 Autumn Exhibition no. 959
Museu Nacional d'Art di Catalunya, Barcelona

Paintings by numbers 1873

		No. of artists	Oils	Works on paper	Sculpture	Total no. of works
Liverpool	*Men*	34	22	66	8	96
	Women	12	5	20	–	25
	Not known	34	15	42	–	57
	Total	80	42	128	8	178
Birkenhead	*Men*	2	1	1	–	2
	Women	2	5	1	–	6
	Not known	2	–	3	–	3
	Total	6	6	5	–	11
Chester	*Men*	1	–	3	–	3
	Women	3	–	5	–	5
	Not known	1	–	1	–	1
	Total	5	–	9	–	9
Wirral excluding Birkenhead	*Men*	–	–	–	–	–
	Women	1	–	3	–	3
	Not known	4	3	7	–	10
	Total	5	3	10	–	13
Manchester	*Men*	1	–	1	–	1
	Women	–	–	–	–	–
	Not known	6	4	7	–	11
	Total	7	4	8	–	12
Lancashire excluding Manchester	*Men*	3	1	6	–	7
	Women	2	–	6	–	6
	Not known	3	2	4	–	6
	Total	8	3	16	–	19
N.W. England excluding Lancashire and Wirral	*Men*	1	2	4	–	6
	Women	–	–	–	–	–
	Not known	9	3	10	–	13
	Total	10	5	14	–	19
North Wales	*Men*	3	–	8	–	8
	Women	–	–	–	–	–
	Not known	3	4	1	–	5
	Total	6	4	9	–	13
Edinburgh	*Men*	10	11	3	–	14
	Women	2	–	2	2	4
	Not known	4	4	3	–	7
	Total	16	15	8	2	25
The rest of Scotland and Ireland	*Men*	5	8	1	–	9
	Women	–	–	–	–	–
	Not known	4	4	–	–	4
	Total	9	12	1	–	13
Birmingham	*Men*	5	7	3	–	10
	Women	1	1	–	–	1
	Not known	8	7	4	–	11
	Total	14	15	7	–	22
South of England	*Men*	12	19	3	1	23
	Women	2	1	4	–	5
	Not known	4	7	2	–	9
	Total	18	27	9	1	37
West of England	*Men*	3	3	2	–	5
	Women	2	–	7	–	7
	Not known	7	5	10	–	15
	Total	12	8	19	–	27

		No. of artists	Oils	Works on paper	Sculpture	Total no. of works
East Anglia and The Midlands	*Men*	3	3	2	–	5
	Women	5	–	9	–	9
	Not known	6	5	4	–	9
	Total	14	8	15	–	23
N.E. England	*Men*	3	2	2	–	4
	Women	–	–	–	–	–
	Not known	6	4	9	–	13
	Total	9	6	11	–	17
Foreign addresses	*Men*	8	14	2	–	16
	Women	–	–	–	–	–
	Not known	–	–	–	–	–
	Total	8	14	2	–	16
No address	*Men*	23	18	7	1	26
	Women	5	5	4	–	9
	Not known	22	13	23	–	36
	Total	50	36	34	1	71
London: Hampstead	*Men*	5	3	4	–	7
	Women	1	–	4	–	4
	Not known	5	4	5	–	9
	Total	11	7	13	–	20
London: Haverstock Hill	*Men*	18	18	23	–	41
	Women	3	–	6	–	6
	Not known	3	3	5	–	8
	Total	24	21	34	–	55
London: St John's Wood	*Men*	11	13	7	–	20
	Women	–	–	–	–	–
	Not known	7	8	8	–	16
	Total	18	21	15	–	36
London: Kensington	*Men*	16	20	5	–	25
	Women	7	6	8	–	14
	Not known	11	15	7	–	22
	Total	34	41	20	–	61
London: Regent's Park	*Men*	7	10	–	–	10
	Women	3	–	9	–	9
	Not known	6	5	1	–	6
	Total	16	15	10	–	25
London: Fitzroy Square	*Men*	5	4	4	–	8
	Women	2	1	2	–	3
	Not known	11	16	10	–	26
	Total	18	21	16	–	37
The rest of inner London	*Men*	57	55	52	22	129
	Women	14	9	24	–	33
	Not known	48	50	57	–	107
	Total	119	114	133	22	269
London: suburbs	*Men*	3	3	6	–	9
	Women	7	3	12	–	15
	Not known	2	–	5	–	5
	Total	12	6	23	–	29
Grand totals	*Men*	239	237	215	32	484
	Women	74	36	126	2	164
**including one anonymous sculpture*	*Not known*	216	181	228	–	409
	Total	**530***	**454**	**569**	**35***	**1058***

1874

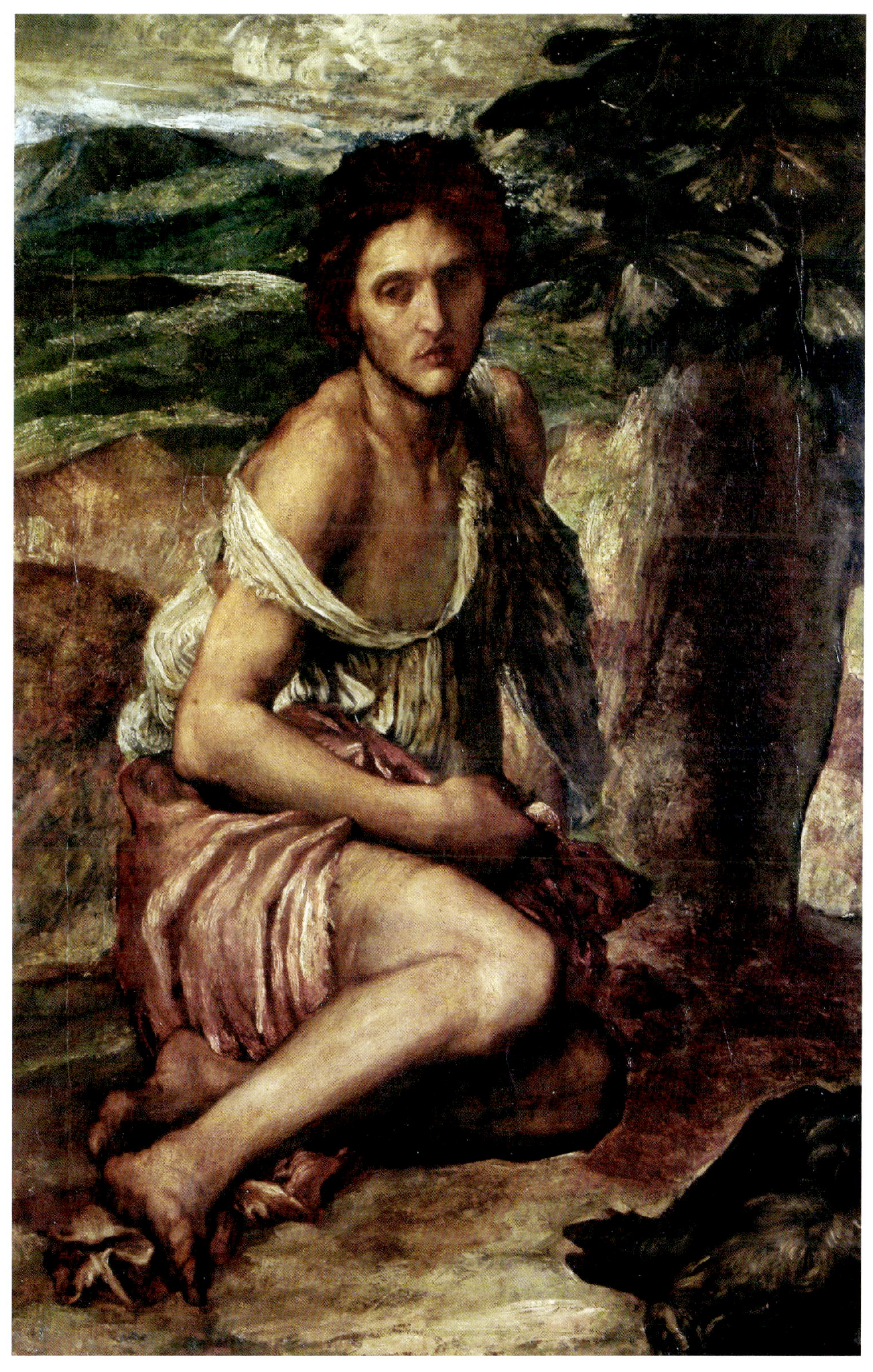

PLATE 45 · *The Prodigal Son* · George Frederick Watts
oil on canvas · 109 x 78.5 cm · 1874 Autumn Exhibition no. 307
© Watts Gallery Trust

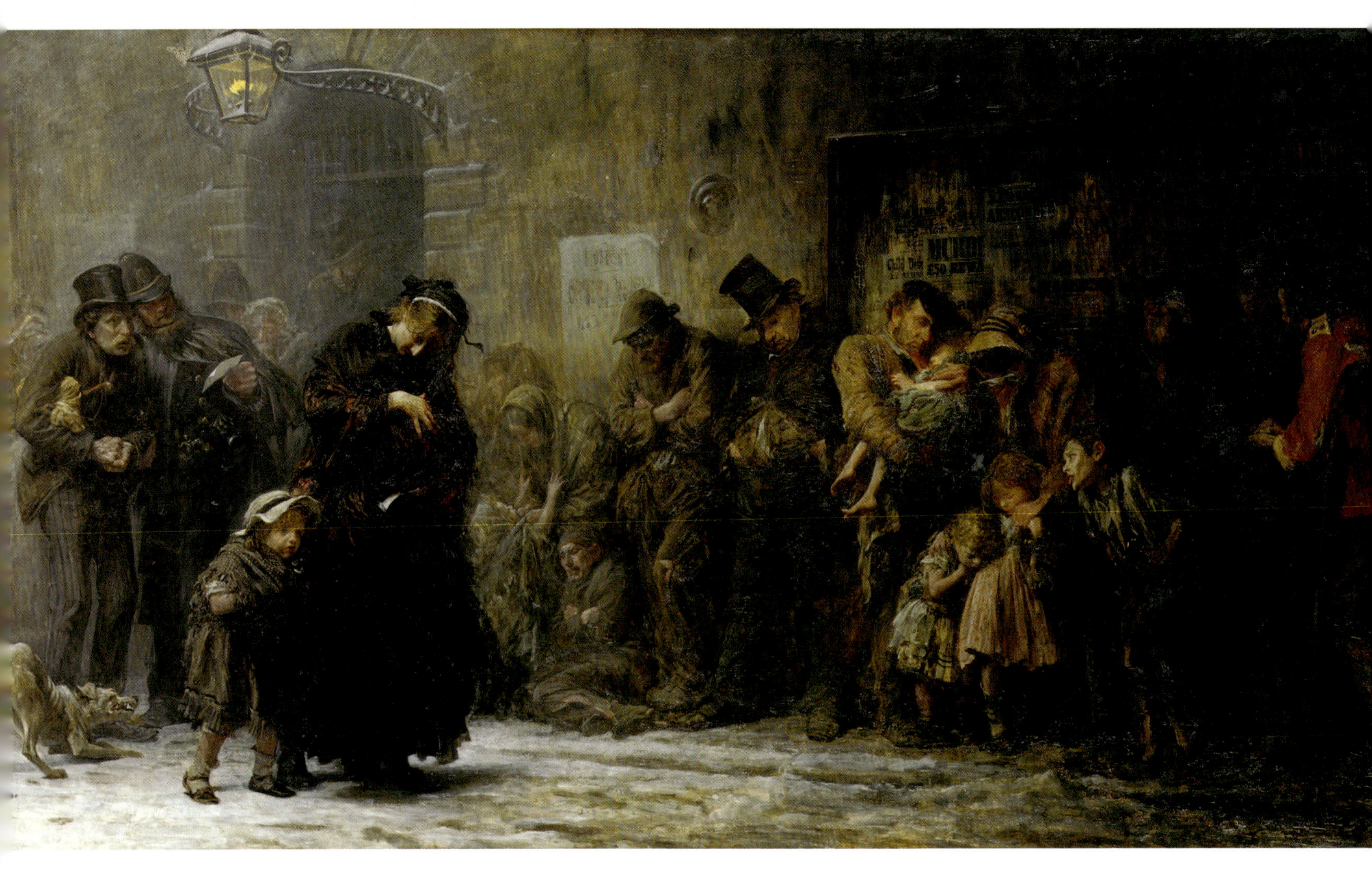

PLATE 46 · ***Applicants for Admission to a Casual Ward*** · Luke Fildes

oil on canvas · 137 x 243.5 cm · 1874 Autumn Exhibition no. 187

© Royal Holloway, University of London

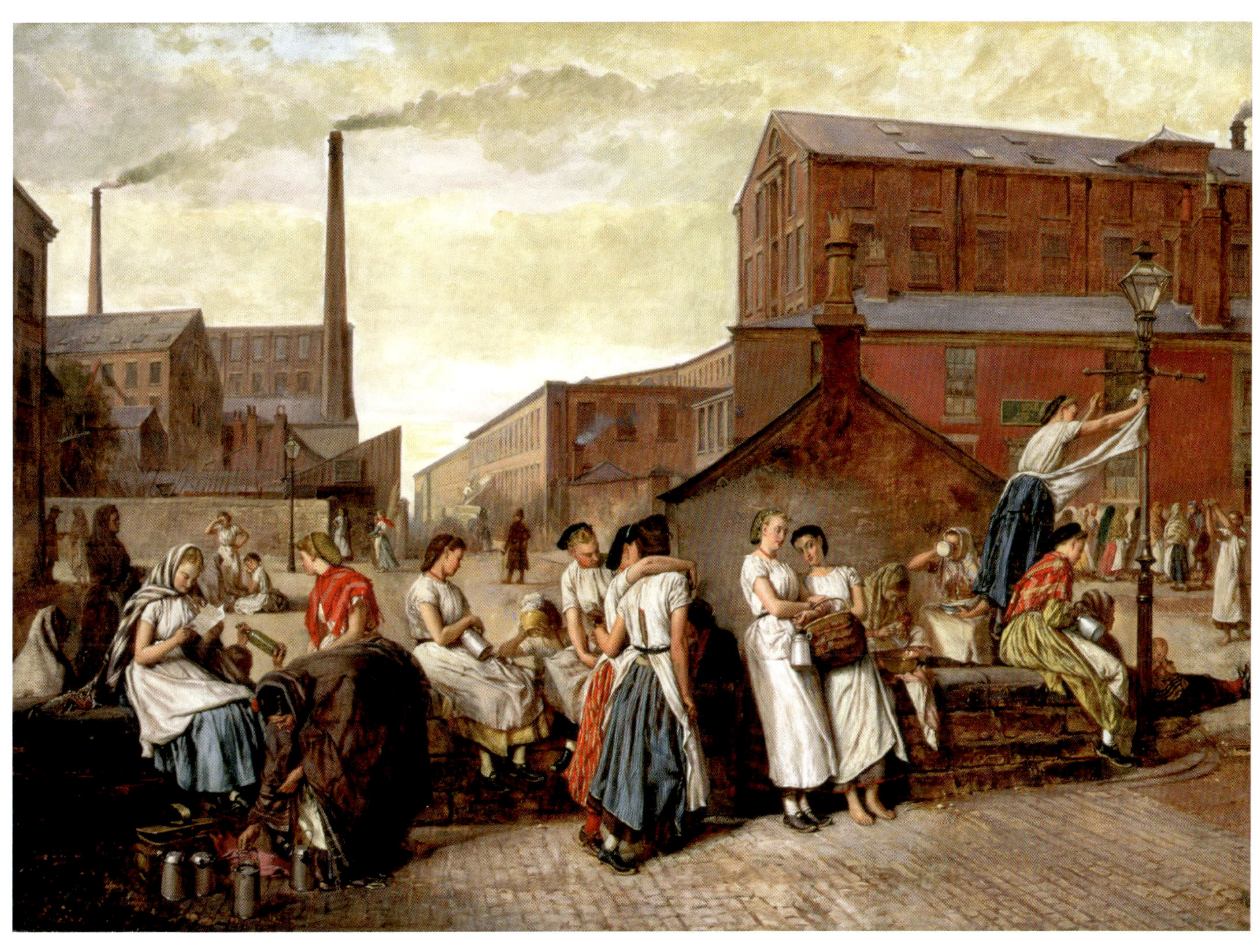

PLATE 47 · *The Dinner Hour at Wigan* · **Eyre Crowe**
oil on canvas · 76.5 x 107 cm · 1874 Autumn Exhibition no. 338
Manchester Art Gallery/Bridgeman Images

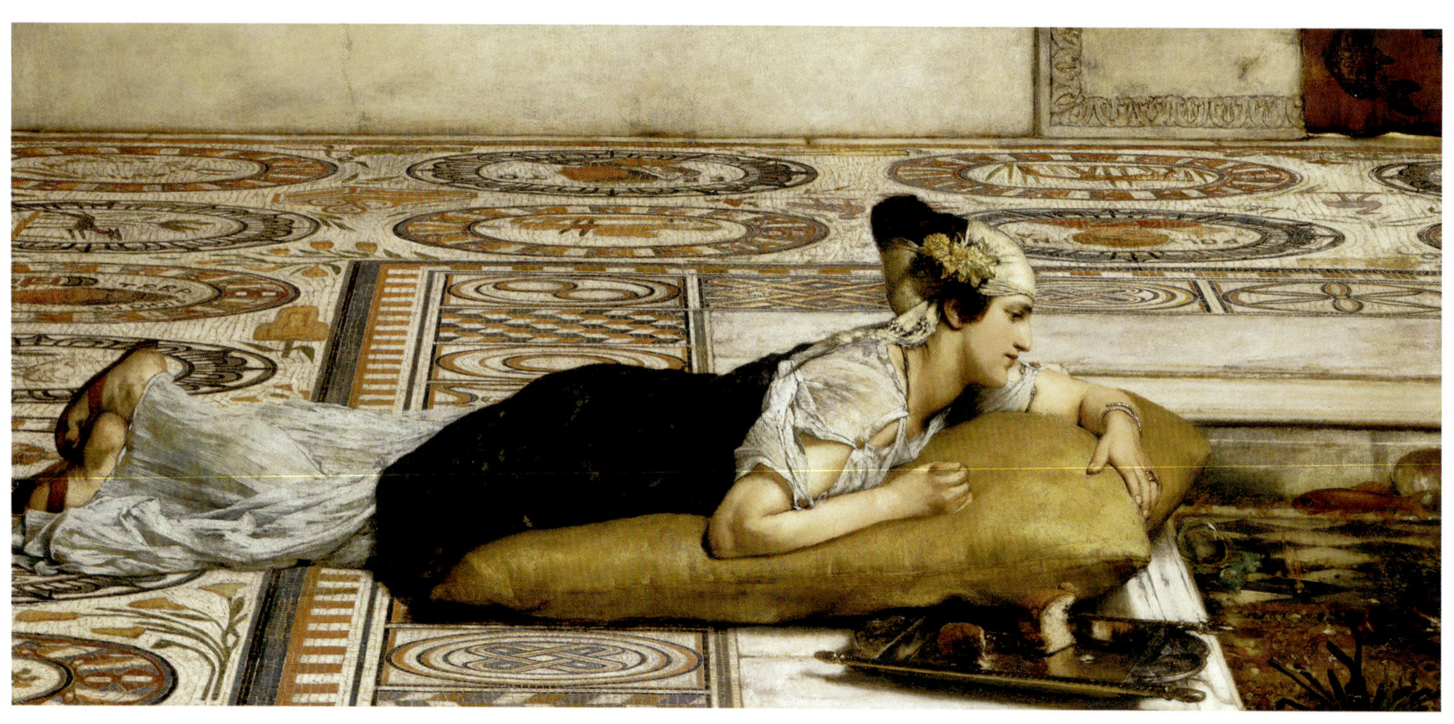

PLATE 48 · *Water-pets* · Lawrence Alma-Tadema
oil on canvas · 67.5 x 142 cm · 1874 Autumn Exhibition no. 65
private collection · photograph © Christie's Images/Bridgeman Images

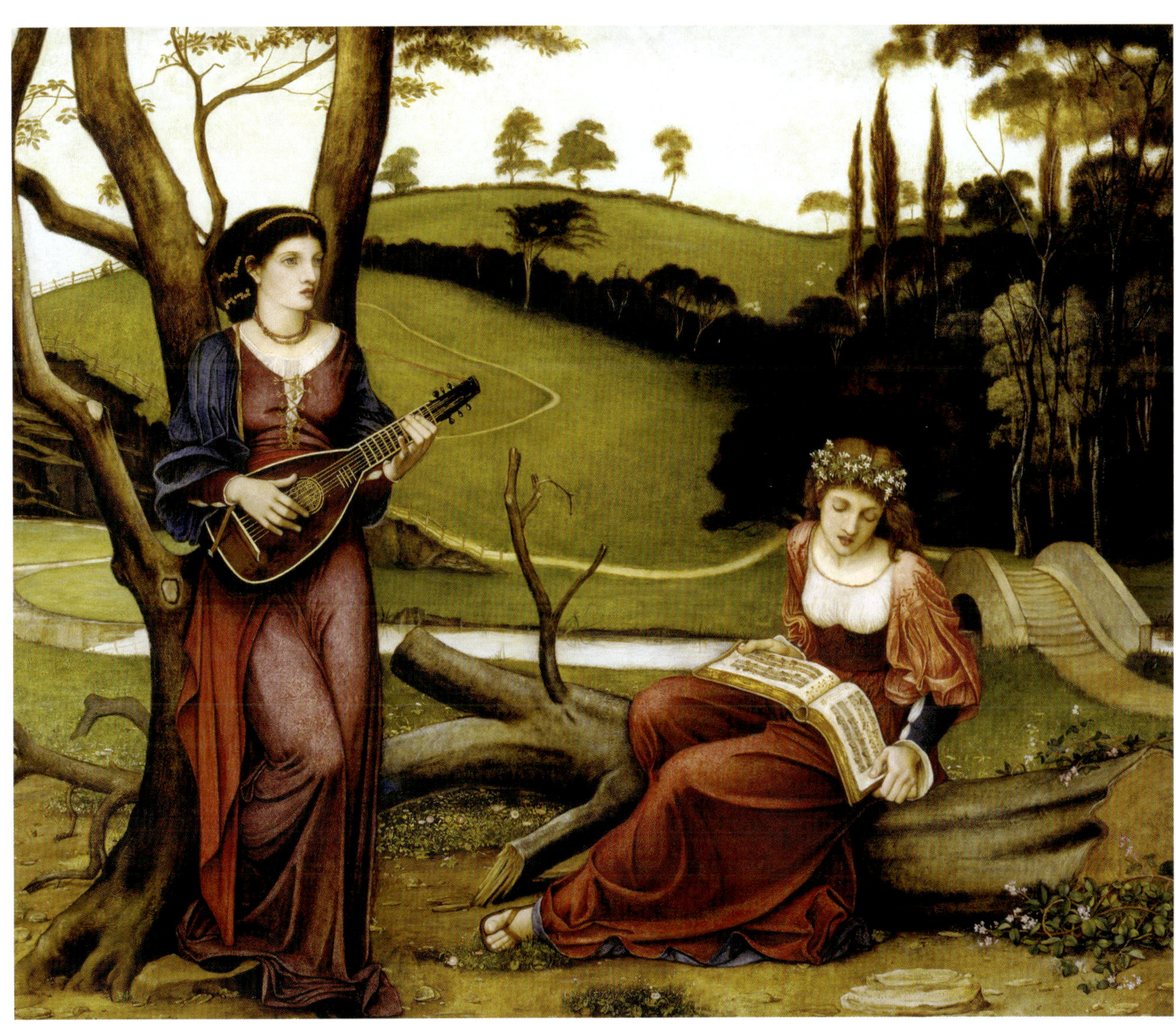

PLATE 49 · *"The gentle music of a byegone day"* · John Roddam Spencer Stanhope
oil on canvas · 97 x 119 cm · 1874 Autumn Exhibition no. 918
Wightwick Manor · © National Trust Images/John Hammond

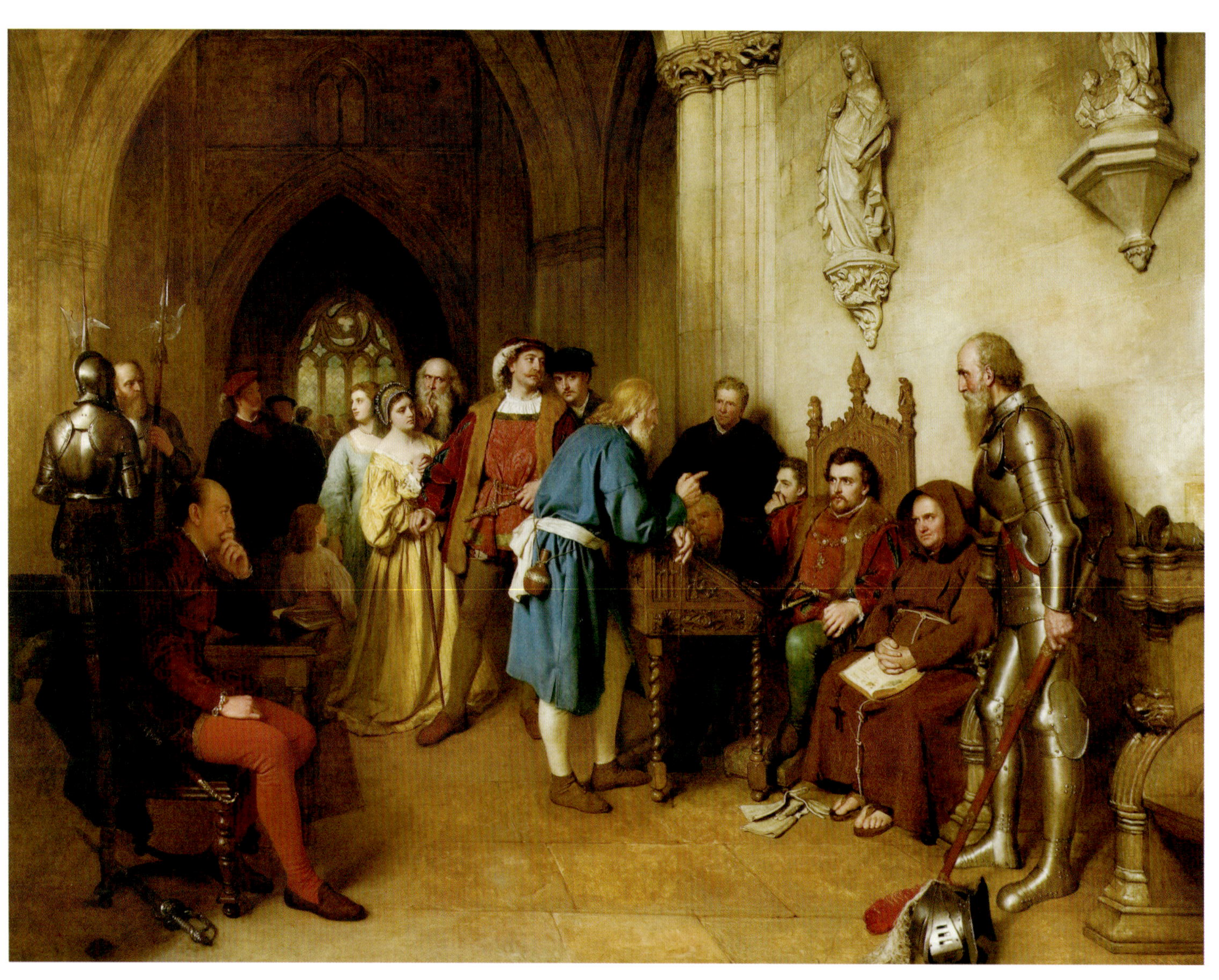

PLATE 50 · *The Morning before Flodden* · John Faed
oil on canvas · 137 x 185 cm · 1874 Autumn Exhibition no. 264
Wolverhampton Art Gallery (Wolverhampton Arts and Heritage)/Bridgeman Images

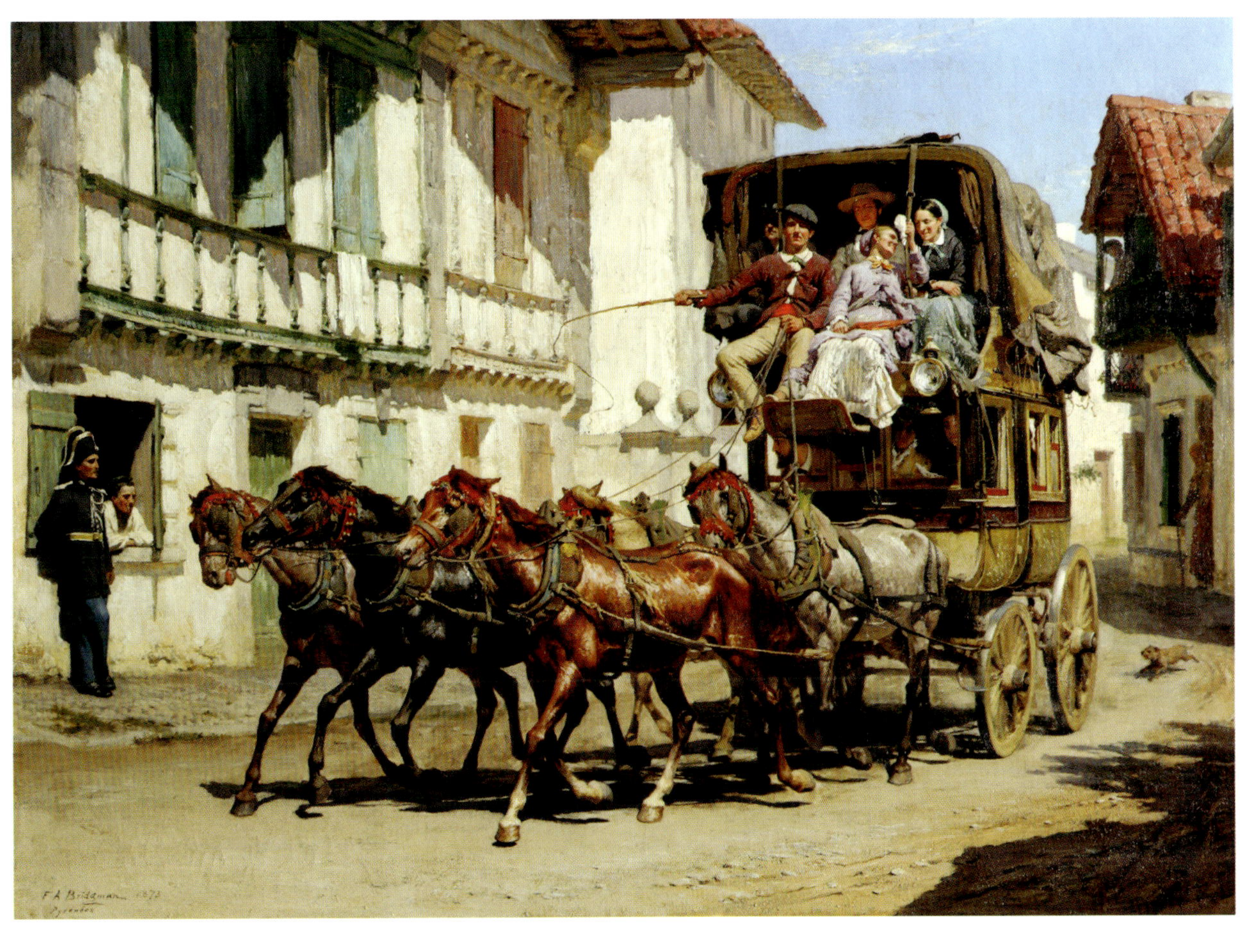

PLATE 51 · *The Diligence* · **Frederick Bridgman**
oil on canvas · 88 x 130.5 cm · 1874 Autumn Exhibition no. 373
National Museums Liverpool (Walker Art Gallery)

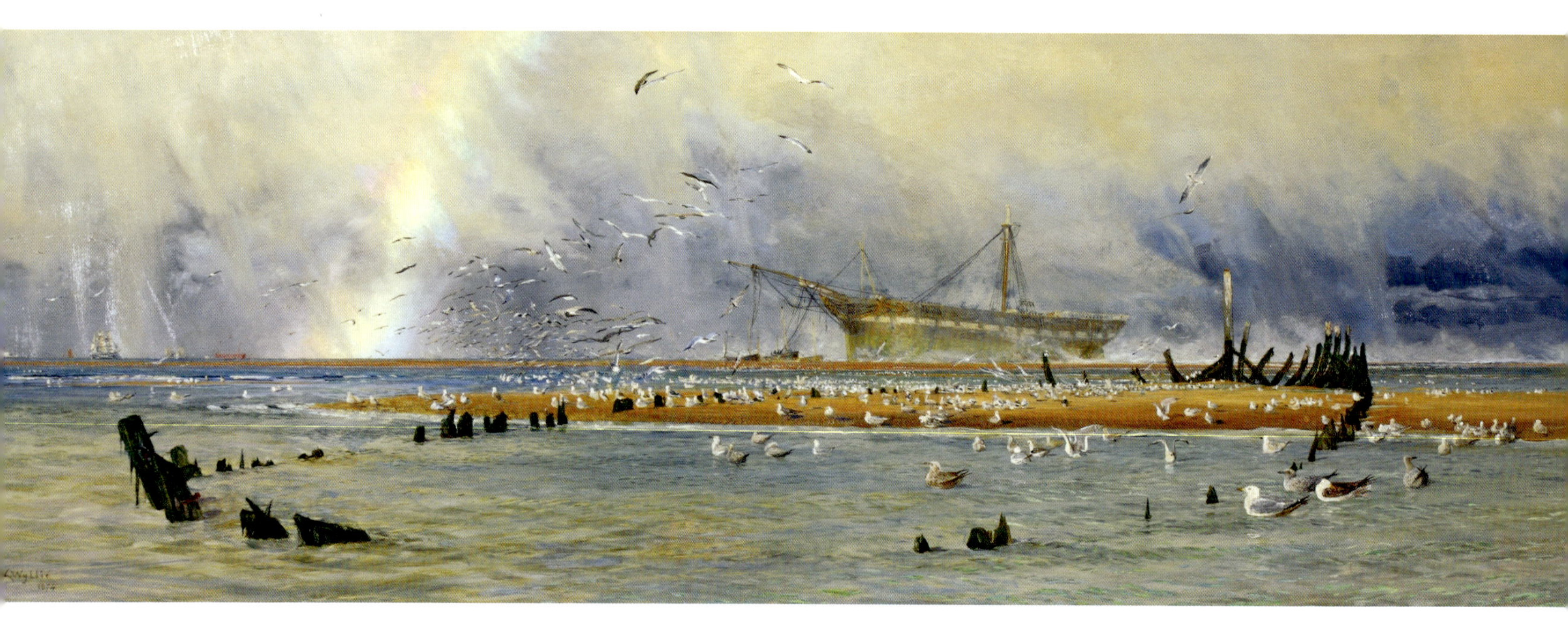

PLATE 52 · ***The Goodwin Sands*** · W.L. Wyllie

oil on canvas · 59.5 x 180 cm · 1874 Autumn Exhibition no. 74

Russell-Cotes Art Gallery & Museum, Bournemouth

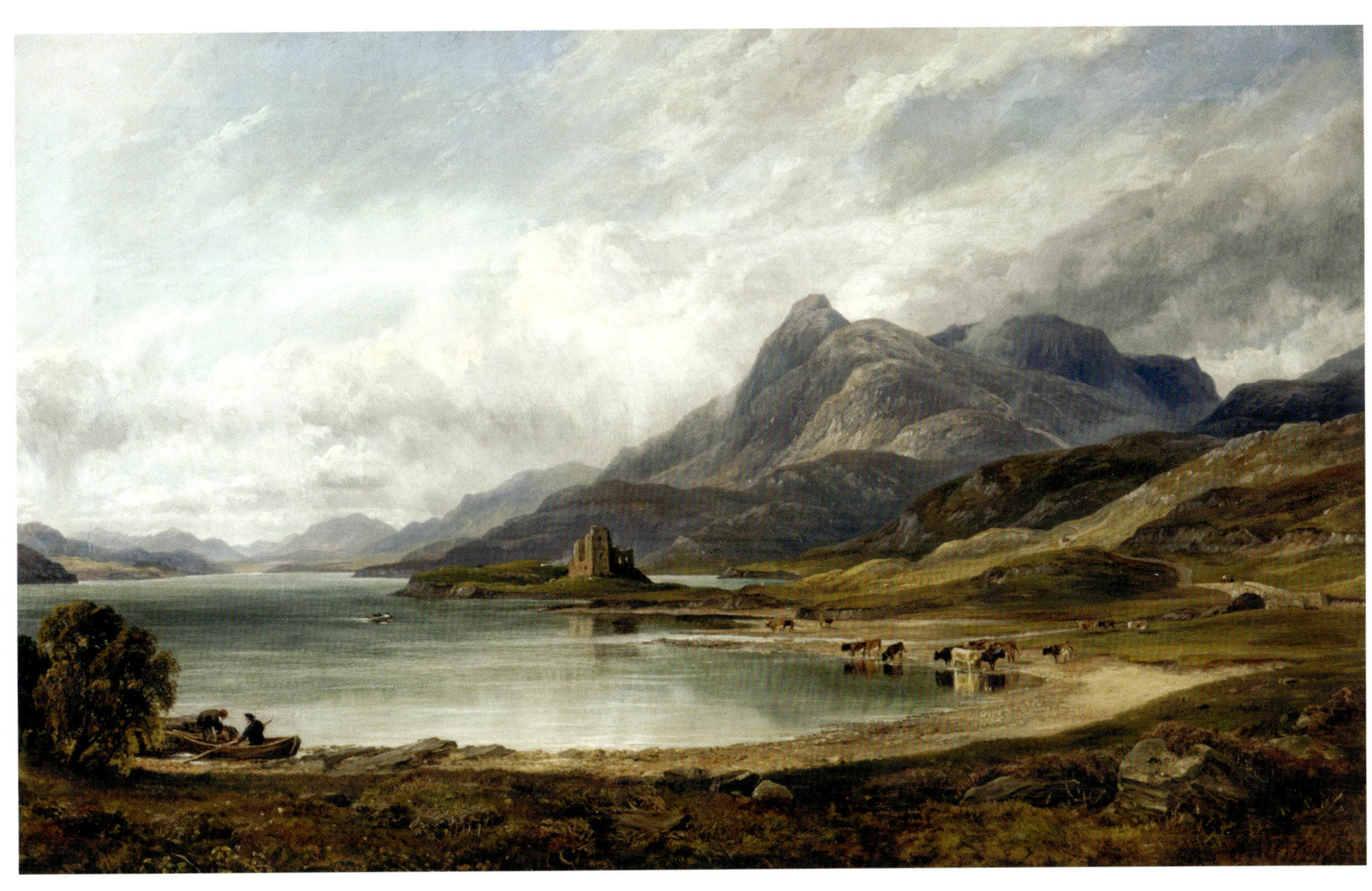

PLATE 53 · *Loch Assynt, Sutherlandshire* · **Arthur Perigal**

oil on canvas · 67 x 111.5 cm · 1874 Autumn Exhibition no. 339

The Dick Institute, Kilmarnock (East Ayrshire Council)

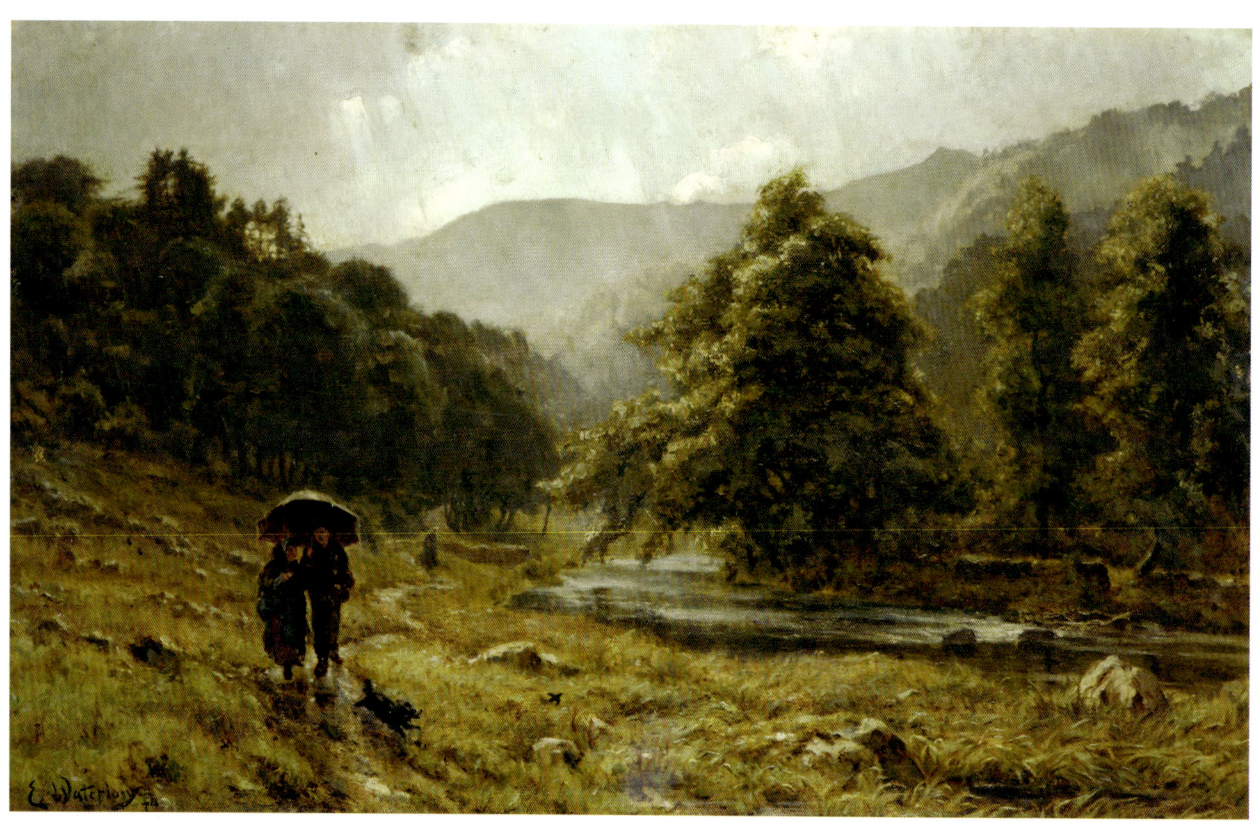

PLATE 54 · *A Summer Shower* · Ernest A. Waterlow
oil on canvas · 61 x 91.5 cm · 1874 Autumn Exhibition no. 66
National Museums Liverpool (Walker Art Gallery)

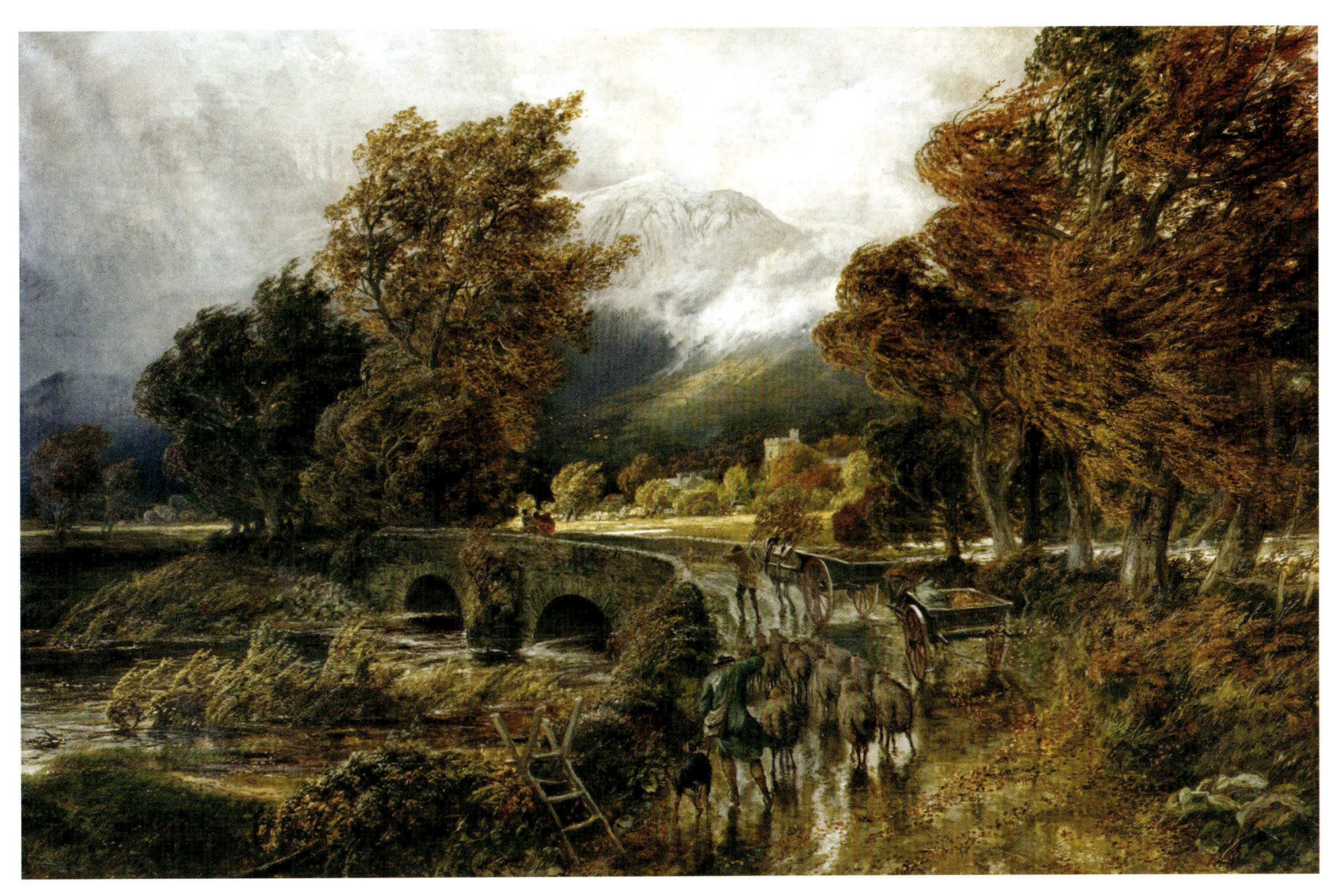

PLATE 55 · *Crossthwaite Bridge, near Keswick* · Sam Bough
oil on canvas · 94 x 155 cm · 1874 Autumn Exhibition no. 157
© CSG CIC Glasgow Museums Collection

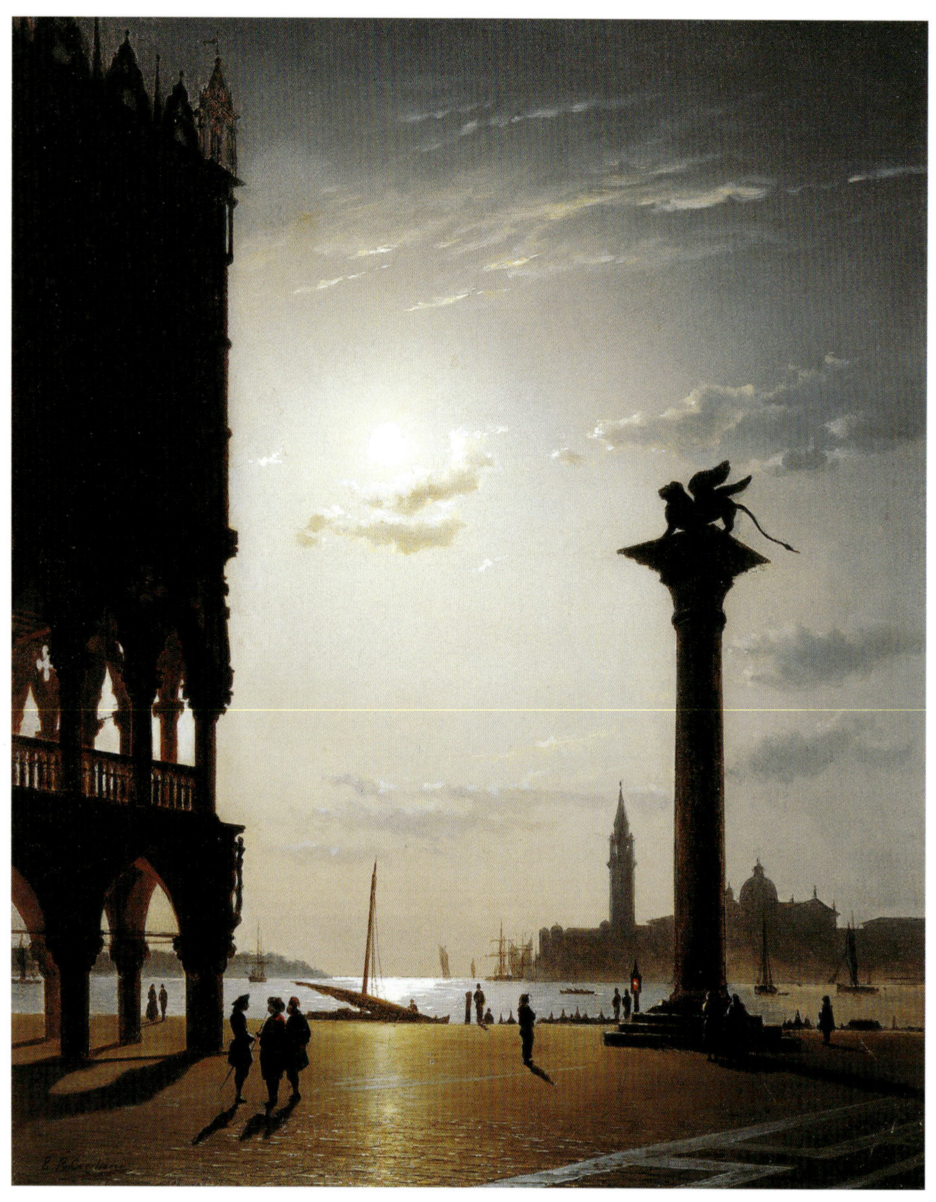

PLATE 56 · *St Mark's Lion, Venice, Moonlight* · Eugenio P. Cecchini
oil on canvas · 48 x 39 cm · 1874 Autumn Exhibition no. 4
Castello Sforzesco, Milan; De Agostini Picture Library/Studio AB/Bridgeman Images

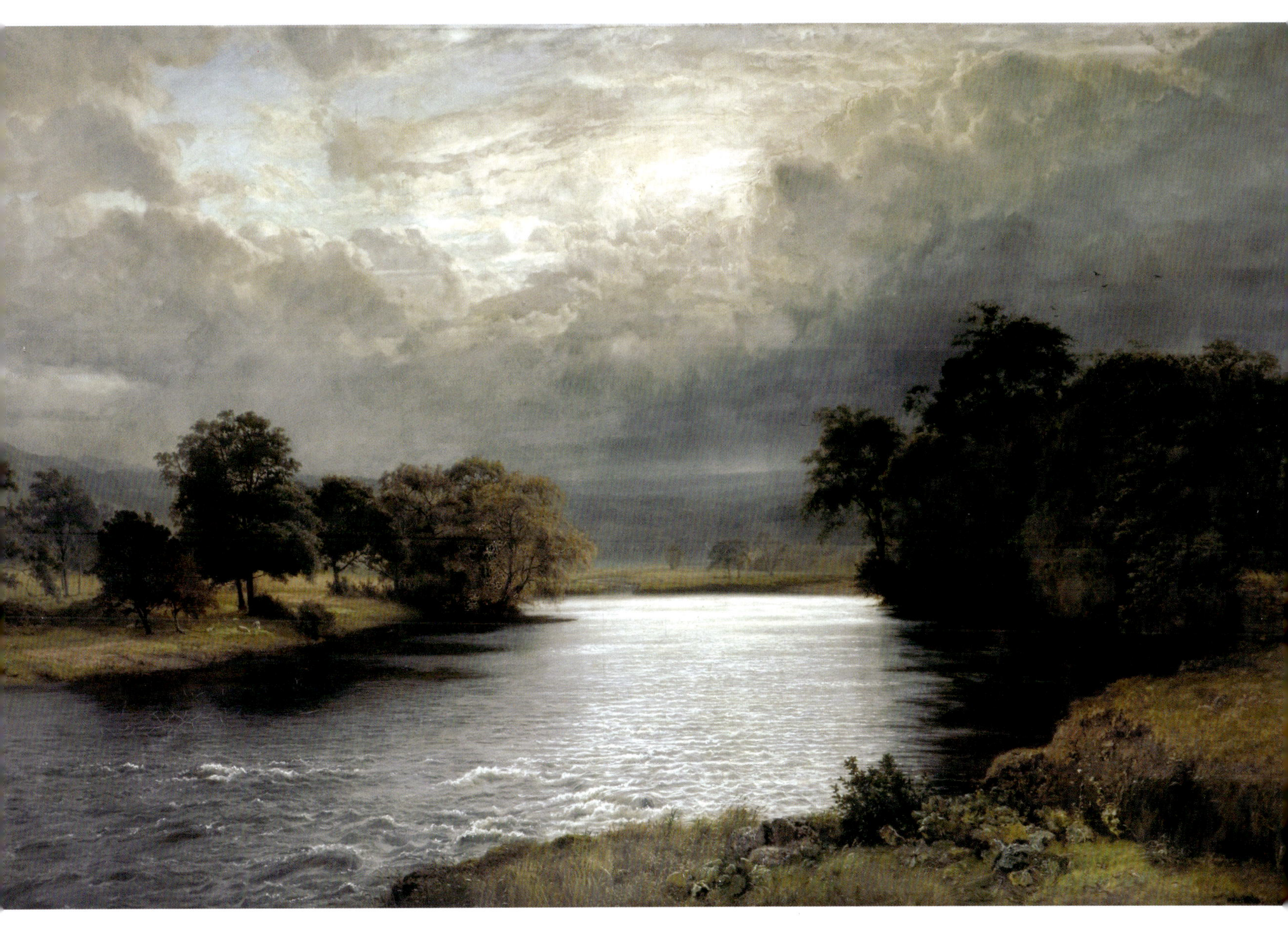

PLATE 57 · *The Diamond Fields* · Richard P. Richards
oil on canvas · 112.5 x 169 cm · 1874 Autumn Exhibition no. 230
National Museums Liverpool (Walker Art Gallery)

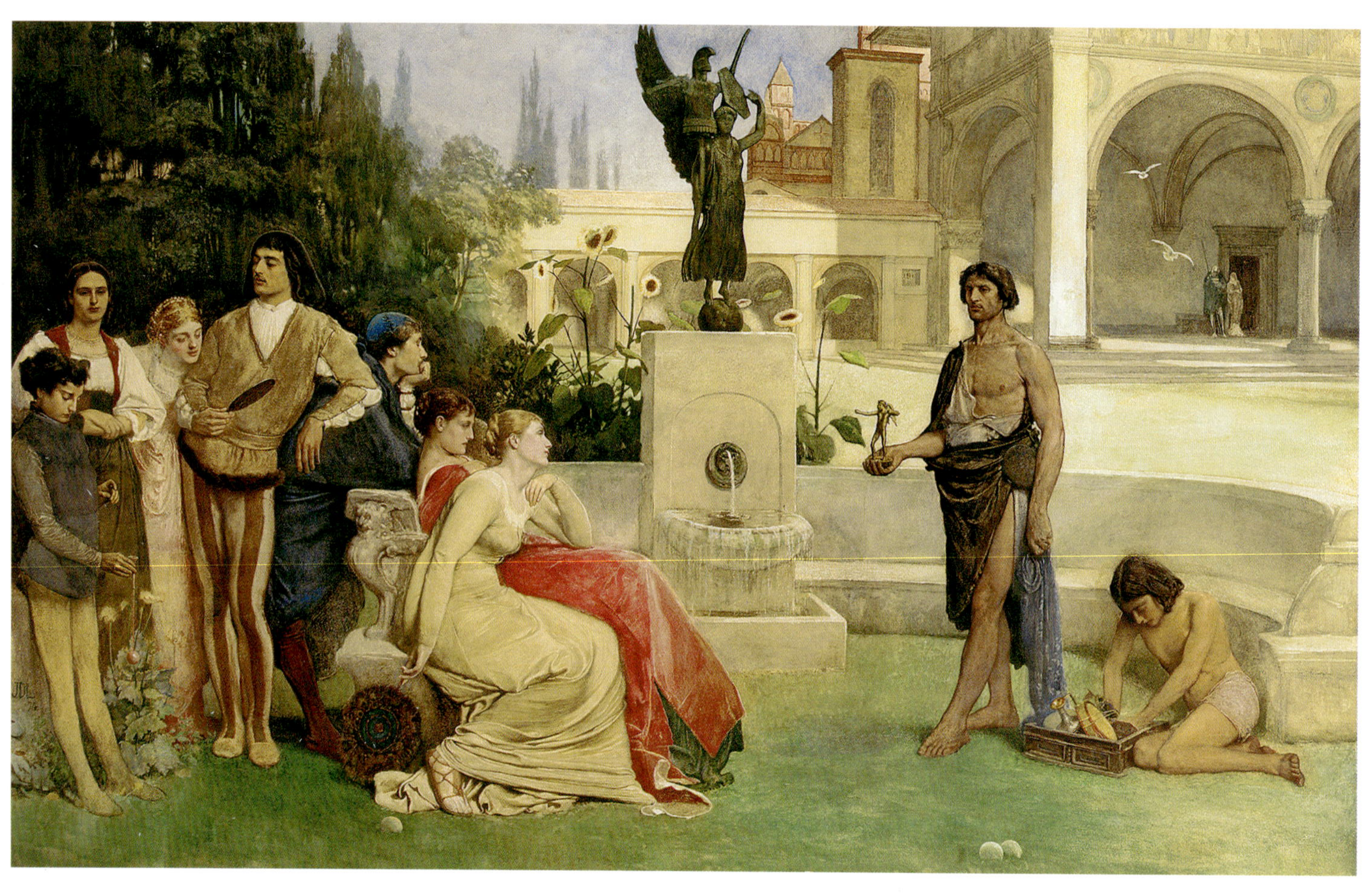

PLATE 58 · *The Lotus Eaters* · James Dromgole Linton
watercolour on paper · 63.5 x 101 cm · 1874 Autumn Exhibition no. 712
Christie's, 29 October 1985 (lot 83) · © 1985 Christie's Images Limited

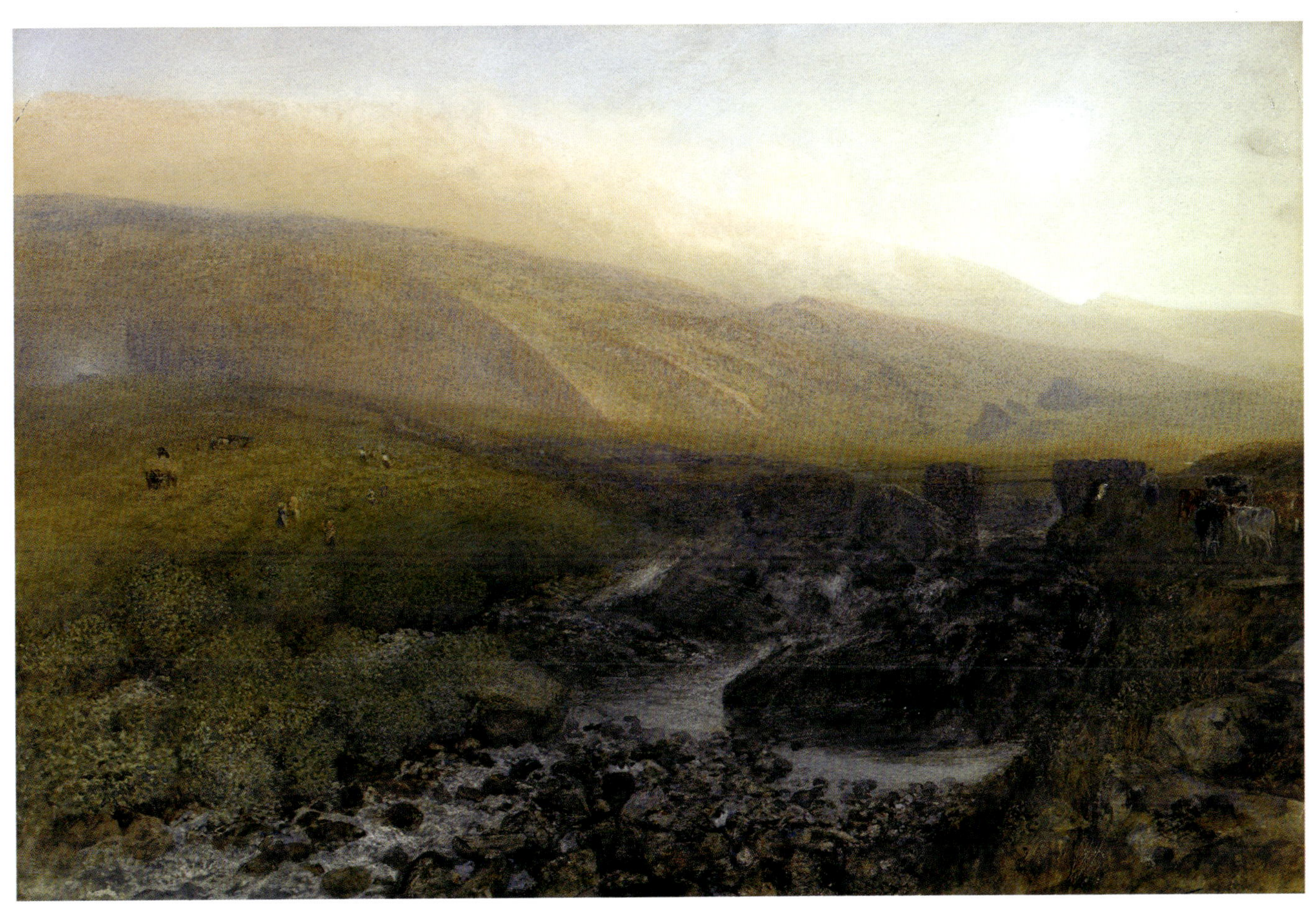

PLATE 59 · *Working Late* · **Alfred W. Hunt**
watercolour on paper · 49.5 x 75 cm · 1874 Autumn Exhibition no. 720
National Museums Liverpool (Walker Art Gallery)

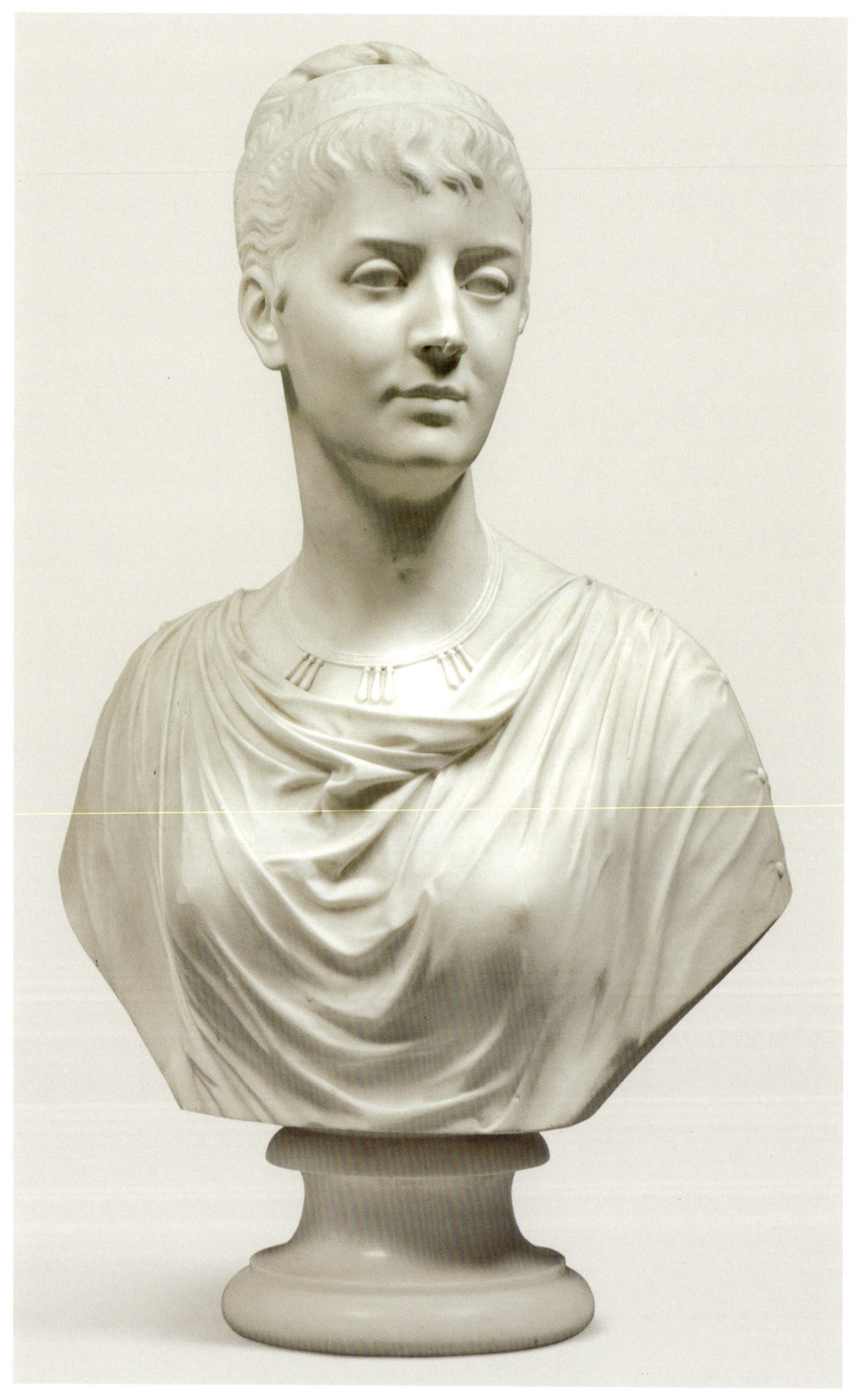

PLATE 60 · *Nellie* · **Edward Davis**

marble · 76 cm high · 1874 Autumn Exhibition no. 1108

Christie's, 31 January 2018 (lot 201) · © 2018 Christie's Images Limited

Paintings by numbers 1874

		No. of artists	Oils	Works on paper	Sculpture	Total no. of works
Liverpool	*Men*	41	28	64	5	97
	Women	15	6	16	–	22
	Not known	21	16	30	1	47
	Total	77	50	110	6	166
Birkenhead	*Men*	4	2	2	–	4
	Women	4	3	4		7
	Not known	6	7	5	1	13
	Total	14	12	11	1	24
Chester	*Men*	3	2	6	–	8
	Women	2	–	3	–	3
	Not known	1	2	–	–	2
	Total	6	4	9	–	13
Wirral excluding Birkenhead	*Men*	4	2	6	–	8
	Women	3	–	3	–	3
	Not known	6	3	6	–	9
	Total	13	5	15	–	20
Manchester	*Men*	1	–	2	–	2
	Women	1	2	–	–	2
	Not known	5	4	3	–	7
	Total	7	6	5	–	11
Lancashire excluding Manchester	*Men*	7	4	13	–	17
	Women	1	–	3	–	3
	Not known	5	1	8	–	9
	Total	13	5	24	–	29
N.W. England excluding Lancashire and Wirral	*Men*	2	1	1	–	2
	Women	–	–	–	–	–
	Not known	3	1	6	–	7
	Total	5	2	7	–	9
North Wales	*Men*	2	–	4	–	4
	Women	–	–	–	–	–
	Not known	6	3	7	–	10
	Total	8	3	11	–	14
Edinburgh	*Men*	11	12	8	–	20
	Women	–	–	–	–	–
	Not known	2	3	–	–	3
	Total	13	15	8	–	23
The rest of Scotland and Ireland	*Men*	4	6	–	5	11
	Women	–	–	–	–	–
	Not known	2	–	3	–	3
	Total	6	6	3	5	14
Birmingham	*Men*	–	–	–	–	–
	Women	–	–	–	–	–
	Not known	2	2	3	–	5
	Total	2	2	3	–	5
South of England	*Men*	18	21	10	–	31
	Women	5	5	6	–	11
	Not known	8	7	11	–	18
	Total	31	33	27	–	60
West of England	*Men*	5	3	11	–	14
	Women	2	–	6	–	6
	Not known	4	4	5	–	9
	Total	11	7	22	–	29

		No. of artists	Oils	Works on paper	Sculpture	Total no. of works
East Anglia and The Midlands	*Men*	4	2	4	–	6
	Women	6	1	11	–	12
	Not known	7	7	2	–	9
	Total	17	10	17	–	27
N.E. England	*Men*	2	1	5	–	6
	Women	1	1	–	–	1
	Not known	3	3	4	–	7
	Total	6	5	9	–	14
Foreign addresses	*Men*	11	16	–	1	17
	Women	2	4	–	–	4
	Not known	–	–	–	–	–
	Total	13	20	–	1	21
No address	*Men*	16	14	4	–	18
	Women	5	2	6	–	8
	Not known	15	9	11	–	20
	Total	36	25	21	–	46
London: Hampstead	*Men*	8	8	9	–	17
	Women	1	1	1	–	2
	Not known	2	2	3	–	5
	Total	11	11	13	–	24
London: Haverstock Hill	*Men*	24	26	21	–	47
	Women	1	–	1	–	1
	Not known	2	1	3	–	4
	Total	27	27	25	–	52
London: St John's Wood	*Men*	14	9	14	–	23
	Women	–	–	–	–	–
	Not known	9	7	14	–	21
	Total	23	16	28	–	44
London: Kensington	*Men*	31	25	17	–	42
	Women	7	9	8	–	17
	Not known	6	7	2	–	9
	Total	44	41	27	–	68
London: Regent's Park	*Men*	8	13	–	3	16
	Women	3	2	3	–	5
	Not known	5	7	1	–	8
	Total	16	22	4	3	29
London: Fitzroy Square	*Men*	6	6	3	3	12
	Women	1	1	1	–	2
	Not known	8	10	2	–	12
	Total	15	17	6	3	26
The rest of inner London	*Men*	86	85	48	12	145
	Women	20	16	24	–	40
	Not known	73	58	74	5	137
	Total	179	159	146	17	322
London: suburbs	*Men*	5	5	7	–	12
	Women	5	3	5	–	8
	Not known	4	–	10	–	10
	Total	14	8	22	–	30
Grand totals	*Men*	317	291	259	29	579
	Women	85	56	101	–	157
	Not known	205	164	213	7	384
	Total	**607**	**511**	**573**	**36**	**1120**

1875

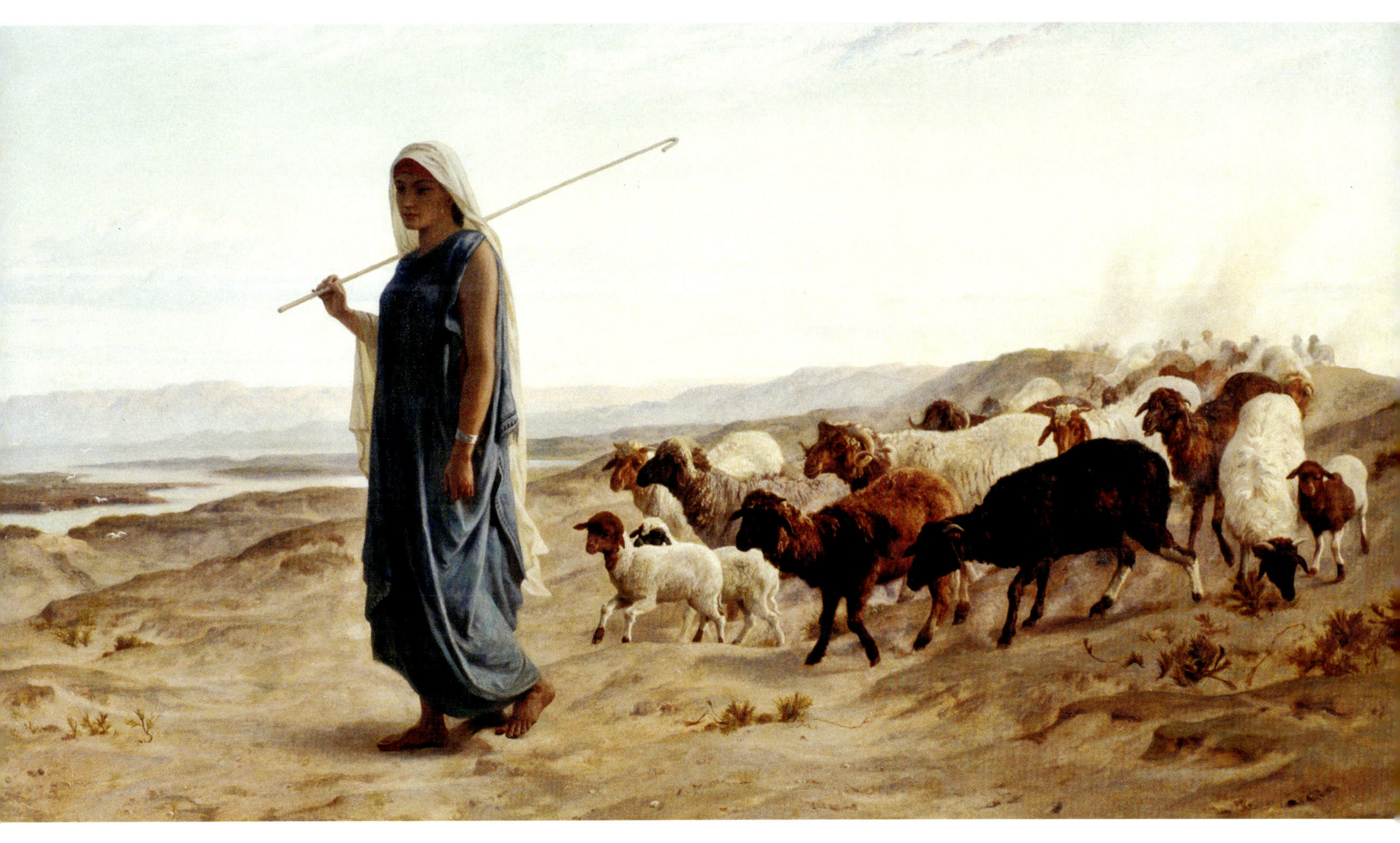

PLATE 61 · _Rachel and her Flock_ · Frederick Goodall
oil on canvas · 97 x 178 cm · 1875 Autumn Exhibition no. 51
courtesy Richard Redding Antiques Ltd

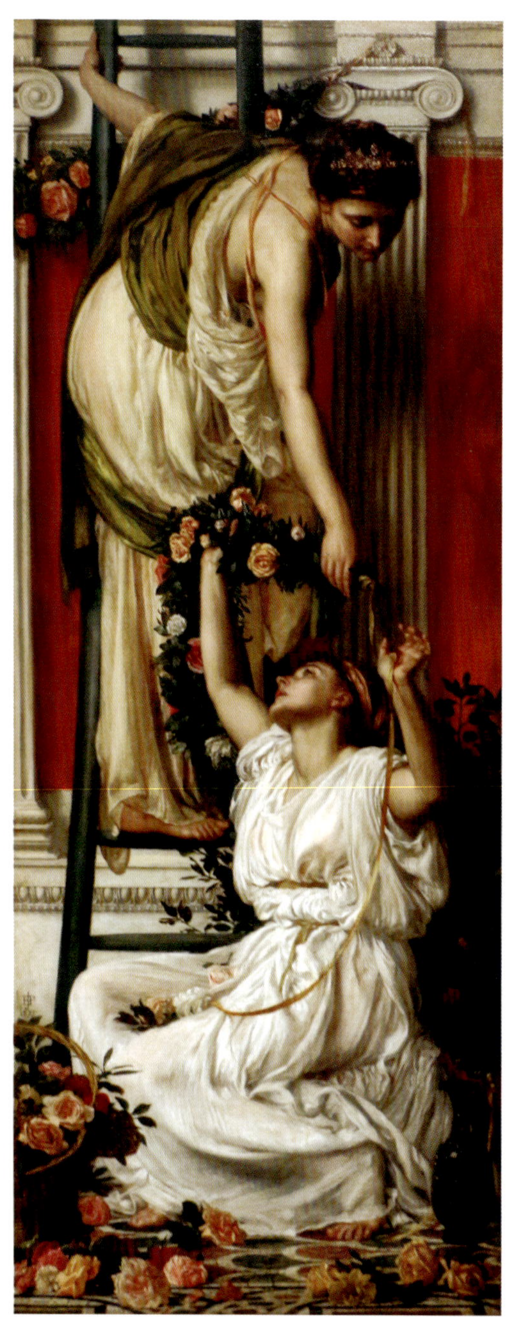

PLATE 62 · *The Festival* · E.J. Poynter
oil on canvas · 137 x 53.5 cm · 1875 Autumn Exhibition no. 99
Art Institute of Chicago, bequest of Suzette Morton Davidson · © 2019 Art Resource NY/Scala, Florence

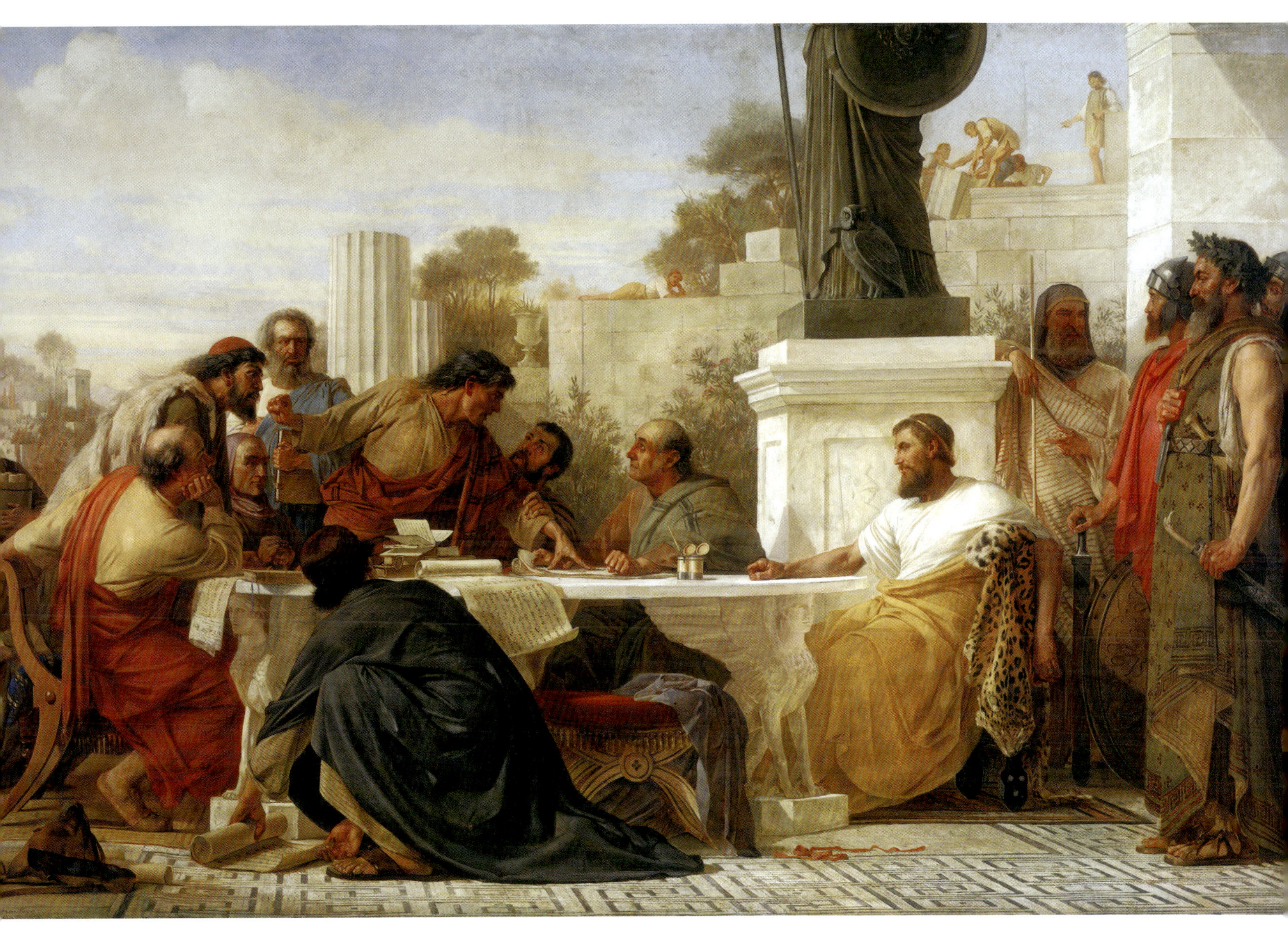

PLATE 63 · *Julian the Apostate Presiding at a Conference of Sectarians* · Edward Armitage
oil on canvas · 174.5 x 272 cm · 1875 Autumn Exhibition no. 172
National Museums Liverpool (Walker Art Gallery)

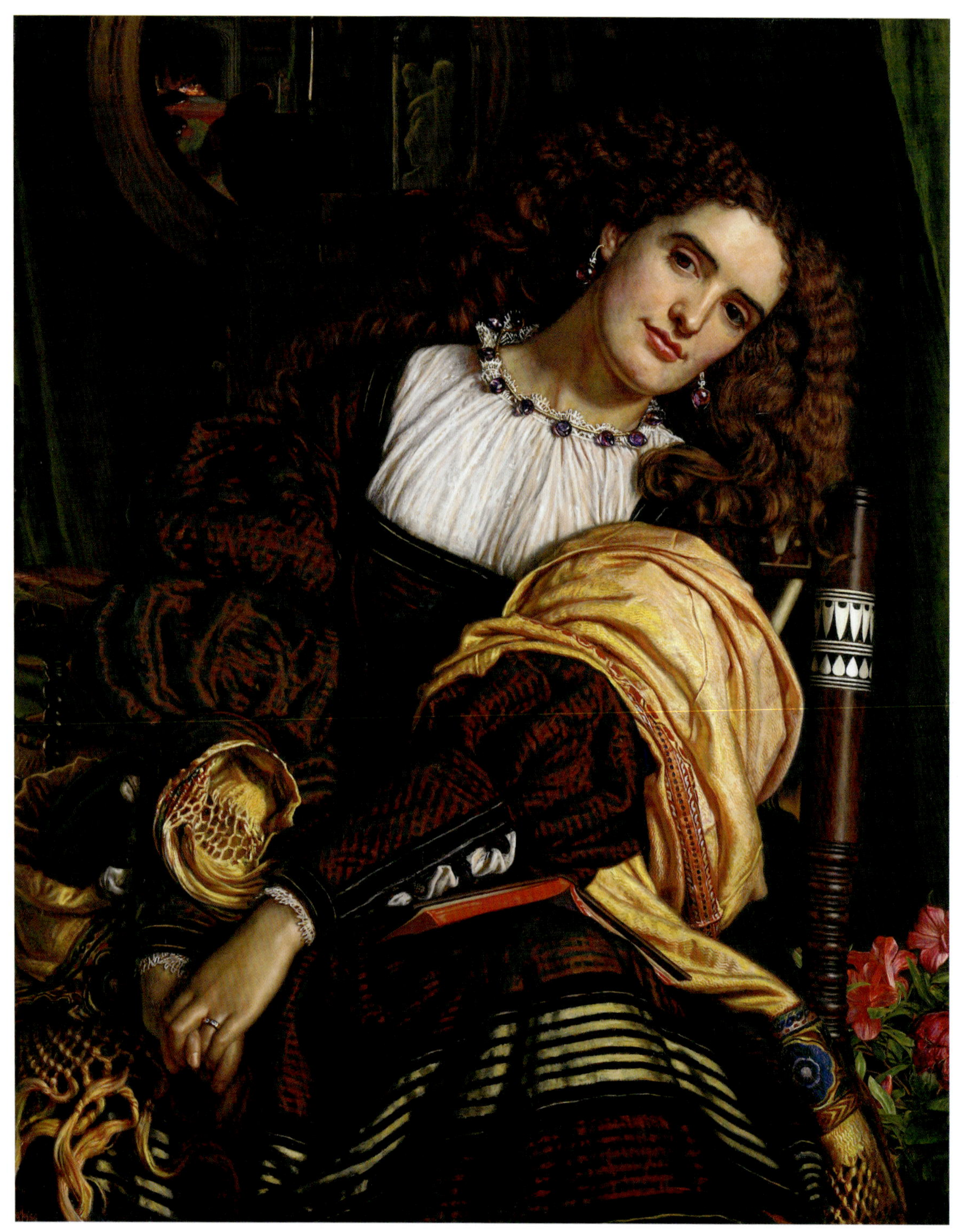

PLATE 64 · *Dolce Far Niente* · William Holman Hunt
oil on canvas · 99.5 x 82 cm · 1875 Autumn Exhibition no. 311
private collection, on loan to National Museums Liverpool (Walker Art Gallery)

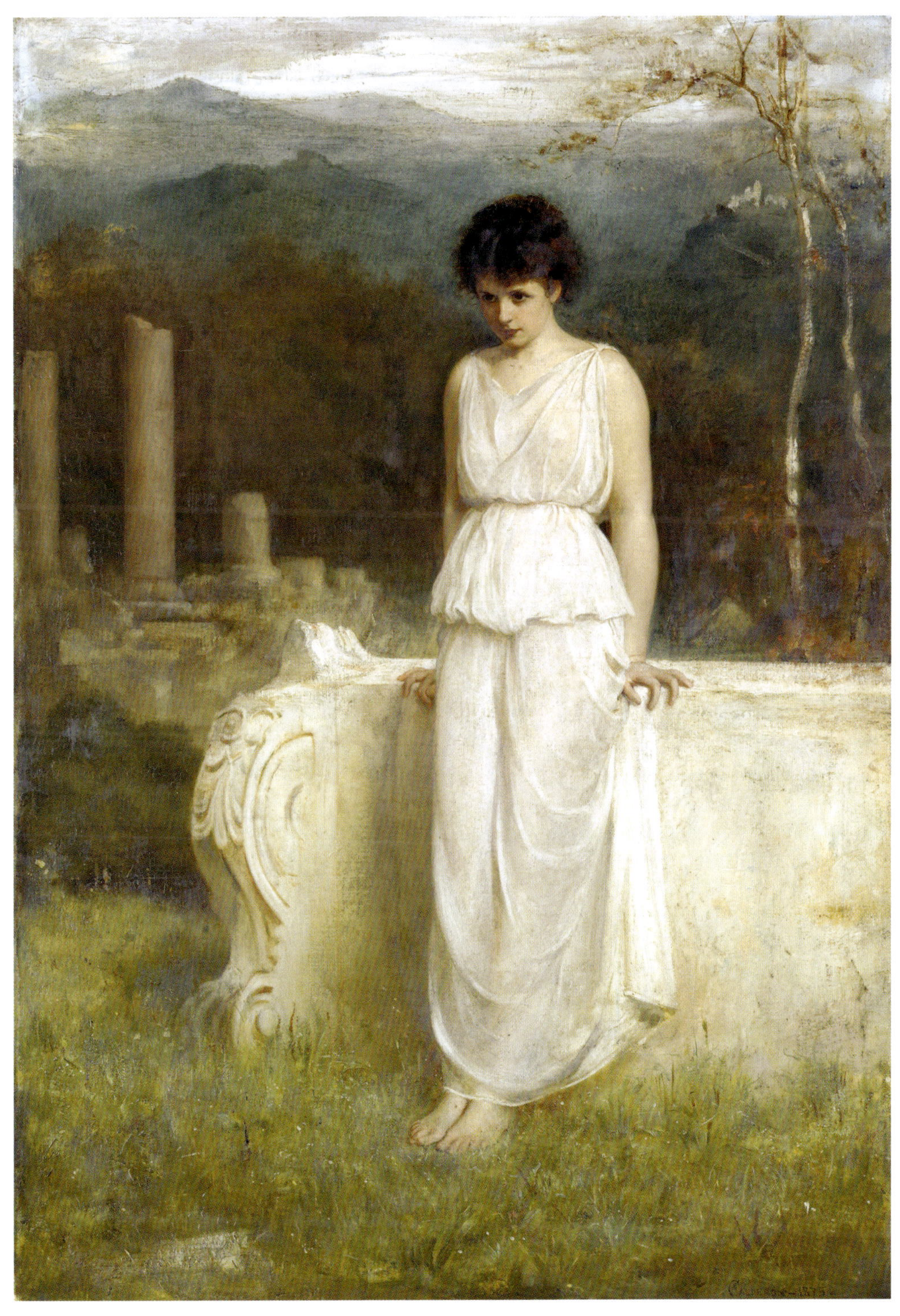

PLATE 65 · *"Her eyes are with her heart, and that is far away"* · Philip H. Calderon
oil on canvas · 92 x 64.5 cm · 1875 Autumn Exhibition no. 106
National Museums Liverpool (Sudley House)

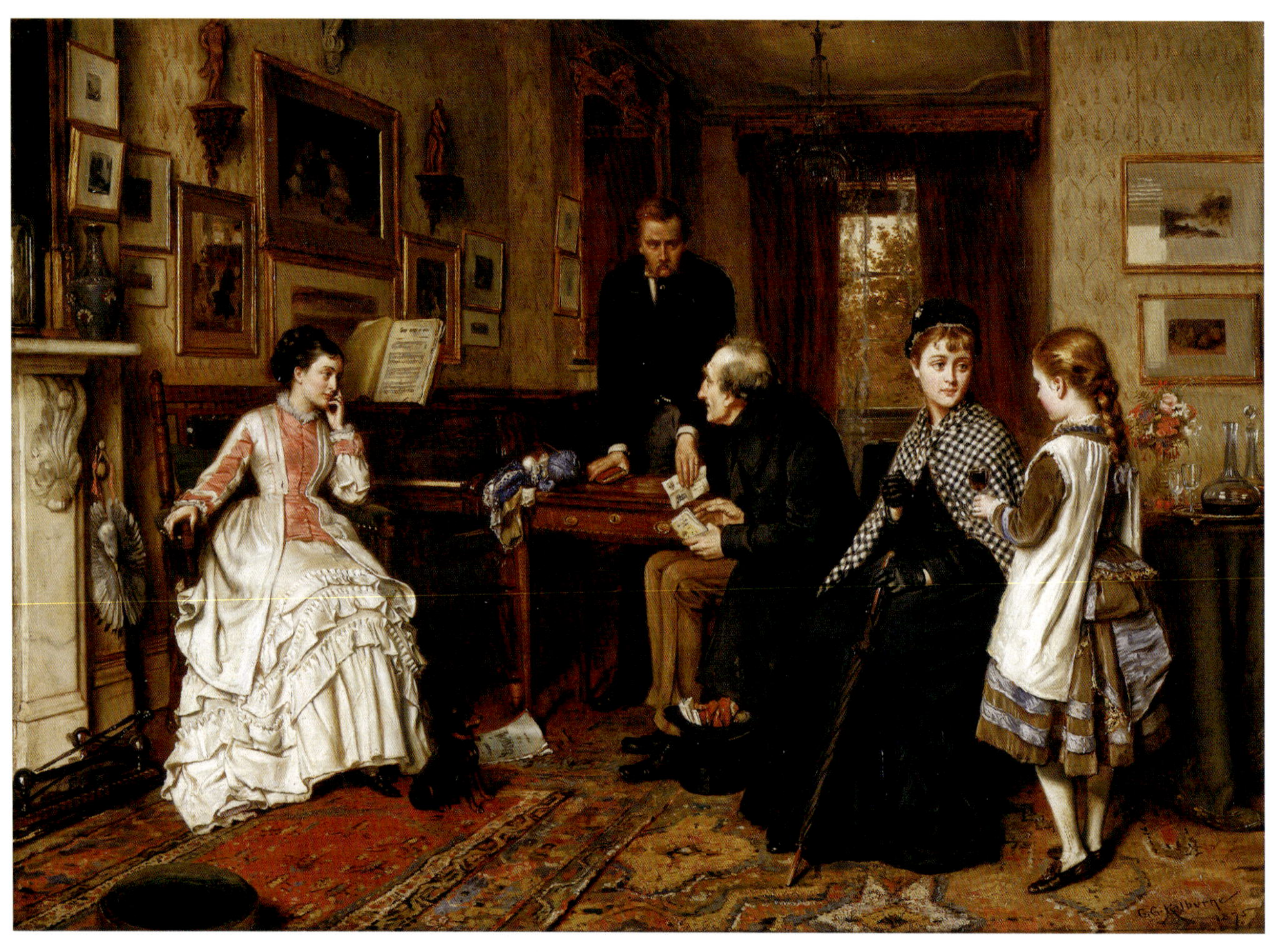

PLATE 66 · *Poor Relations* · **George Goodwin Kilburne**
oil on canvas · 76.5 x 107 cm · 1875 Autumn Exhibition no. 119
National Museums Liverpool (Walker Art Gallery)

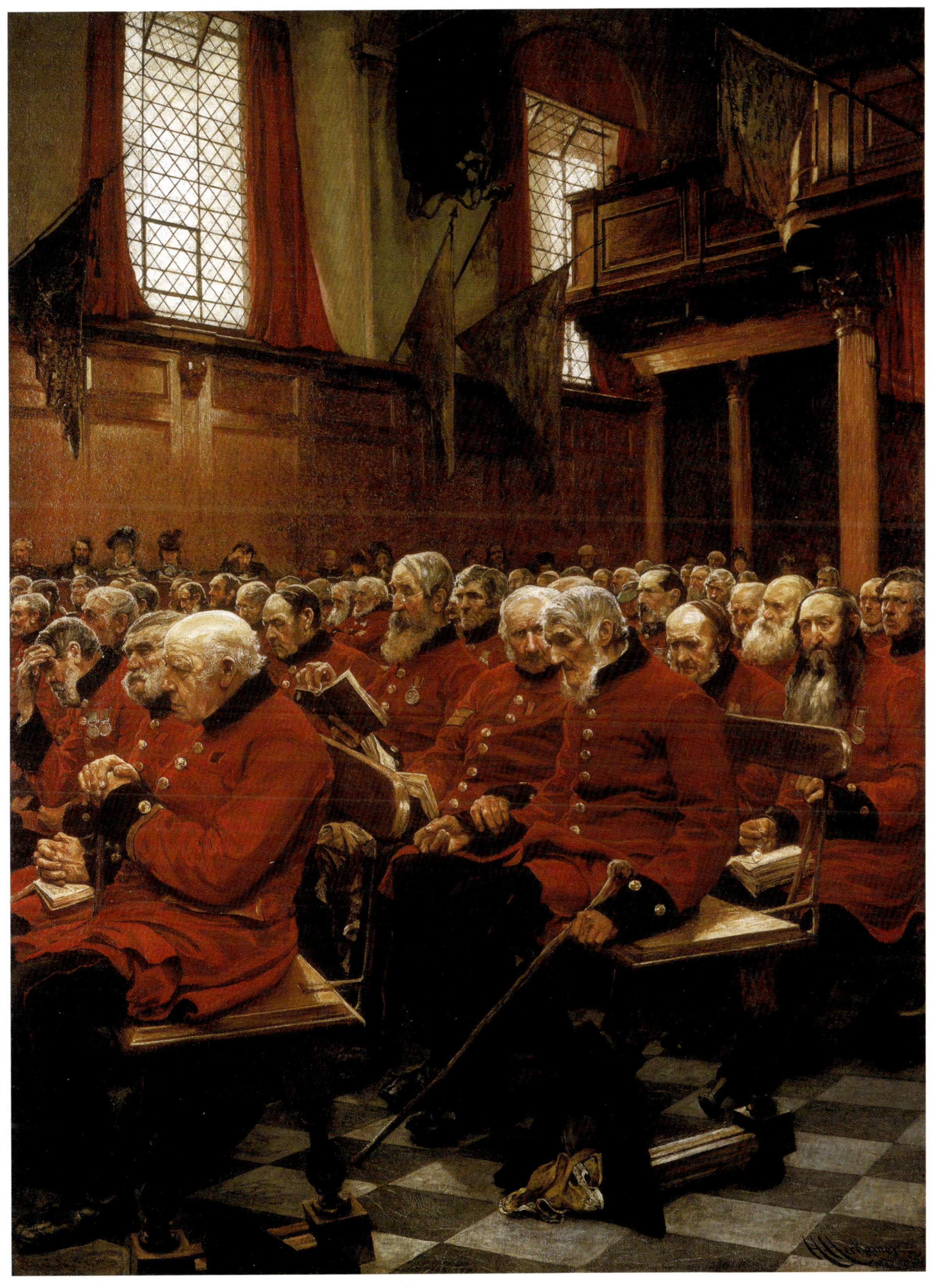

PLATE 67 · *The Last Muster: Sunday at the Royal Hospital, Chelsea* · Hubert von Herkomer
oil on canvas · 214.5 x 159 cm · 1875 Autumn Exhibition no. 292
National Museums Liverpool (Lady Lever Art Gallery)

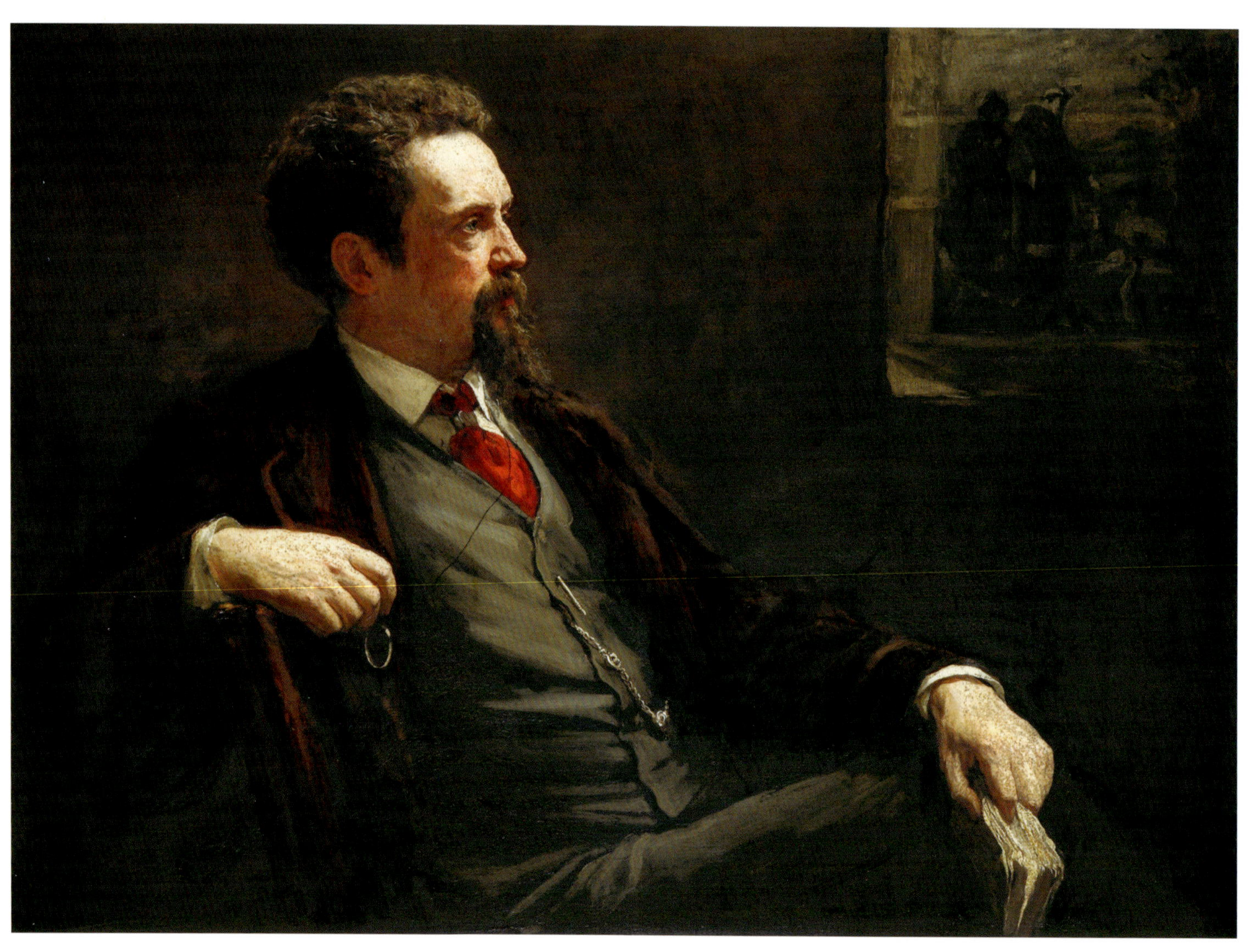

PLATE 68 · *H.S. Marks, Esq.,* A.R.A. · W.W. Ouless
oil on canvas · 87.5 x 113 cm · 1875 Autumn Exhibition no. 73
National Museums Liverpool (Walker Art Gallery)

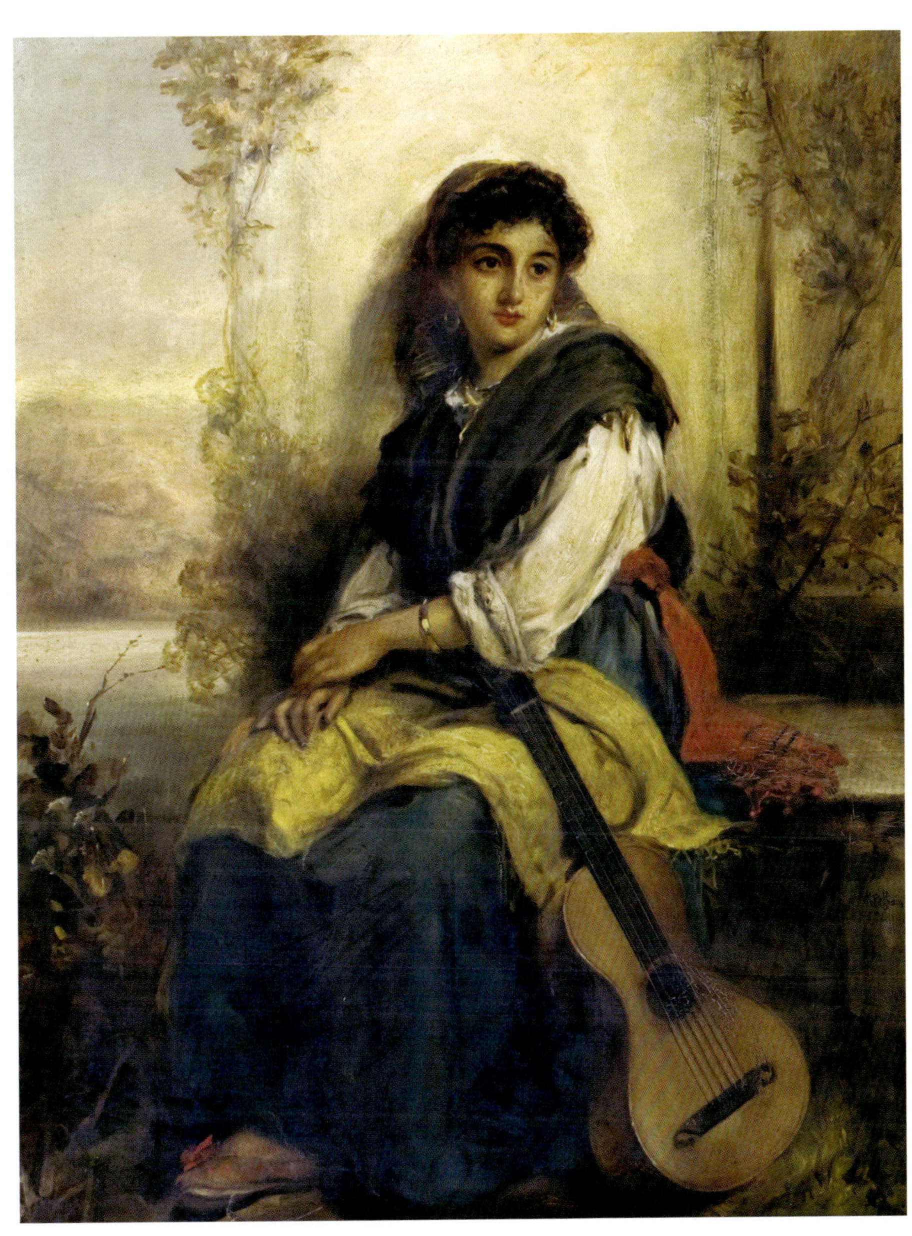

PLATE 69 · *A Minstrel of the Basque Provinces* · T.K. Pelham
oil on canvas · 91.5 x 72 cm · 1875 Autumn Exhibition no. 403
Orchar Collection, Broughty Castle Museum (Leisure and Culture Dundee)

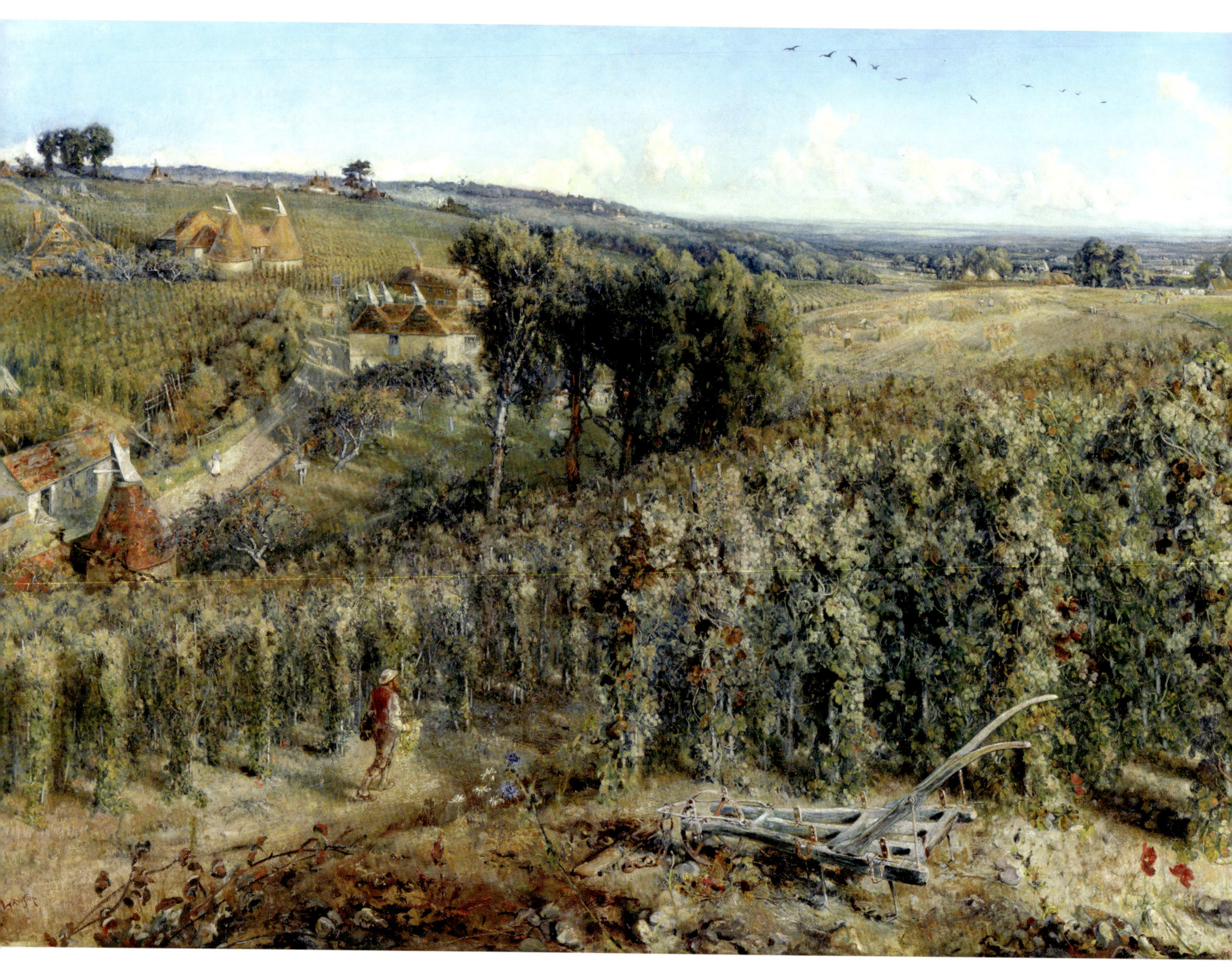

PLATE 70 · *The Hop Gardens of England* · Cecil Gordon Lawson

oil on canvas · 153.5 x 213.5 cm · 1875 Autumn Exhibition no. 100

Tate · © Tate, London 2019

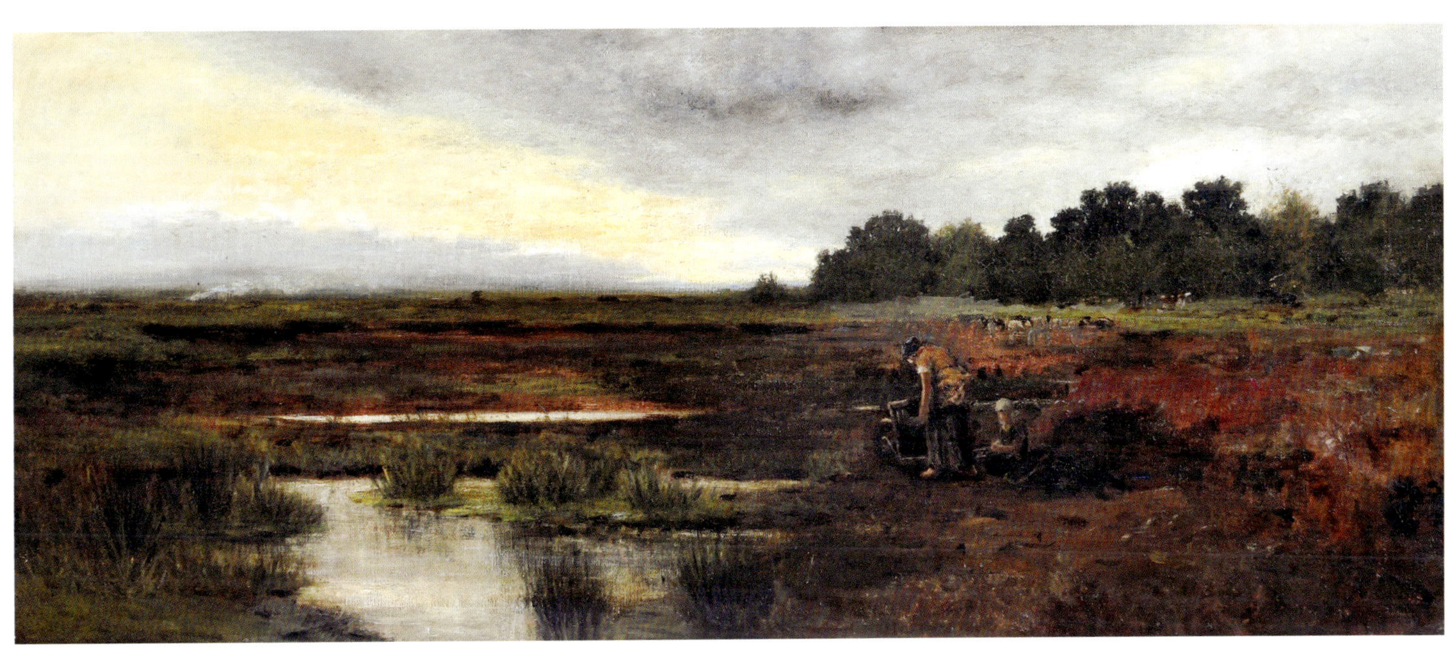

PLATE 71 · *Peat Moss, Scotland* · Leslie Thomson
oil on canvas · 50 x 121 cm · 1875 Autumn Exhibition no. 217
Bangor University

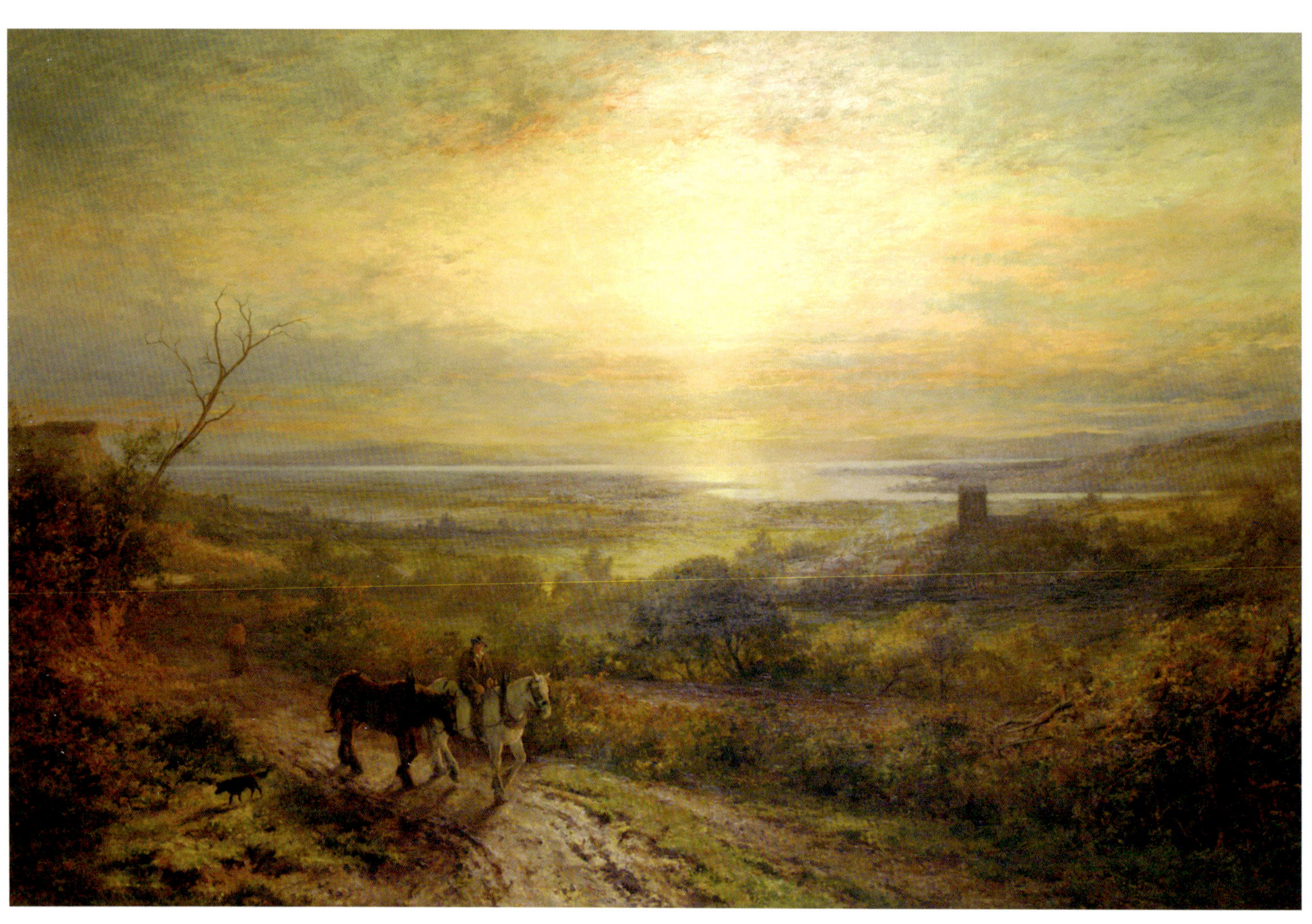

PLATE 72 · *Meeting of the Rivers Mersey and Weaver* · John Finnie

oil on canvas · 118 x 180 cm · 1875 Autumn Exhibition no. 41

reproduced by kind permission of Portsmouth Museums Service, Portsmouth City Council

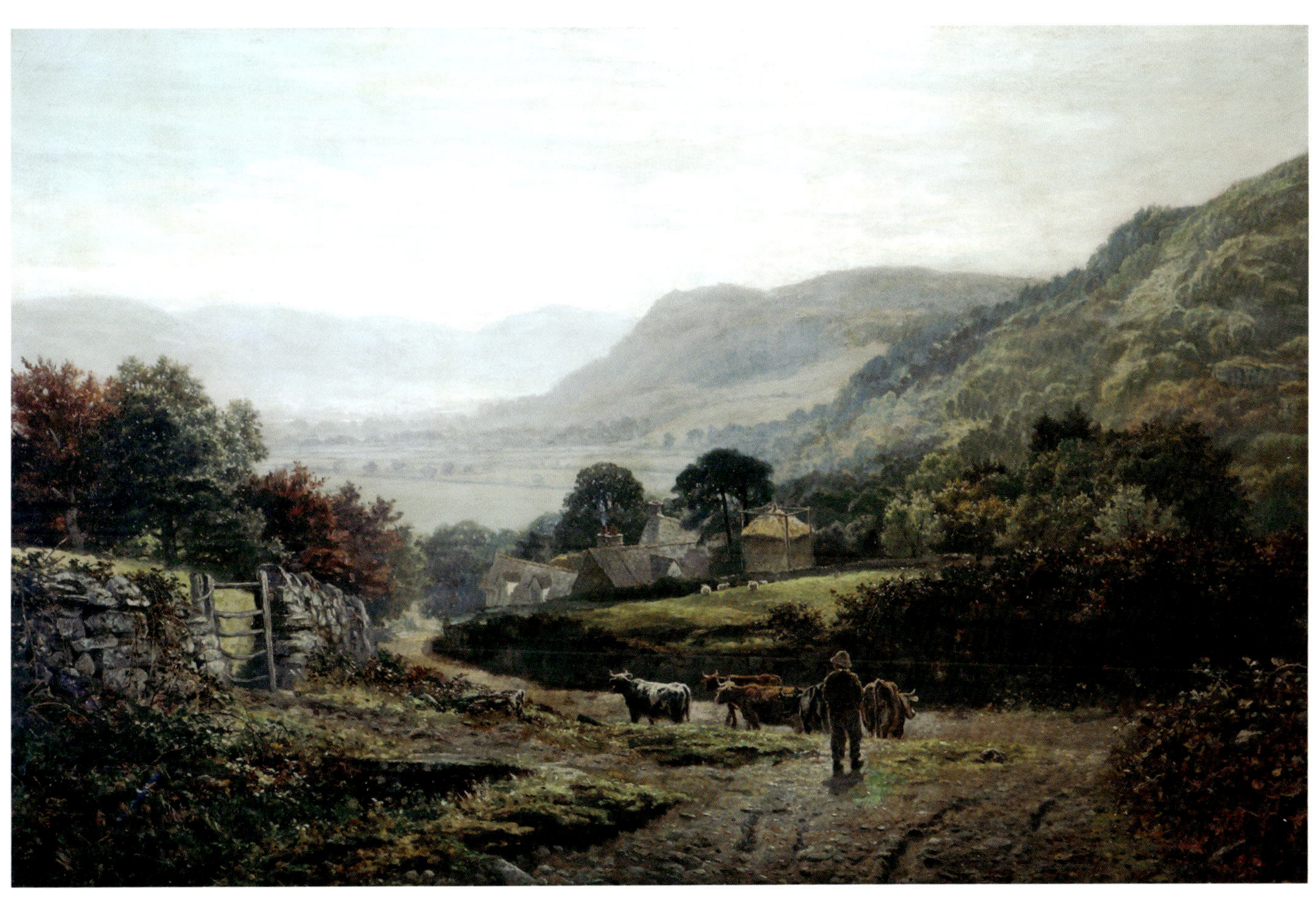

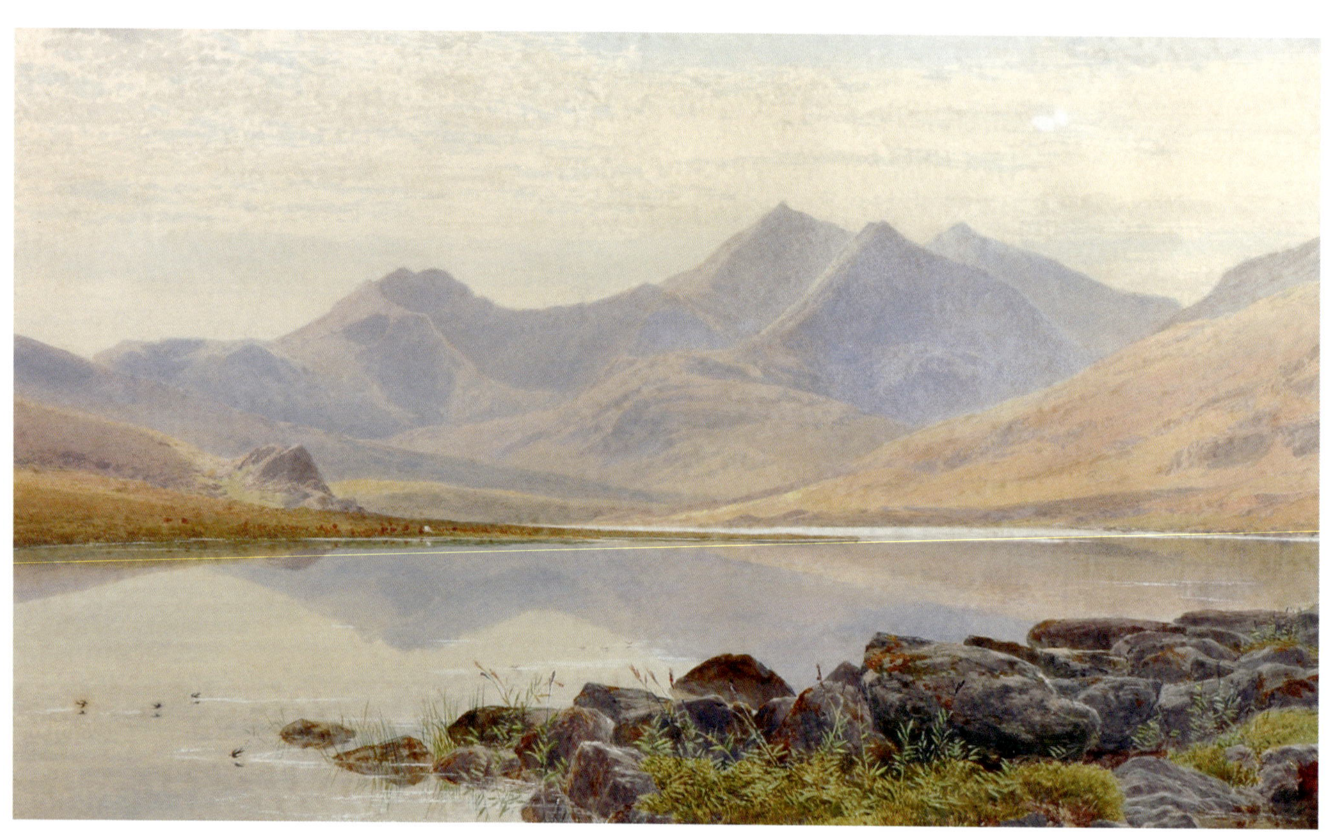

PLATE 74 · *Snowdon* · James Jackson Curnock
watercolour on paper · 35.5 x 59.5 cm · 1875 Autumn Exhibition no. 543
John Nicholson's, Haslemere, 15 June 2016 (lot 140) · image courtesy John Nicholson's Auction Rooms

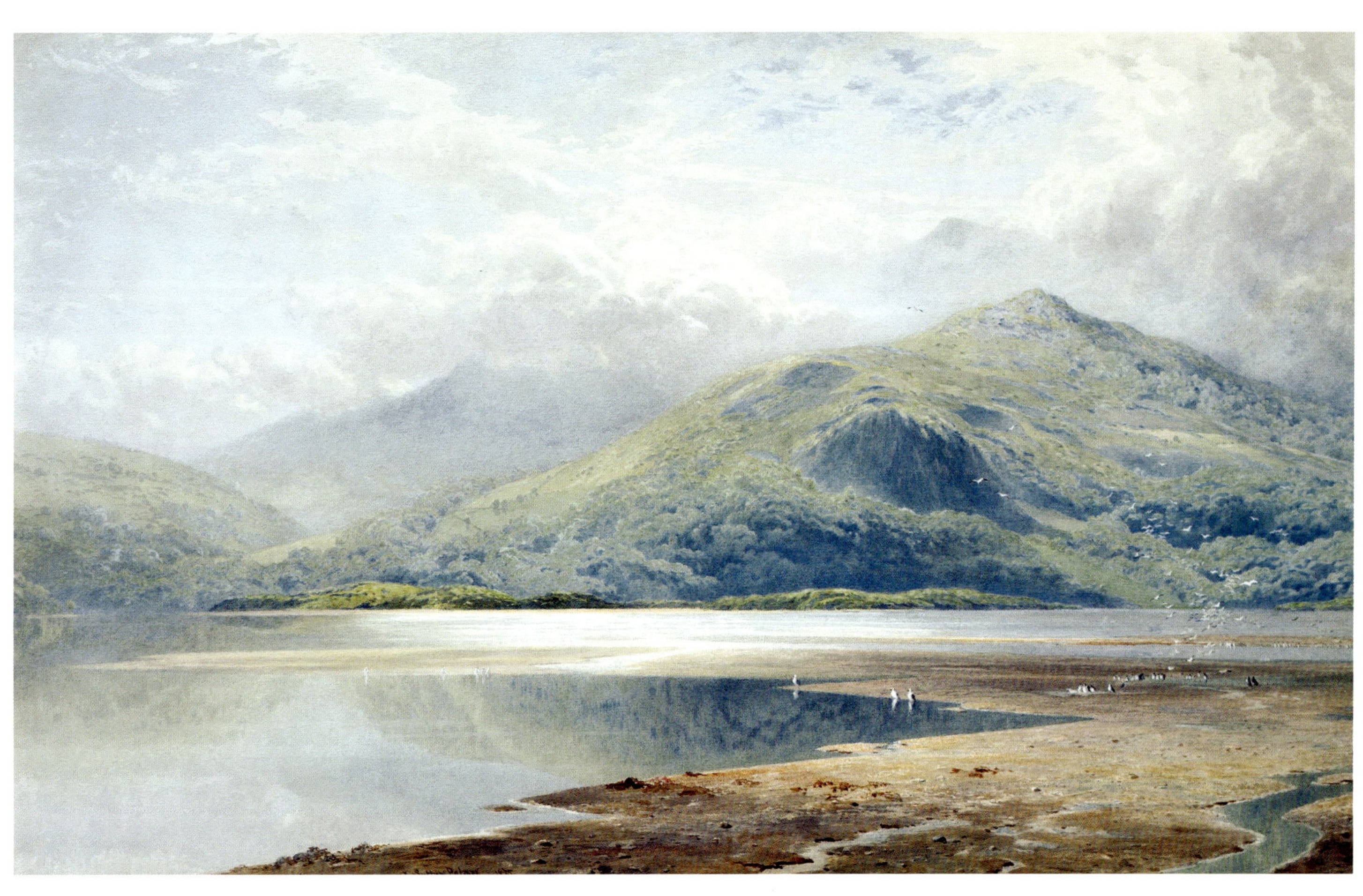

PLATE 75 · *Cader Idris, North Wales – Early Morning* · Harry Sutton Palmer
watercolour on paper · 47 x 76 cm · 1875 Autumn Exhibition no. 584
Christie's South Kensington, 7 July 2016 (lot 71) · © 2016 Christie's Images Limited

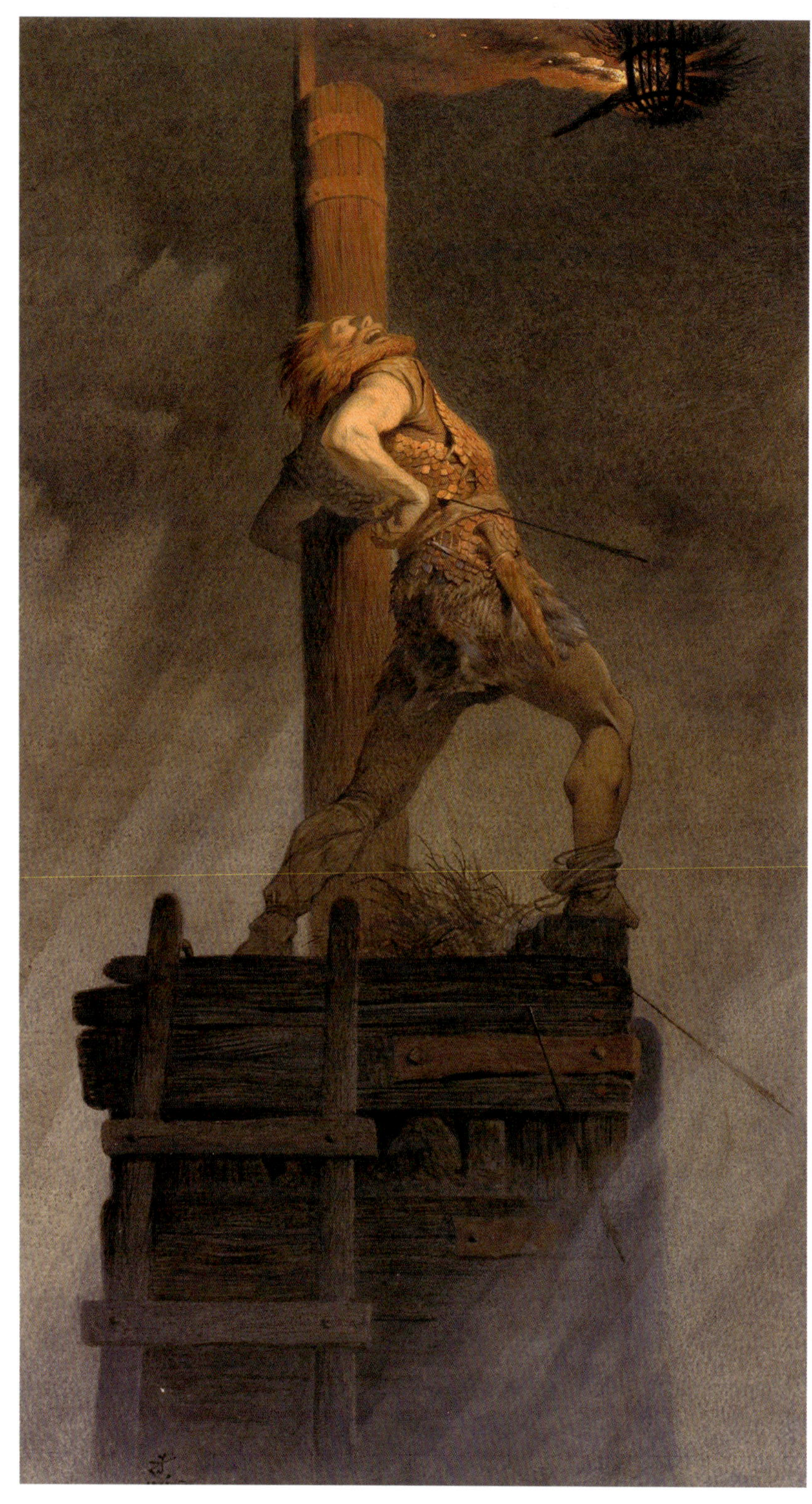

PLATE 76 · *Lighting the Beacon* · John Tenniel
watercolour on paper · 64.5 x 38.5 cm · 1875 Autumn Exhibition no. 993
National Museums Liverpool (Walker Art Gallery)

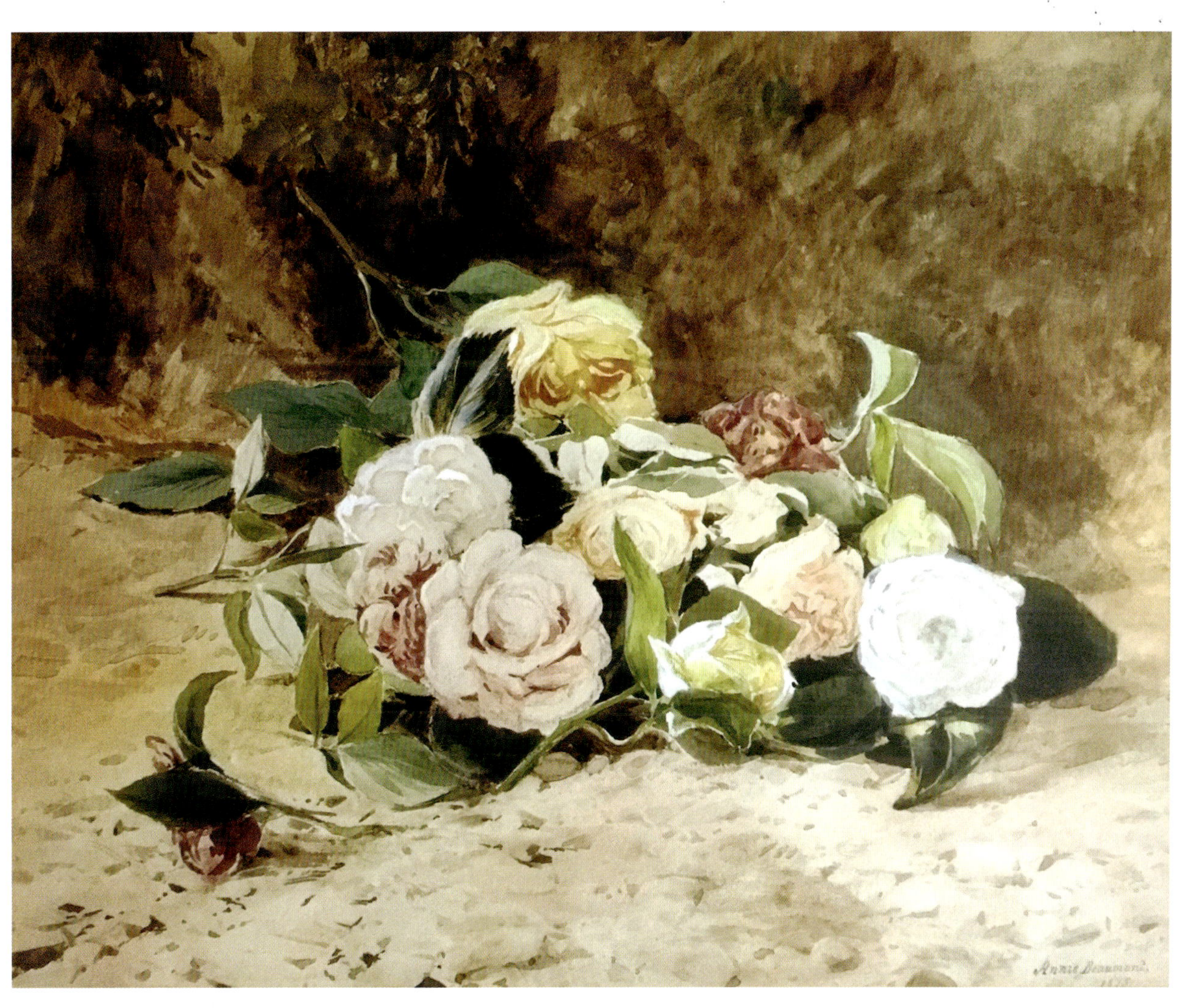

PLATE 77 · *Roses and Camellias* · Annie Beaumont
watercolour on paper · 37.5 x 46 cm · 1875 Autumn Exhibition no. 653
private collection, Liverpool

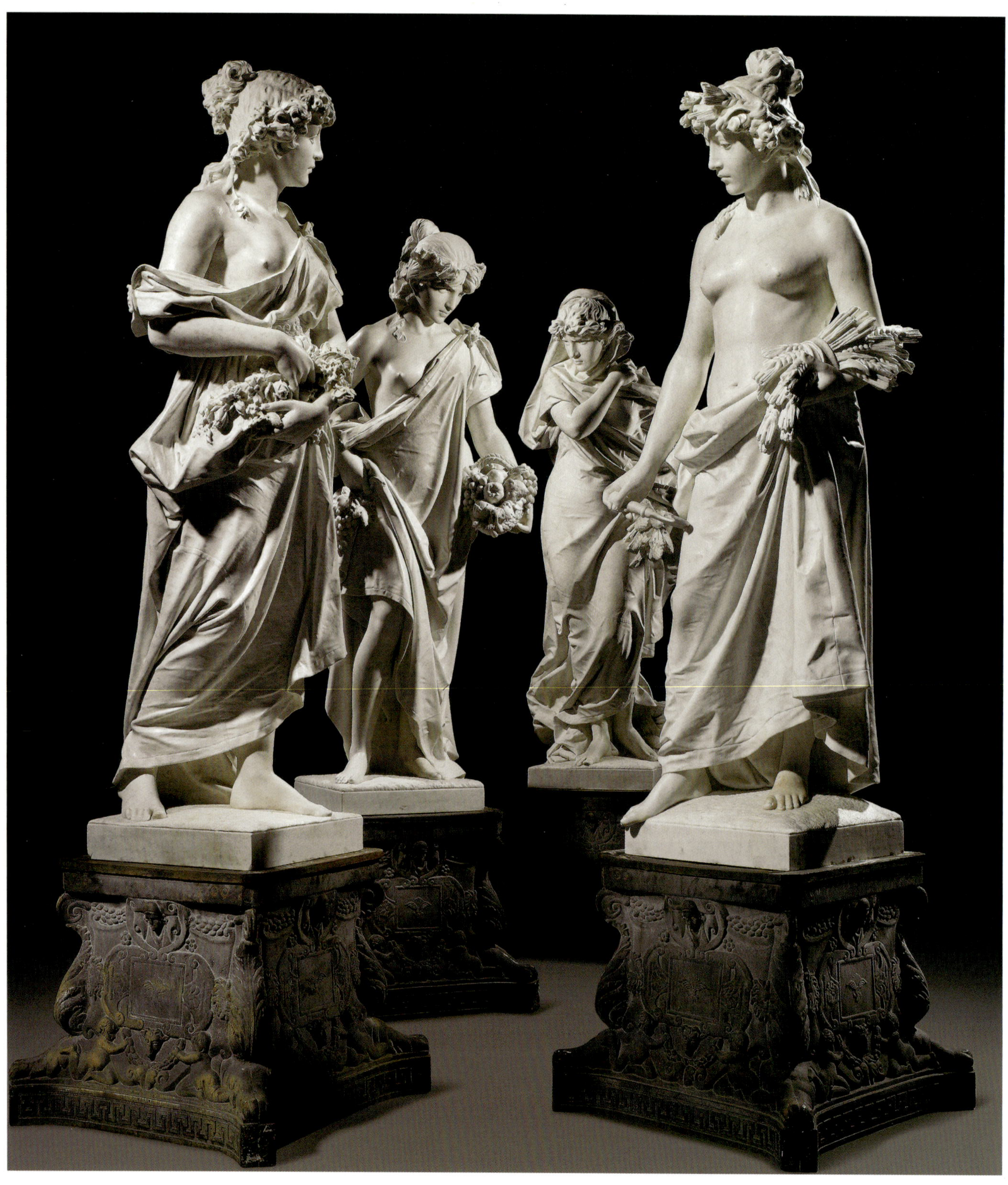

PLATE 78 · *Four Seasons* · Carlo Nicoli
marble · each 166–9 cm high · 1875 Autumn Exhibition nos 1081 (*Spring*), 1083 (*Summer*), 1097 (*Autumn*) and 1101 (*Winter*)
Christie's, 7 June 2016 (lot 150) · © 2016 Christie's Images Limited

Paintings by numbers 1875

		No. of artists	Oils	Works on paper	Sculpture	Total no. of works
Liverpool	Men	43	47	73	5	125
	Women	11	2	18	—	20
	Not known	16	12	26	—	38
	Total	70	61	117	5	183
Birkenhead	Men	5	1	11	—	12
	Women	4	3	5	—	8
	Not known	5	6	3	—	9
	Total	14	10	19	—	29
Chester	Men	2	1	5	—	6
	Women	2	—	7	—	7
	Not known	—	—	—	—	—
	Total	4	1	12	—	13
Wirral excluding Birkenhead	Men	6	—	10	—	10
	Women	3	—	7	—	7
	Not known	3	4	1	—	5
	Total	12	4	18	—	22
Manchester	Men	3	2	1	—	3
	Women	3	4	—	—	4
	Not known	5	3	3	—	6
	Total	11	9	4	—	13
Lancashire excluding Manchester	Men	7	3	15	—	18
	Women	4	1	6	—	7
	Not known	3	2	2	—	4
	Total	14	6	23	—	29
N.W. England excluding Lancashire and Wirral	Men	2	2	2	—	4
	Women	1	1	—	—	1
	Not known	4	2	7	—	9
	Total	7	5	9	—	14
North Wales	Men	3	3	3	—	6
	Women	1	1	1	—	2
	Not known	4	—	8	—	8
	Total	8	4	12	—	16
Edinburgh	Men	12	13	—	2	15
	Women	—	—	—	—	—
	Not known	1	2	—	—	2
	Total	13	15	—	2	17
The rest of Scotland and Ireland	Men	4	5	—	—	5
	Women	—	—	—	—	—
	Not known	2	2	—	—	2
	Total	6	7	—	—	7
Birmingham	Men	2	—	2	—	2
	Women	—	—	—	—	—
	Not known	1	2	1	—	3
	Total	3	2	3	—	5
South of England	Men	16	24	10	—	34
	Women	9	7	8	—	15
	Not known	5	6	5	—	11
	Total	30	37	23	—	60
West of England	Men	6	7	10	—	17
	Women	4	—	8	—	8
	Not known	4	3	4	—	7
	Total	14	10	22	—	32

		No. of artists	Oils	Works on paper	Sculpture	Total no. of works
East Anglia and The Midlands	Men	4	2	3	—	5
	Women	3	—	7	—	7
	Not known	5	5	4	—	9
	Total	12	7	14	—	21
N.E. England	Men	2	1	6	—	7
	Women	2	1	1	—	2
	Not known	5	3	6	—	9
	Total	9	5	13	—	18
Foreign addresses	Men	5	10	1	—	11
	Women	2	6	—	—	6
	Not known	—	—	—	—	—
	Total	7	16	1	—	17
No address	Men	19	8	12	5	25
	Women	7	5	5	—	10
	Not known	9	5	5	—	10
	Total	35	18	22	5	45
London: Hampstead	Men	5	5	4	—	9
	Women	2	—	2	1	3
	Not known	2	1	3	—	4
	Total	9	6	9	1	16
London: Haverstock Hill	Men	24	24	23	—	47
	Women	1	—	2	—	2
	Not known	5	4	2	—	6
	Total	30	28	27	—	55
London: St John's Wood	Men	21	19	9	—	28
	Women	2	—	3	—	3
	Not known	4	2	4	—	6
	Total	27	21	16	—	37
London: Kensington	Men	17	19	14	—	33
	Women	8	8	7	—	15
	Not known	7	8	11	—	19
	Total	32	35	32	—	67
London: Regent's Park	Men	6	7	2	1	10
	Women	2	3	3	—	6
	Not known	1	1	—	—	1
	Total	9	11	5	1	17
London: Fitzroy Square	Men	10	15	2	2	19
	Women	—	—	—	—	—
	Not known	9	17	4	—	21
	Total	19	32	6	2	40
The rest of inner London	Men	89	97	65	19	181
	Women	19	18	28	—	46
	Not known	67	42	61	—	103
	Total	175	157	154	19	330
London: suburbs	Men	9	6	10	—	16
	Women	5	2	7	1	10
	Not known	3	5	2	—	7
	Total	17	13	19	1	33
Grand totals	Men	322	321	293	34	648
	Women	95	62	125	2	189
	Not known	170	137	162	—	299
	Total	**587**	**520**	**580**	**36**	**1136**

1876

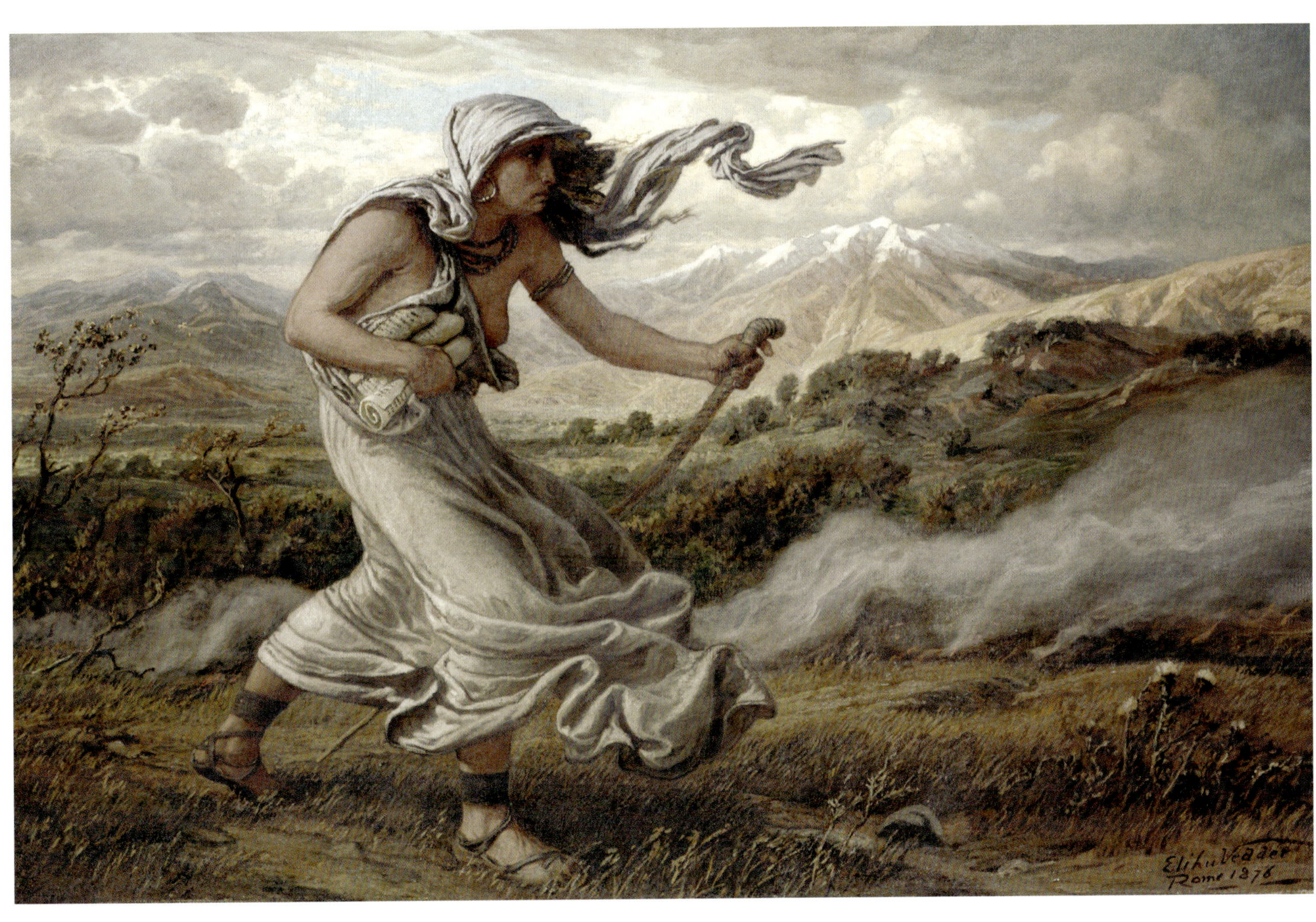

PLATE 79 · *The Cumaean Sibyl returning with the last of the Sibylline Books to Tarquin* · Elihu Vedder
oil on canvas · 96.5 x 150 cm · 1876 Autumn Exhibition no. 163
Detroit Institute of Arts, USA/Bridgeman Images

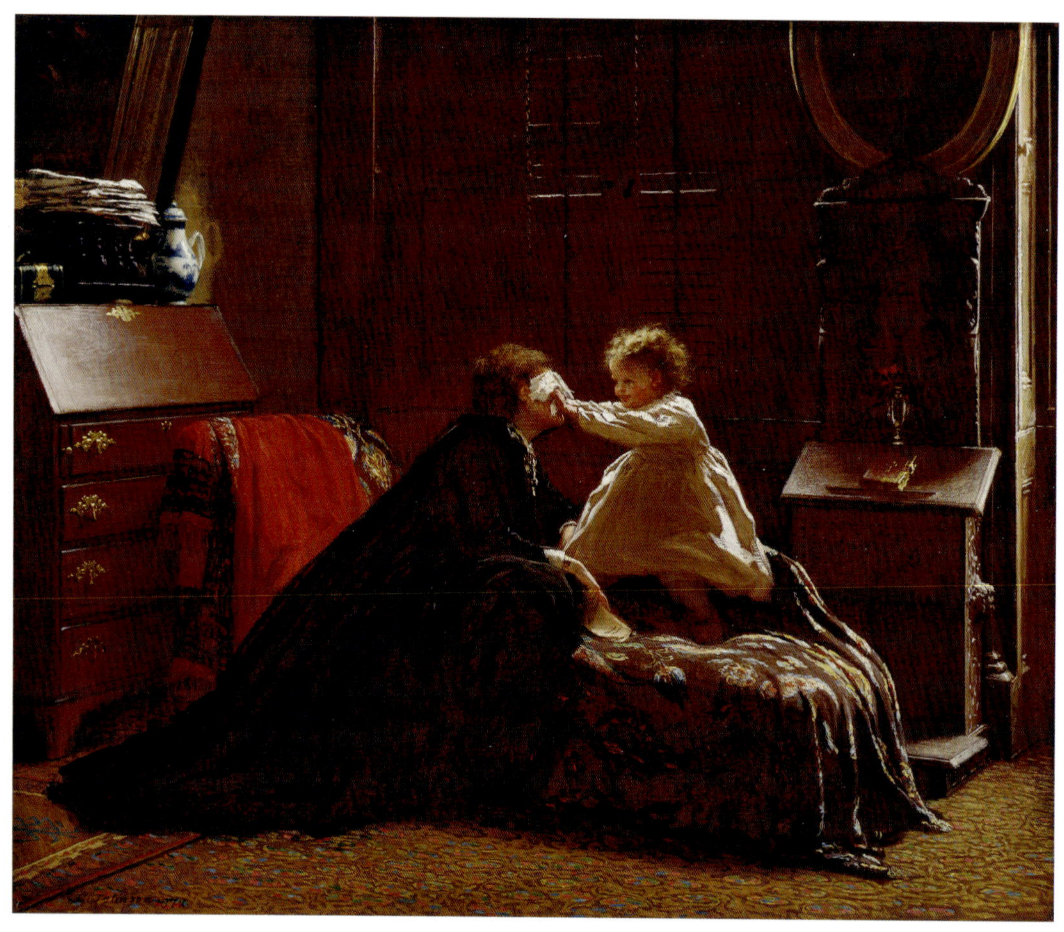

PLATE 80 · ***Bo Peep!*** · **Eastman Johnson**
oil on board on panel · 56 x 67.5 cm · 1876 Autumn Exhibition no. 8
Amon Carter Museum of American Art, Fort Worth, TX

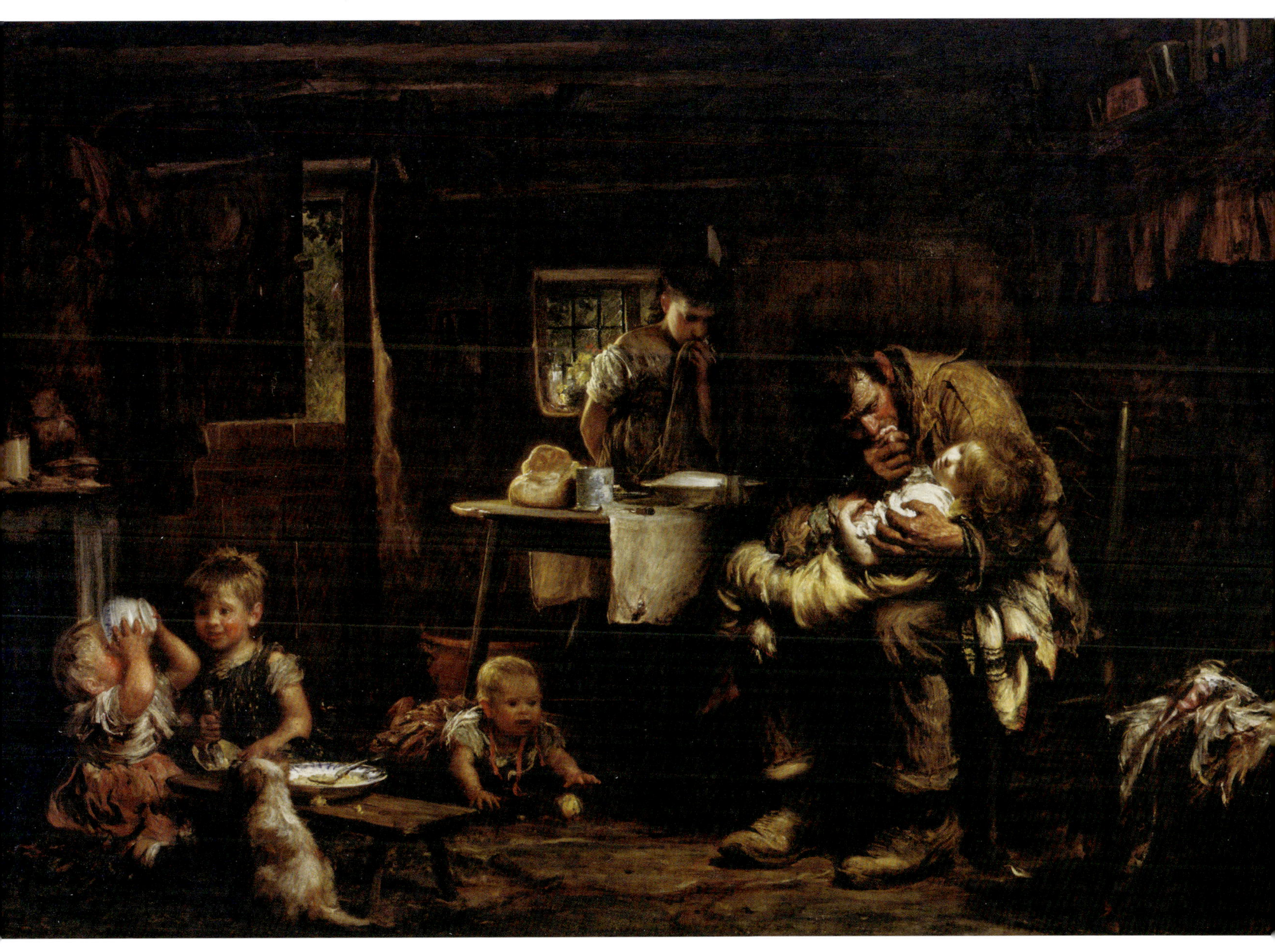

PLATE 81 · *The Widower* · Luke Fildes
oil on canvas · 169 x 248.5 cm · 1876 Autumn Exhibition no. 54
Art Gallery of New South Wales · photo AGNSW

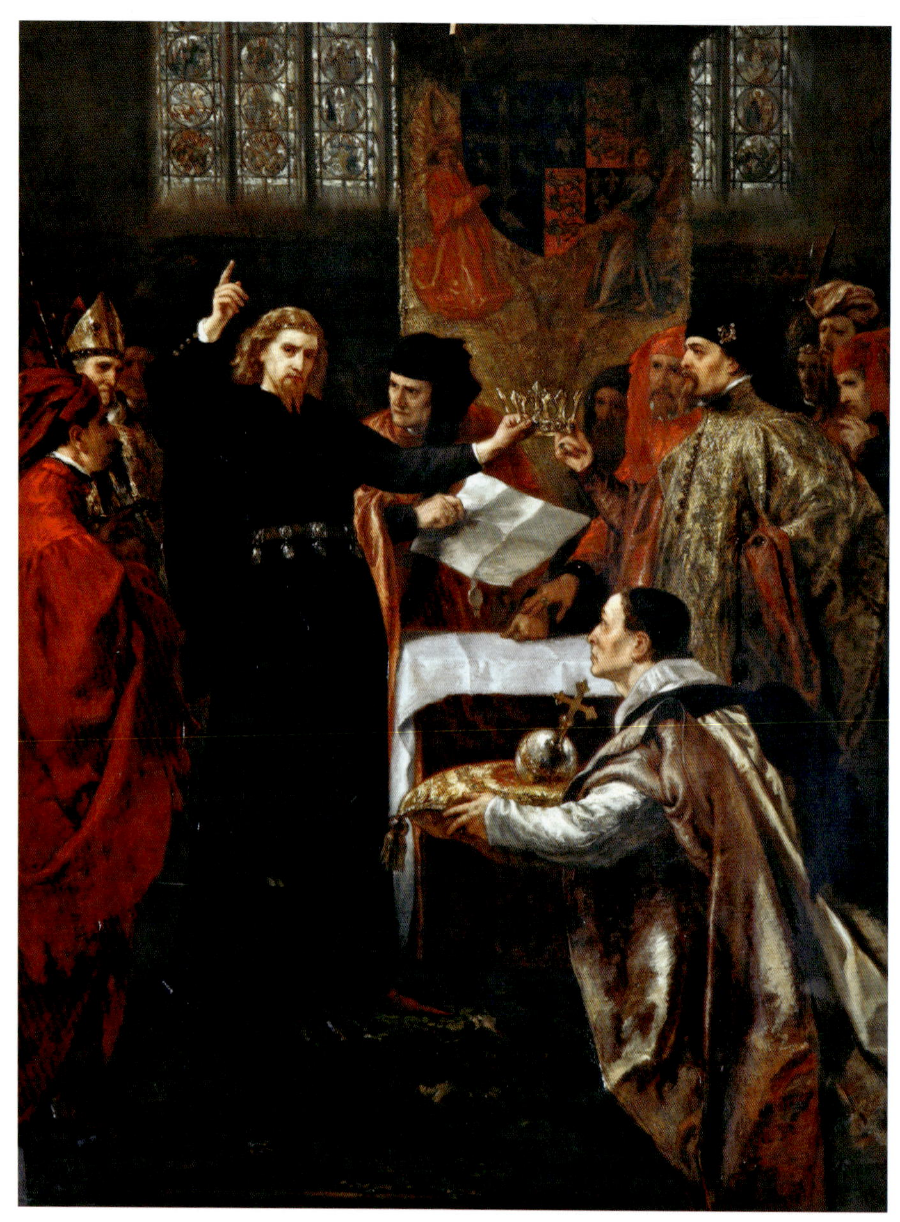

PLATE 82 · *Richard II Resigning the Crown to Bolingbroke* · Sir John Gilbert
oil on canvas · 161.5 x 123 cm · 1876 Autumn Exhibition no. 333
National Museums Liverpool (Walker Art Gallery)

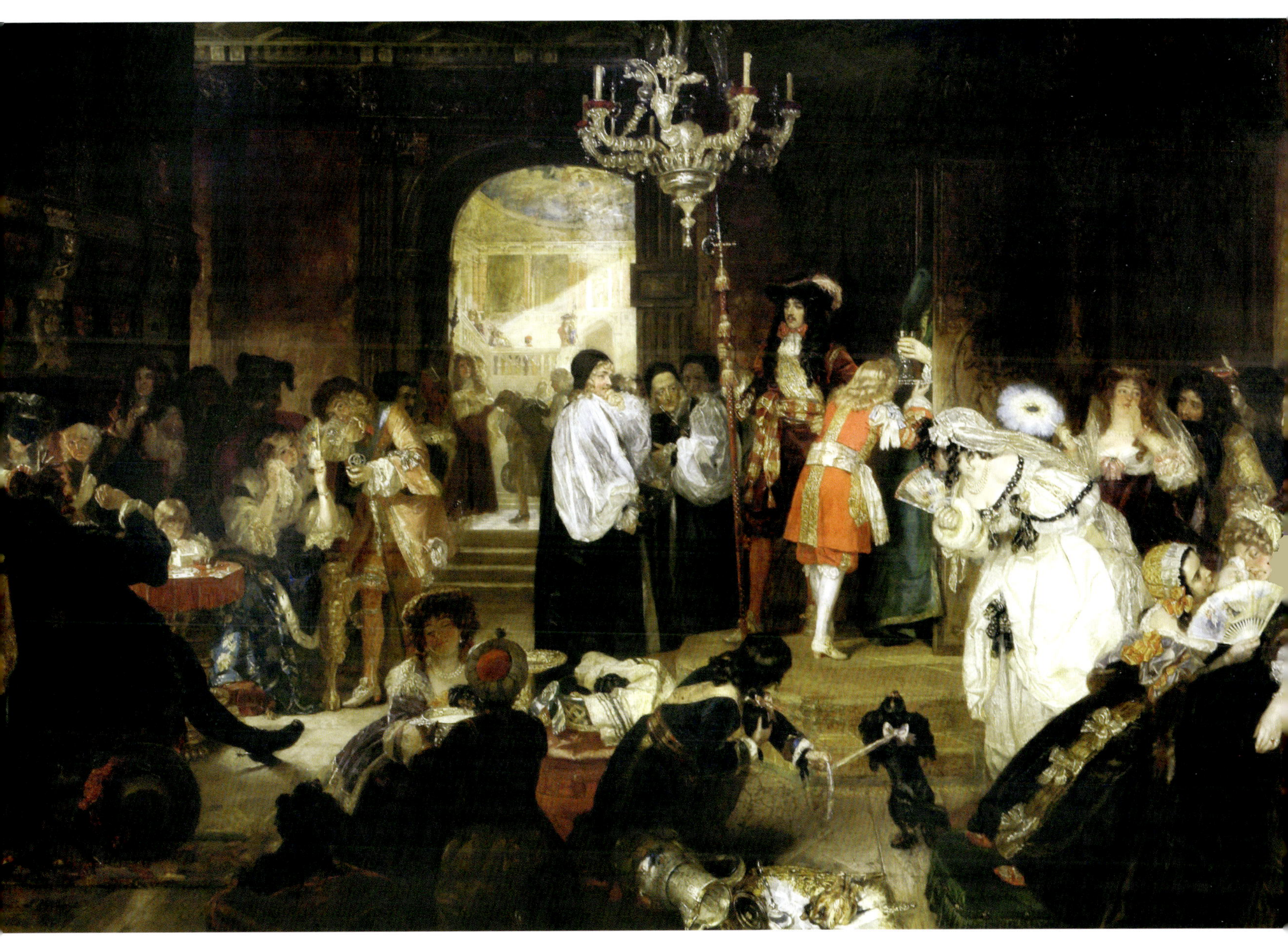

PLATE 83 · *Antechamber at Whitehall, during the Dying Moments of Charles II. The Glass of Water* · E.M. Ward
oil on canvas · 160.5 x 229 cm · 1876 Autumn Exhibition no. 156
National Museums Liverpool (Walker Art Gallery)

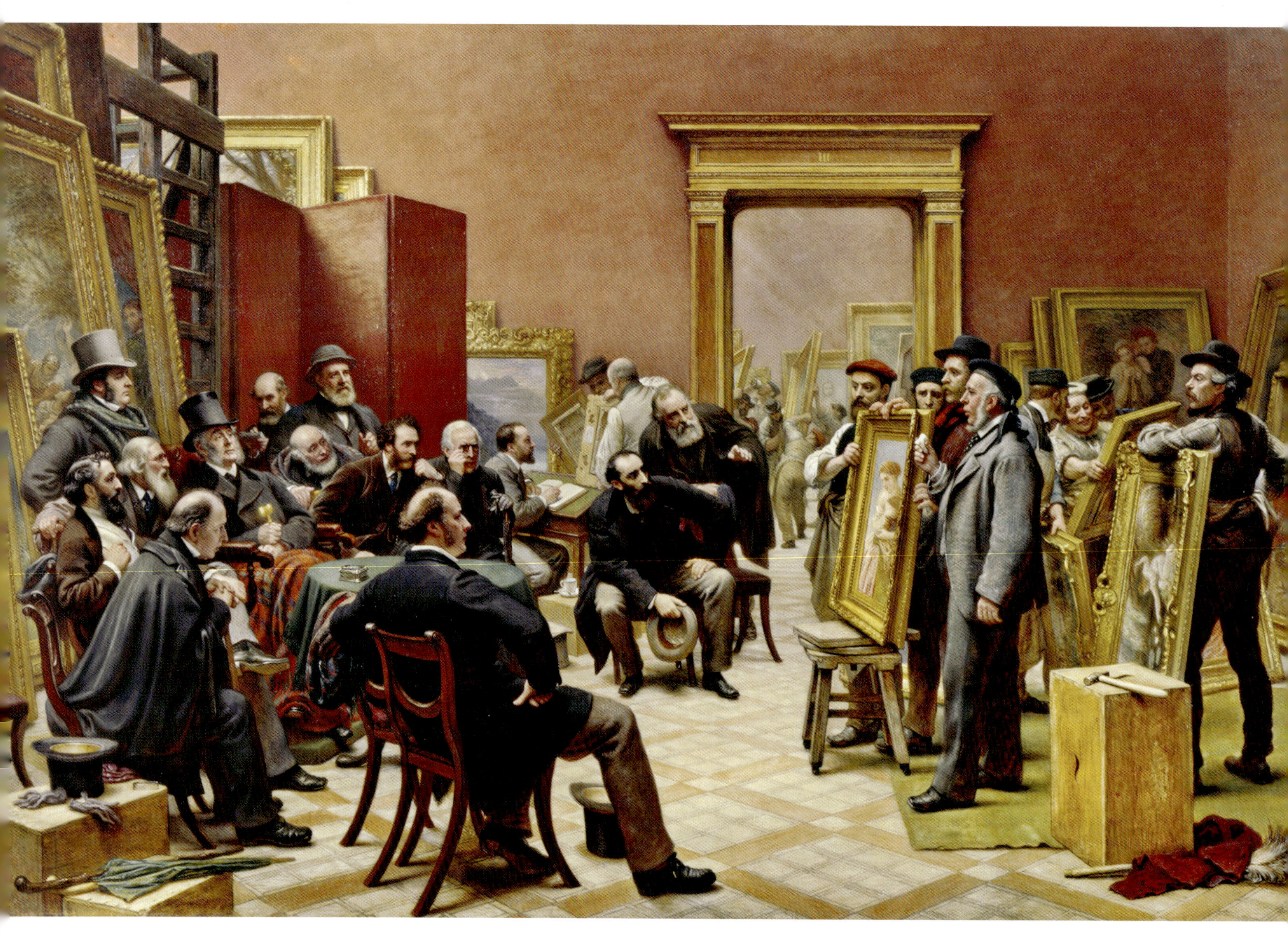

PLATE 84 · *Selecting Pictures for the Royal Academy Exhibition* · C.W. Cope
oil on canvas · 145 x 220 cm · 1876 Autumn Exhibition no. 202
Royal Academy of Arts, London

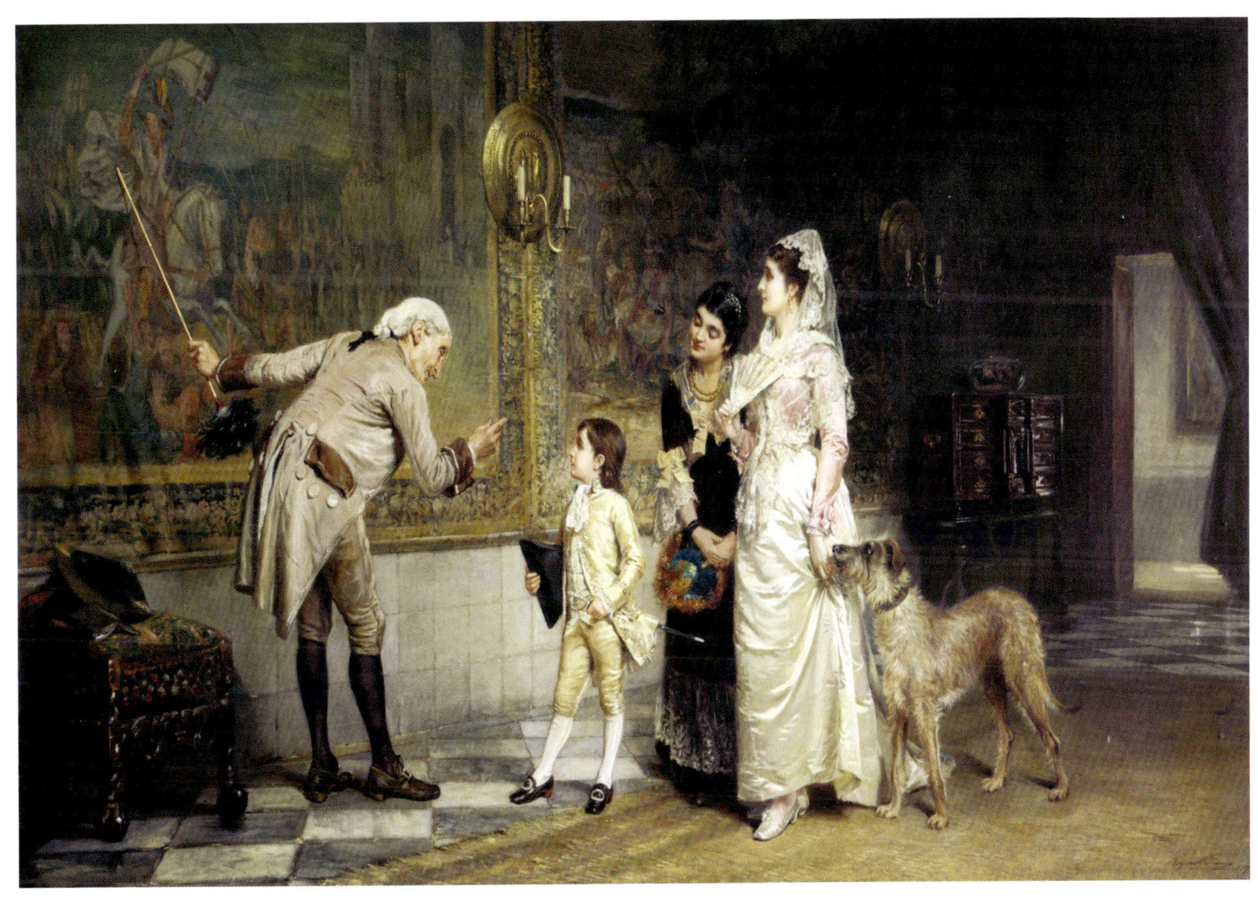

PLATE 85 · ***The Ancestor on the Tapestry*** · **Haynes Williams**
oil on canvas · 92 x 155.5 cm · 1876 Autumn Exhibition no. 24
National Museums Liverpool (Walker Art Gallery)

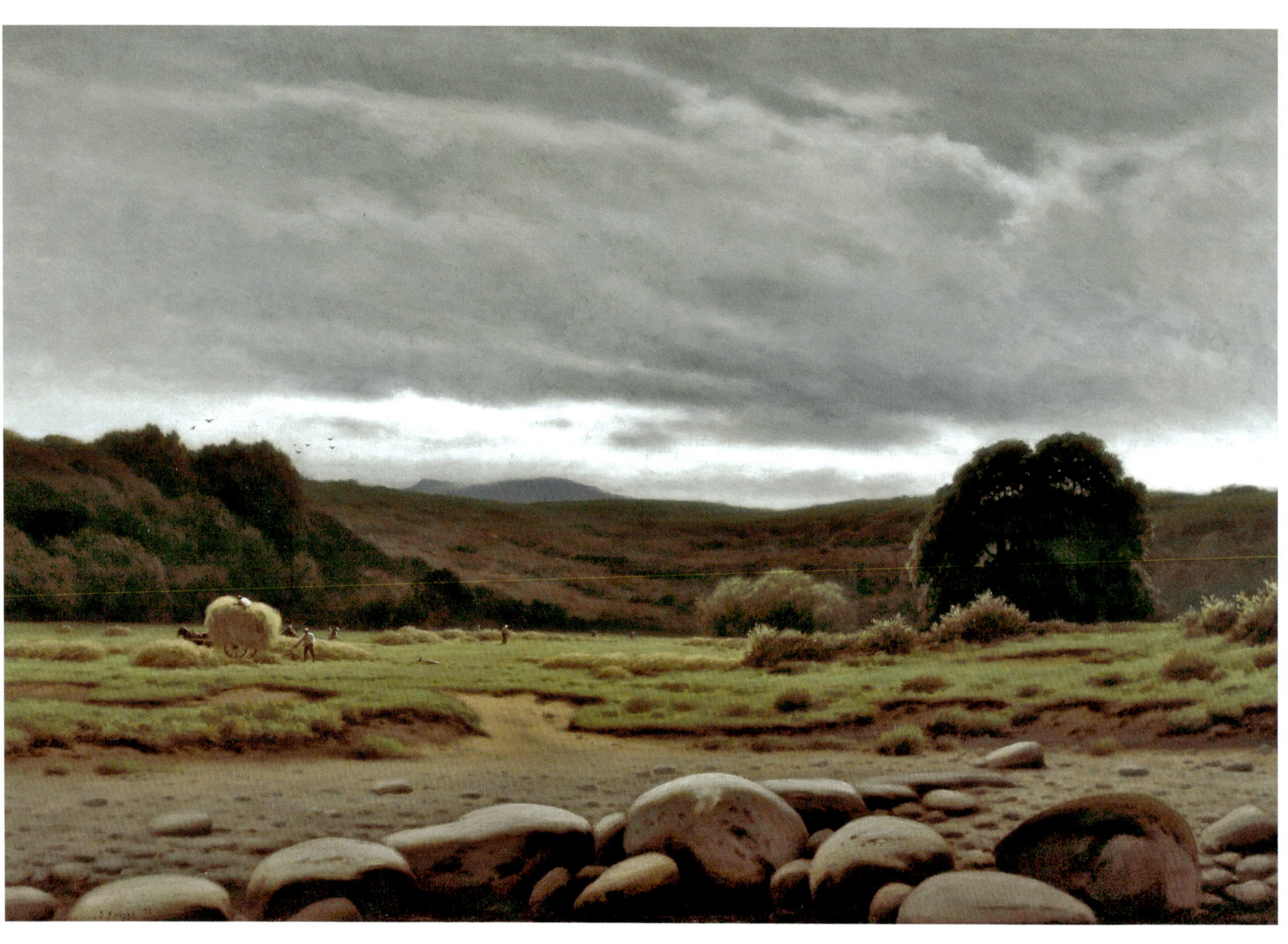

PLATE 86 · *Showery Weather* · Joseph Knight

oil on canvas · 87.5 x 128 cm · 1876 Autumn Exhibition no. 44

National Museums Liverpool (Walker Art Gallery)

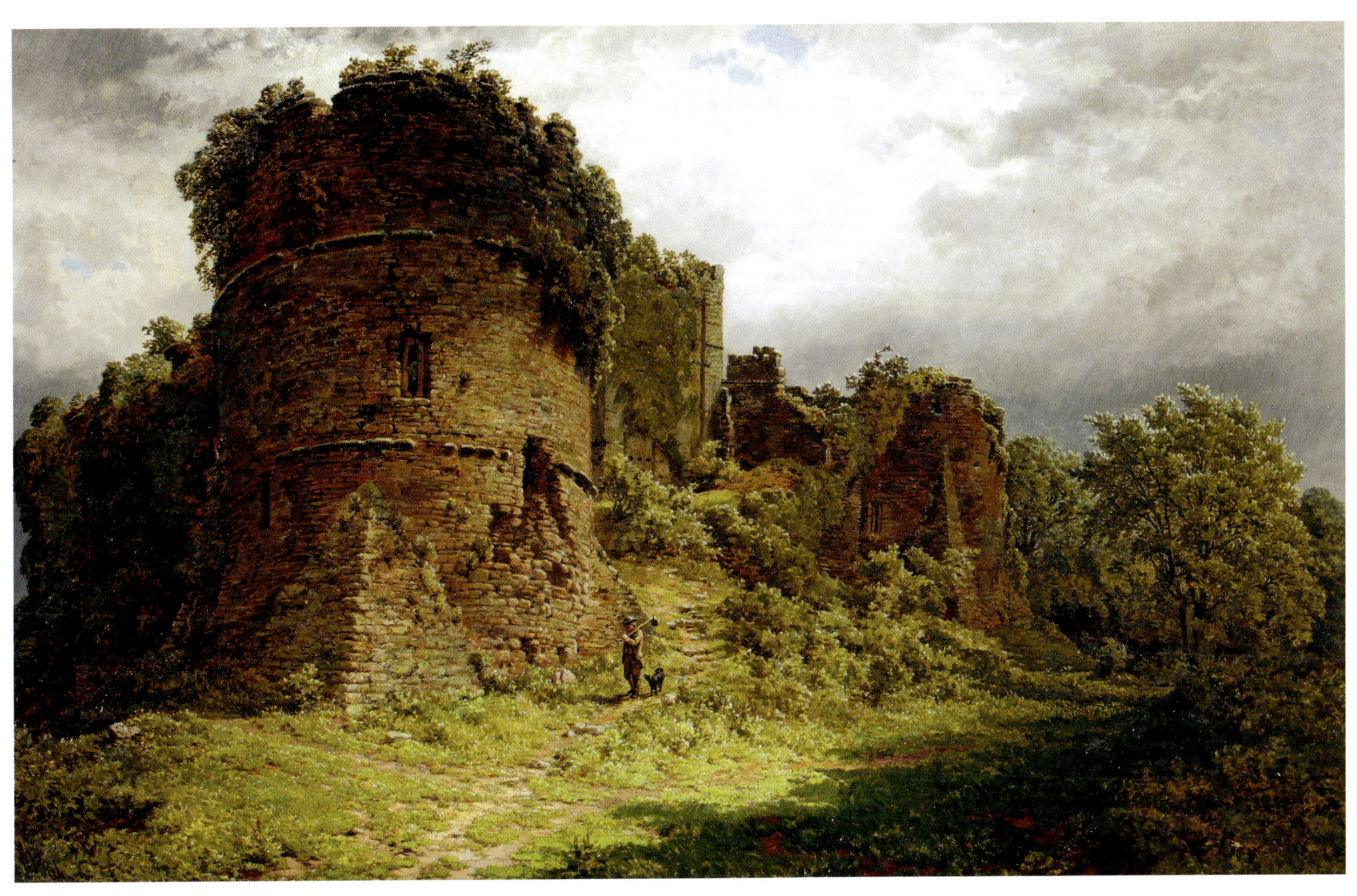

PLATE 87 · *Goodrich Castle* · Samuel H. Baker
oil on canvas · 68.5 x 109.5 cm · 1876 Autumn Exhibition no. 13
Newport Museum and Art Gallery/Bridgeman Images

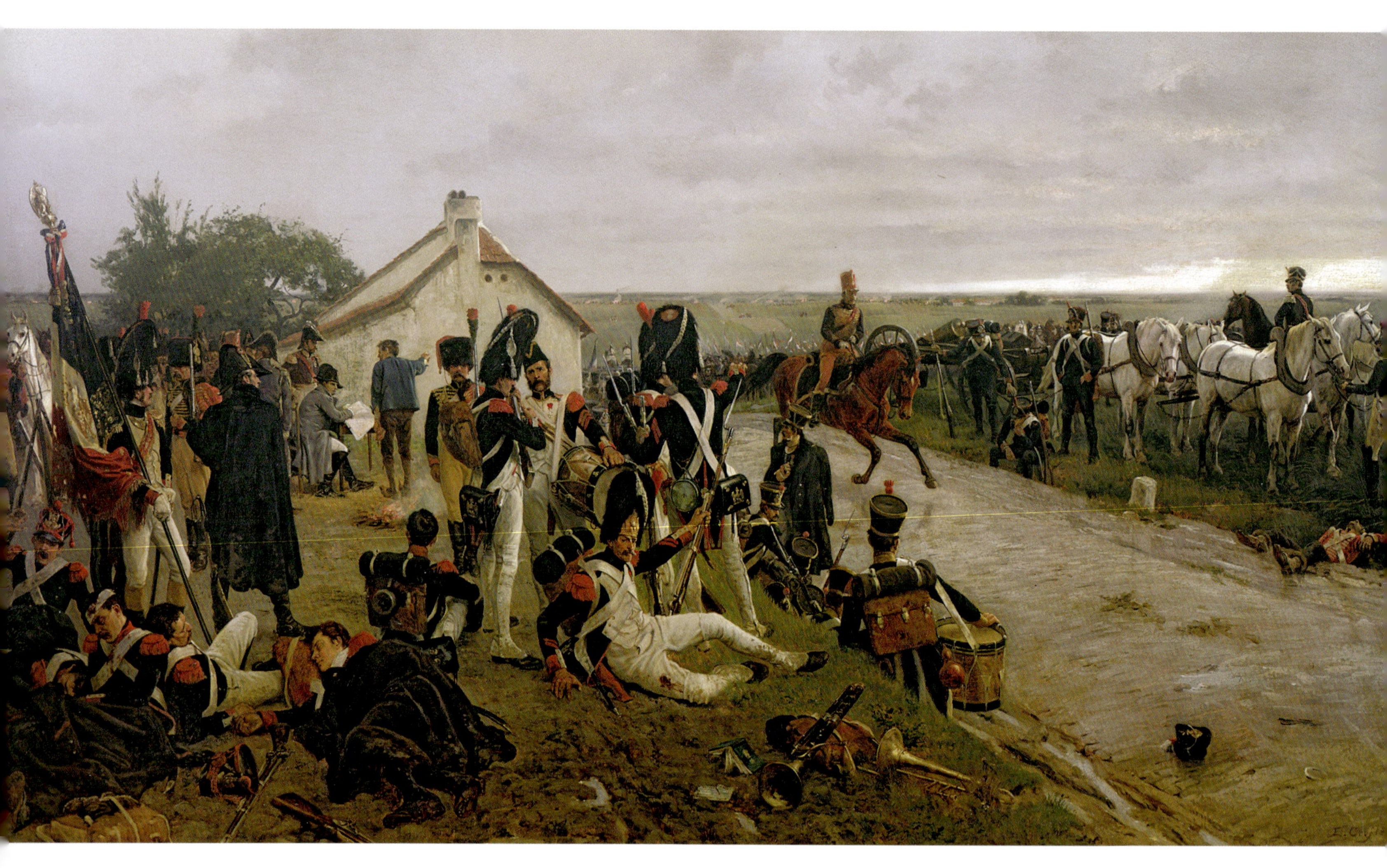

PLATE 88 · *On the Morning of the Battle of Waterloo* · Ernest W. Crofts
oil on canvas · 99.5 x 178 cm · 1876 Autumn Exhibition no. 241
Museums Sheffield/Bridgeman Images

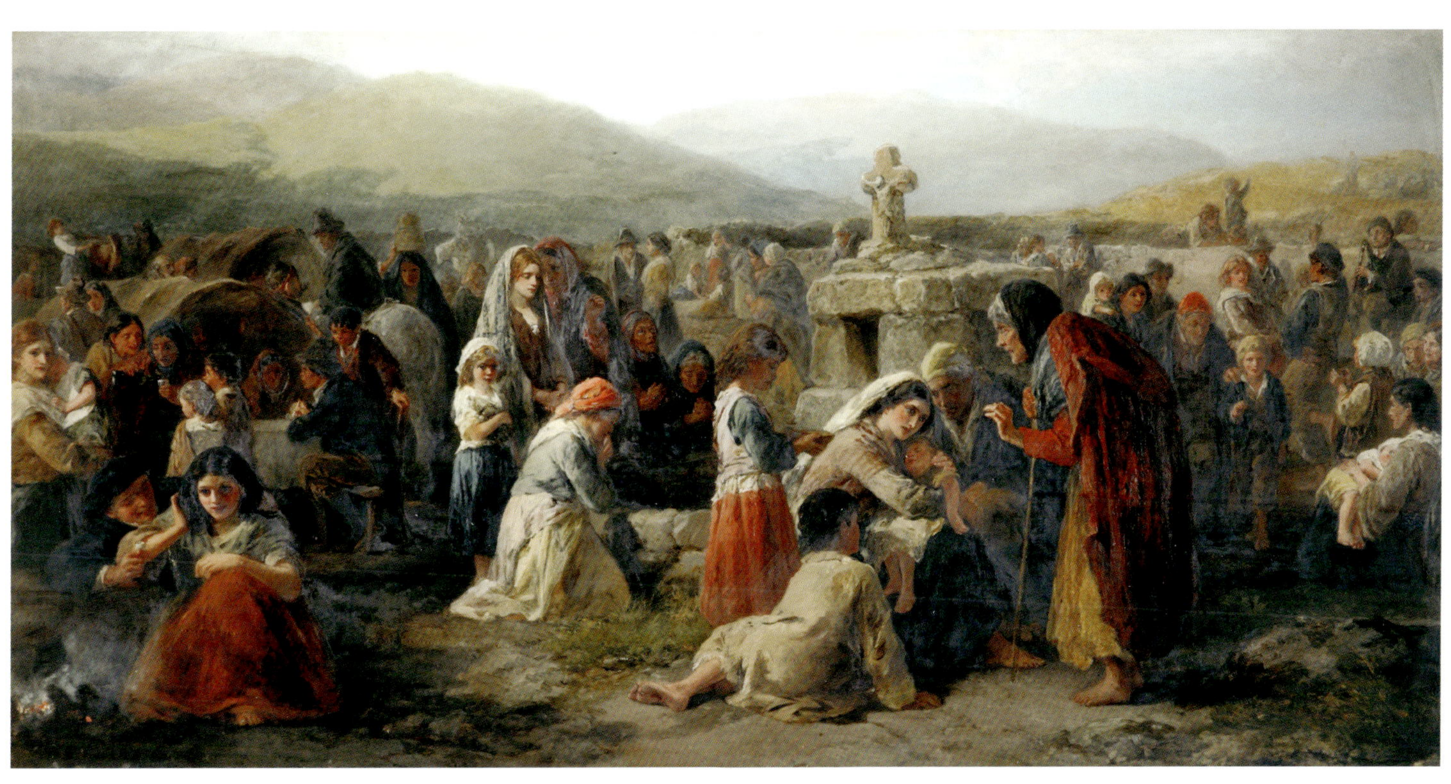

PLATE 89 · *The Morning of the Pattern* · Francis W. Topham
oil on canvas · 76 x 152.5 cm · 1876 Autumn Exhibition no. 805
National Museums Liverpool (Walker Art Gallery)

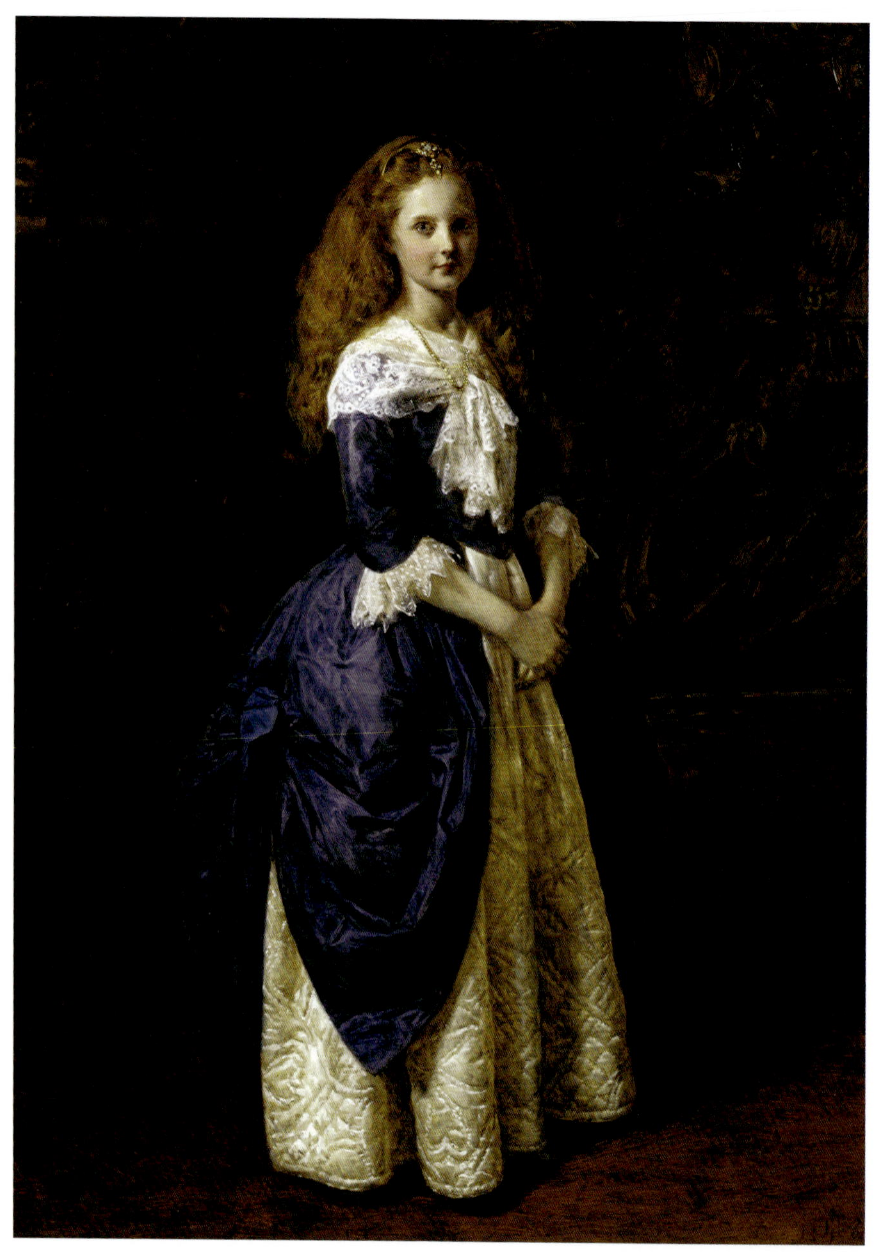

PLATE 90 · *My Great Grandmother* · James Archer
oil on canvas · 61 x 46 cm · 1876 Autumn Exhibition no. 250
Guildhall Art Gallery, City of London

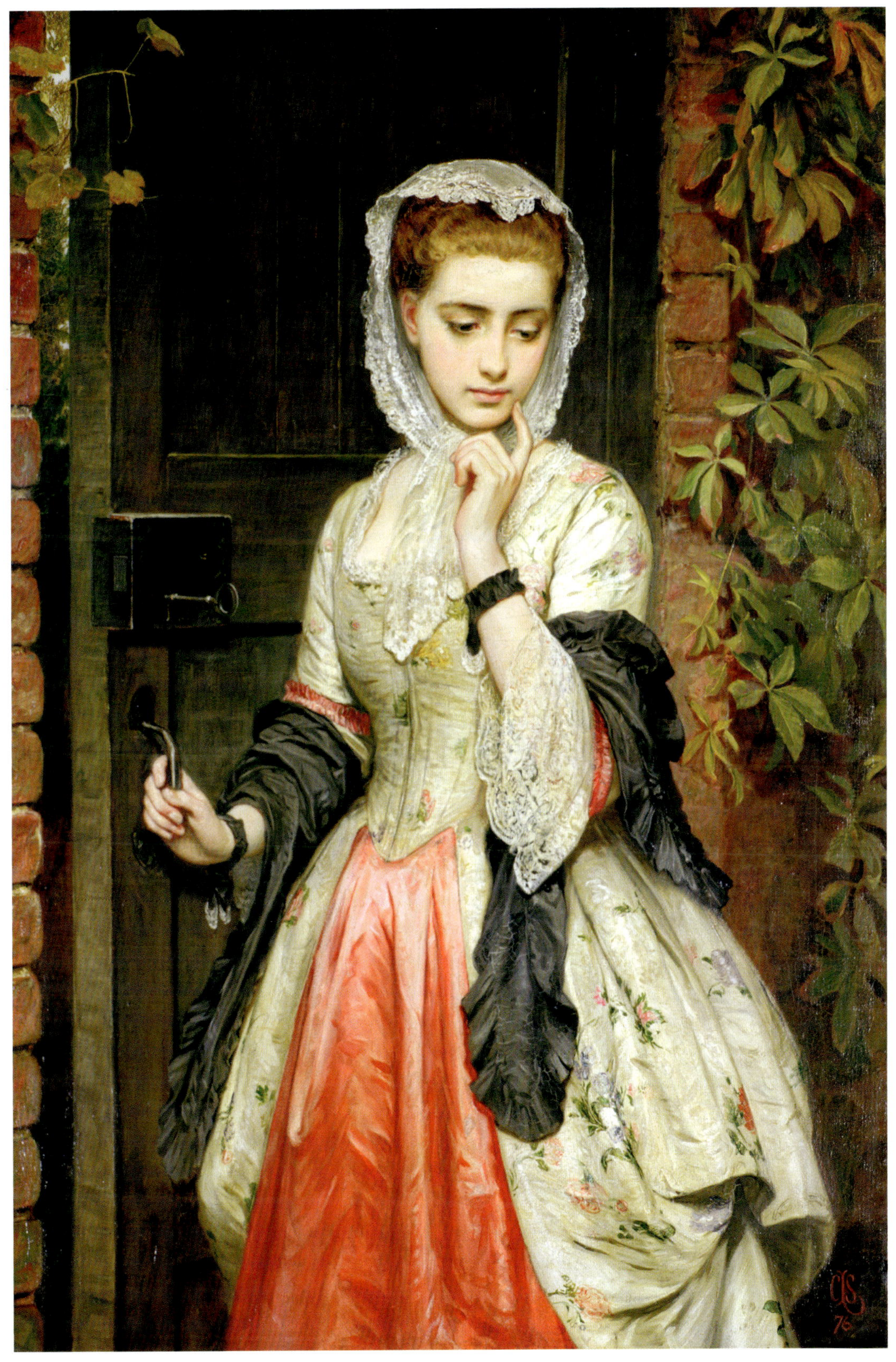

PLATE 91 · *Rejected Addresses* · C.S. Lidderdale
oil on canvas · 128 x 86.5 cm · 1876 Autumn Exhibition no. 393
Cartwright Hall Art Gallery, Bradford (Bradford Museums and Galleries)/Bridgeman Images

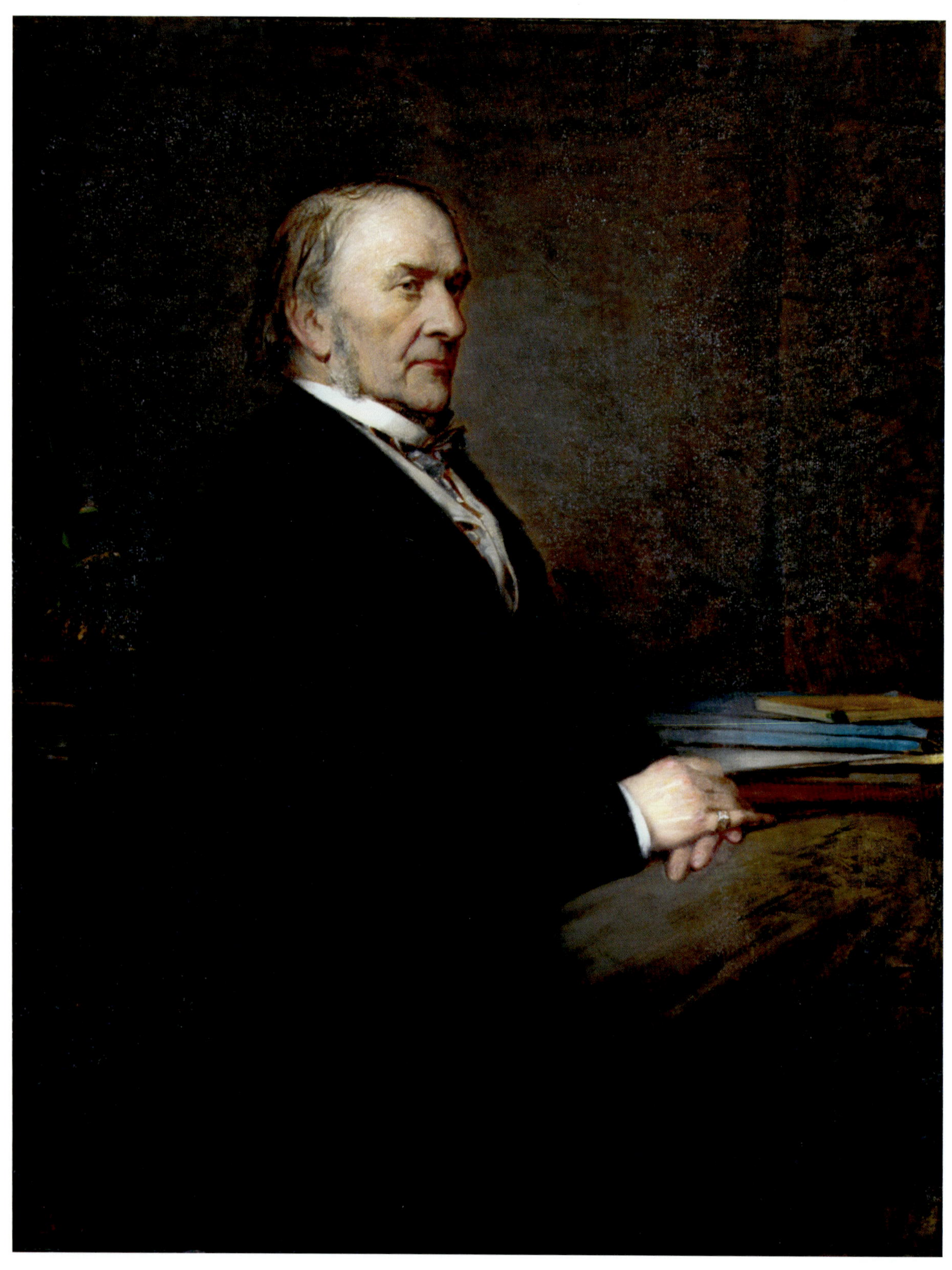

PLATE 92 · *Right Hon. W.E. Gladstone, M.P.* · Lowes Cato Dickinson
oil on canvas · 126.5 x 98.5 cm · 1876 Autumn Exhibition no. 69
reproduced with the kind consent of the Trustees of the Liverpool College Foundation · photograph by Steve Judson

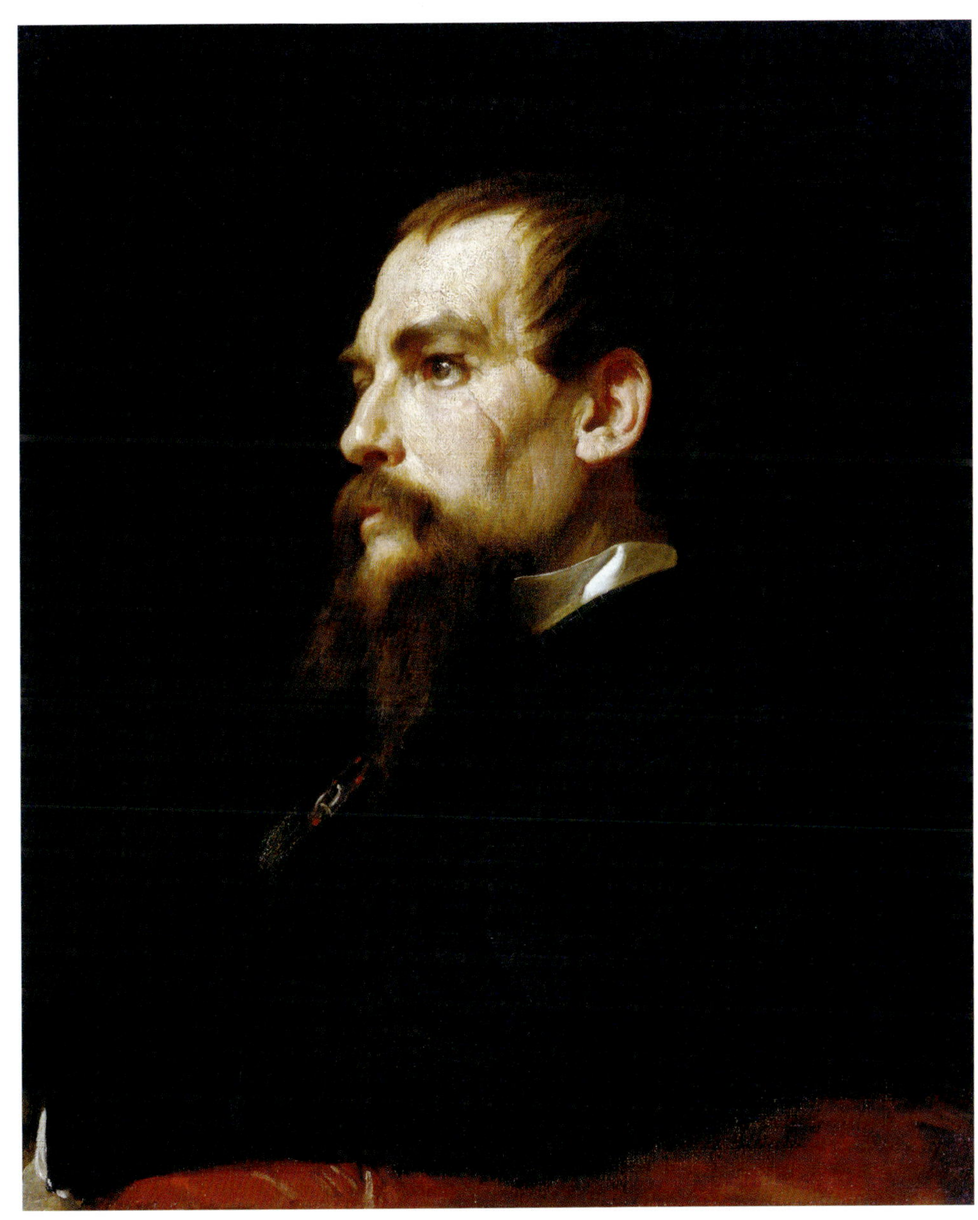

PLATE 93 · *Captain Richard Burton, H.M.'s Consul at Trieste* · Frederic Leighton
oil on canvas · 61 x 51 cm · 1876 Autumn Exhibition no. 289
National Portrait Gallery, London

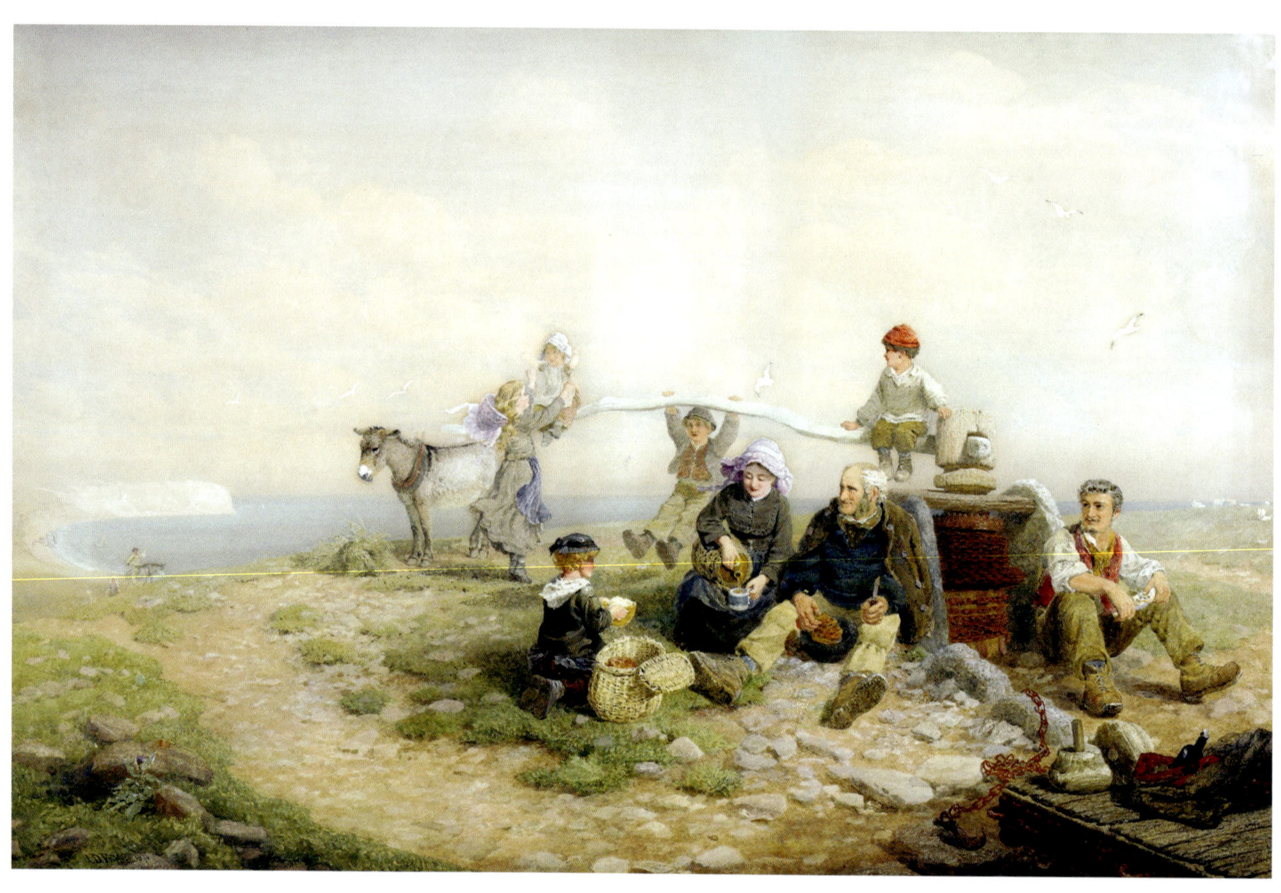

PLATE 94 · *Dinner Time at the Quarries – Purbeck* · Alfred D. Fripp
watercolour and gouache on paper · 63 x 98.5 cm · 1876 Autumn Exhibition no. 1045
National Museums Liverpool (Walker Art Gallery)

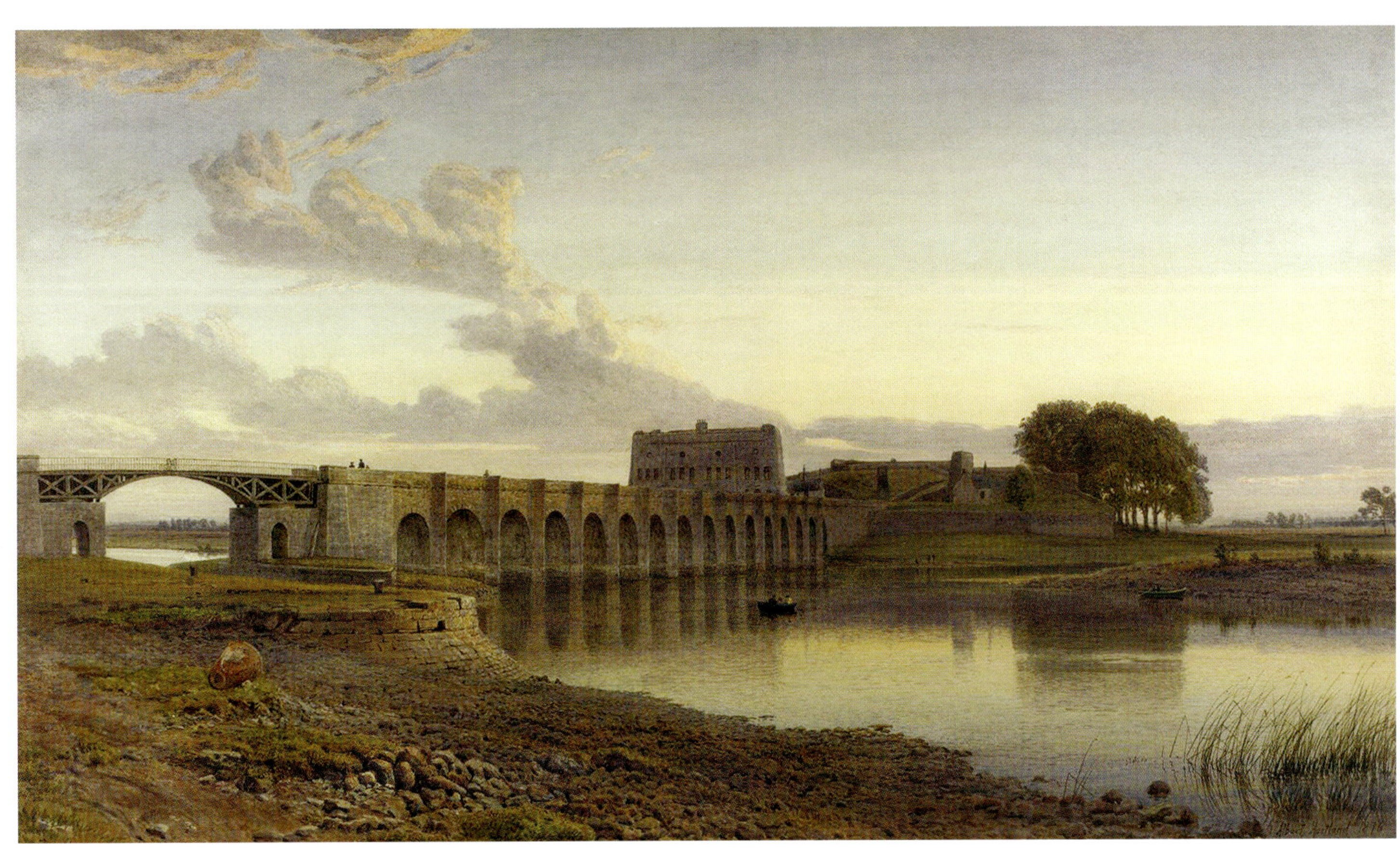

PLATE 95 · *The Last Ray of Evening – Shannon Bridge* · Albert Hartland
watercolour on paper · 58.5 x 103 cm · 1876 Autumn Exhibition no. 1085
Victoria & Albert Museum

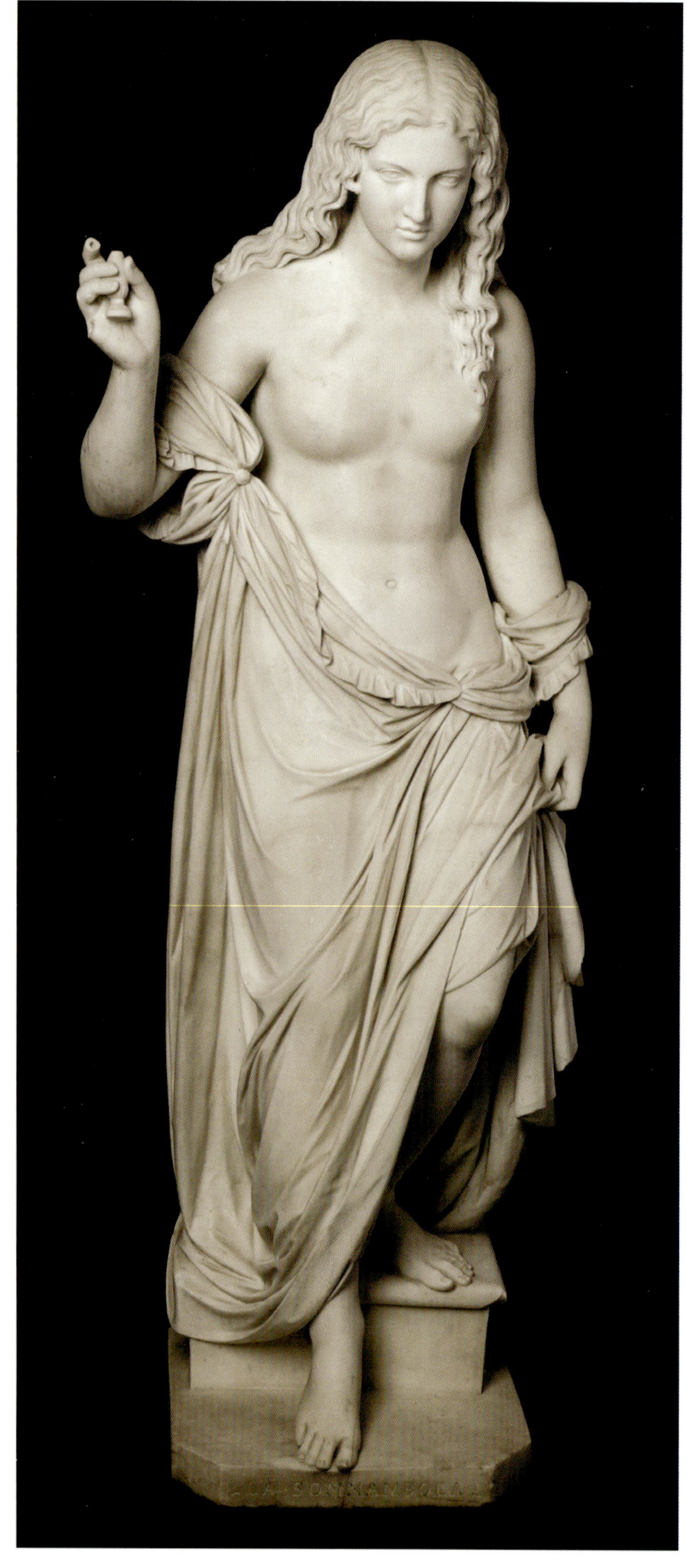

PLATE 96 · *La Somnambula* · **Giovanni Fontana**
marble · 155 cm high · 1876 Autumn Exhibition no. 1143
Art Gallery of New South Wales · photo AGNSW

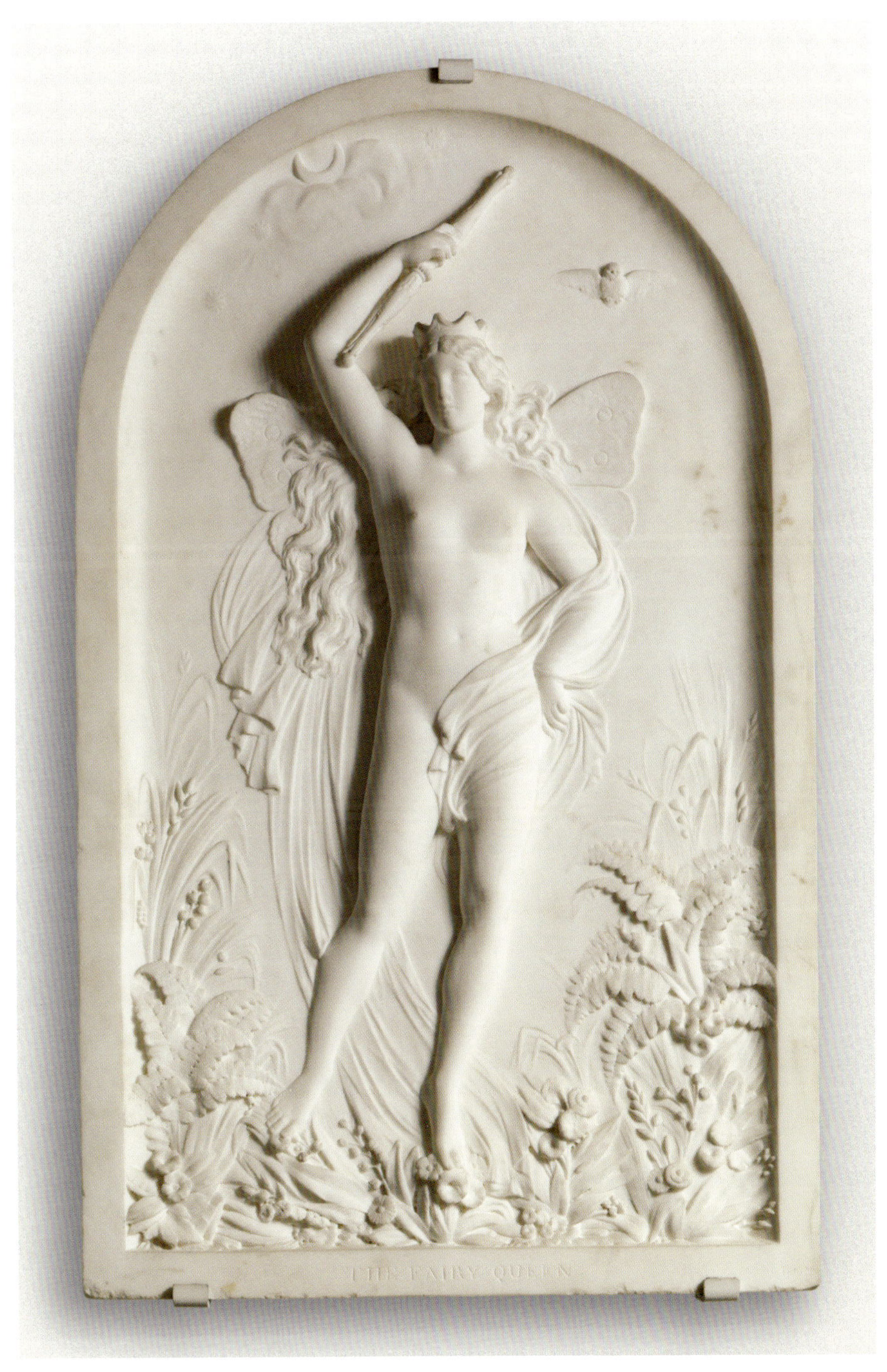

PLATE 97 · *The Fairie Queen* · **Giovanni Fontana**
marble · 106.5 x 66 cm · 1876 Autumn Exhibition no. 1139
National Museums Liverpool (Walker Art Gallery)

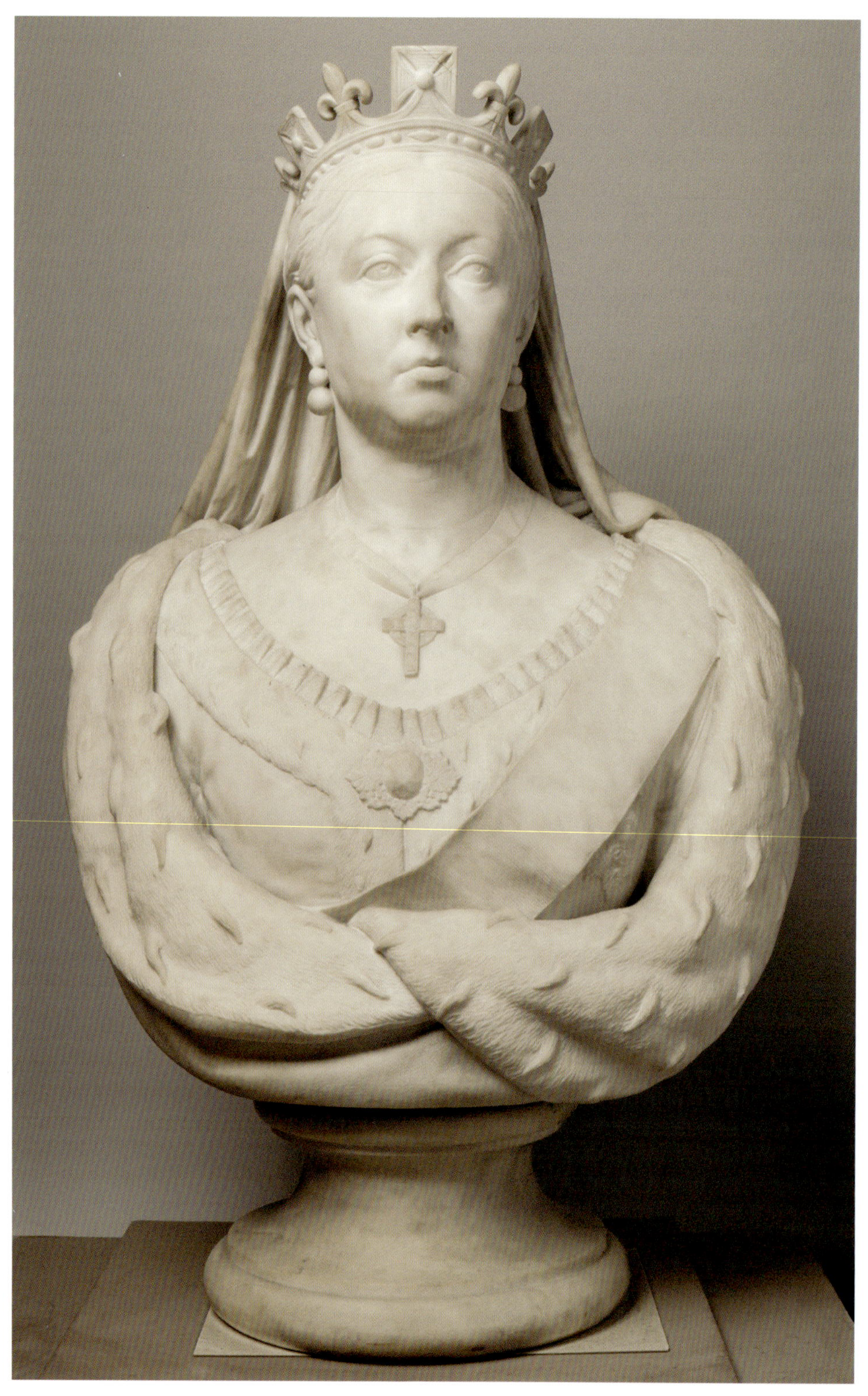

PLATE 98 · *Her Majesty the Queen* · **Count Gleichen (Prince Victor of Hohenlohe-Langenburg)**
marble · 91.5 cm high · 1876 Autumn Exhibition no. 1114
National Museums Liverpool (Walker Art Gallery)

Paintings by numbers 1876

		No. of artists	Oils	Works on paper	Sculpture	Total no. of works
Liverpool	*Men*	54	46	72	4	122
	Women	11	3	15	–	18
	Not known	21	17	29	–	46
	Total	86	66	116	4	186
Birkenhead	*Men*	3	1	3	–	4
	Women	4	1	6	–	7
	Not known	4	7	4	–	11
	Total	11	9	13	–	22
Chester	*Men*	2	1	3	–	4
	Women	2	–	3	–	3
	Not known	1	1	–	–	1
	Total	5	2	6	–	8
Wirral excluding Birkenhead	*Men*	5	–	15	–	15
	Women	1	–	2	–	2
	Not known	4	3	3	–	6
	Total	10	3	20	–	23
Manchester	*Men*	6	3	4	2	9
	Women	5	4	1	–	5
	Not known	5	5	3	–	8
	Total	16	12	8	2	22
Lancashire excluding Manchester	*Men*	5	2	13	–	15
	Women	5	1	6	–	7
	Not known	3	3	2	–	5
	Total	13	6	21	–	27
N.W. England excluding Lancashire and Wirral	*Men*	2	–	5	–	5
	Women	2	1	5	–	6
	Not known	2	–	3	–	3
	Total	6	1	13	–	14
North Wales	*Men*	4	4	3	–	7
	Women	1	–	1	–	1
	Not known	3	–	9	–	9
	Total	8	4	13	–	17
Edinburgh	*Men*	13	14	1	2	17
	Women	–	–	–	–	–
	Not known	4	3	3	–	6
	Total	17	17	4	2	23
The rest of Scotland and Ireland	*Men*	8	9	–	–	9
	Women	–	–	–	–	–
	Not known	8	6	2	–	8
	Total	16	15	2	–	17
Birmingham	*Men*	5	4	2	–	6
	Women	–	–	–	–	–
	Not known	2	7	–	–	7
	Total	7	11	2	–	13
South of England	*Men*	24	33	21	–	54
	Women	9	3	15	–	18
	Not known	8	5	5	–	10
	Total	41	41	41	–	82
West of England	*Men*	5	7	8	–	15
	Women	4	1	6	2	9
	Not known	4	5	3	–	8
	Total	13	13	17	2	32

		No. of artists	Oils	Works on paper	Sculpture	Total no. of works
East Anglia and The Midlands	*Men*	–	–	–	–	–
	Women	2	–	4	–	4
	Not known	7	3	10	–	13
	Total	9	3	14	–	17
N.E. England	*Men*	2	3	2	–	5
	Women	1	–	2	–	2
	Not known	–	–	–	–	–
	Total	3	3	4	–	7
Foreign addresses	*Men*	6	5	4	–	9
	Women	1	3	–	–	3
	Not known	2	2	1	–	3
	Total	9	10	5	–	15
No address	*Men*	40	38	14	3	55
	Women	8	10	2	–	12
	Not known	14	10	5	2	17
	Total	62	58	21	5	84
London: Hampstead	*Men*	4	2	2	–	4
	Women	1	–	1	–	1
	Not known	3	–	4	–	4
	Total	8	2	7	–	9
London: Haverstock Hill	*Men*	22	23	20	–	43
	Women	–	–	–	–	–
	Not known	6	5	3	–	8
	Total	28	28	23	–	51
London: St John's Wood	*Men*	13	12	6	–	18
	Women	3	1	4	–	5
	Not known	12	15	6	–	21
	Total	28	28	16	–	44
London: Kensington	*Men*	19	26	11	2	39
	Women	4	3	5	–	8
	Not known	8	10	6	–	16
	Total	31	39	22	2	63
London: Regent's Park	*Men*	6	8	6	–	14
	Women	2	4	4	–	8
	Not known	7	5	10	–	15
	Total	15	17	20	–	37
London: Fitzroy Square	*Men*	2	2	–	–	2
	Women	2	1	3	–	4
	Not known	8	9	5	–	14
	Total	12	12	8	–	20
The rest of inner London	*Men*	91	100	64	12	176
	Women	23	16	32	–	48
	Not known	63	50	52	–	102
	Total	177	166	148	12	326
London: suburbs	*Men*	8	8	5	–	13
	Women	4	2	5	1	8
	Not known	4	6	–	–	6
	Total	16	16	10	1	27
Grand totals	*Men*	349	351	284	25	660
	Women	95	54	122	3	179
	Not known	203	177	168	2	347
	Total	**647**	**582**	**574**	**30**	**1186**

APPENDICES

APPENDIX 1

Artists whose works were included in all six Autumn Exhibitions, 1871–76, and their total number of exhibited works.

S.H. Baker · 19
J.J. Bannatyne · 23
W.D. Barker · 15
Annie Beaumont · 19
W.R. Beverley · 13
Henry Birtles · 13
W.J. Bishop · 25
George Bonavia · 11
W.J.J.C. Bond · 17
John R. Brown · 13
Charles Cattermole · 9
Ellen Clacy · 19
Alfred Clint · 13
E.J. Cobbett · 11
James Cole · 11
William Collingwood · 26
Thomas Daniels · 7
Jane Deakin · 8
Peter Deakin · 17
Thomas C. Dibdin · 20
Fred Dimes · 12
A.B. Donaldson · 24
Robert Dudley · 18
Allan Duncan · 13
Edward Duncan · 8
Charles Earle · 18
William Eden · 26
Mary Ensor · 20
Walter Field · 7
John Finnie · 30
Giovanni Fontana · 14
G.H. Garraway · 18
Arthur Gilbert · 11
Edith Gittins · 17
J. Godet · 12
Towneley Green · 10
W.H. Haines · 14
Edwin Hayes · 14
James Hayllar · 12
W. Henry · 7
J.A. Houston · 10
Thomas Huson · 25

Fanny Jolly · 24
J.M. Jopling · 20
W.L. Kerry · 31
G.G. Kilburne · 9
W.W. Laing · 15
Frederic Leighton · 6
A. Durer Lucas · 32
J.A.P. Macbride · 21
Jessie Macgregor · 16
Thomas R. Macquoid · 31
Agnes MacWhirter · 12
Edith Martineau · 11
Gertrude Martineau · 16
John Mogford · 24
J.H. Mole · 12
Alfred P. Newton · 12
Richard Norbury · 14
Emma Oliver · 13
John Pedder · 21
G. Pope · 11
Sam Pride · 30
Ephraim Pugh · 13
R.P. Richards · 14
H.B. Roberts · 23
Charles Robertson · 10
A.M. Rossi · 14
F. Smallfield · 14
Charles Smith · 16
James Smith · 15
W.J. Smith · 26
Charles Thornely · 22
F.W.W. Topham · 15
Thomas Wade · 25
J.W. Walker · 22
Pauline Walker · 18
George Stanfield Walters · 14
Frank Walton · 14
S.S. Warren · 15
A.W. Weedon · 12
A. Whittle · 20
L. Pinhorn Wood · 13

APPENDIX 2

Artworks (oils unless otherwise indicated) purchased from the exhibitions for the Liverpool permanent collection (excludes works purchased privately for immediate donation to the permanent collection).
*watercolour †sculpture

1871
Sophie Anderson: *Elaine*
catalogue £420; bought for £315
John Finnie: *Snowdon*
catalogue £100; bought for £80
J.M. Jopling:
*"Sweet eyes of starry tenderness"**
catalogue £136 10s; bought for £100

1872
J.W. Oakes:
A North Devon Glen – Autumn
catalogue £367 10s; bought for £300
F.W.W. Topham: *The Fall of Rienzi, the Last Roman Tribune*
catalogue £367 10s; bought for £300

1873
Mark Anthony: *Evensong*
catalogue £525; bought for £420
E.A. Goodall:
The Pescheria in the Ghetto – Rome
catalogue £210; bought for £157 10s
Louisa Starr: *Sintram*
catalogue £315; bought for £210

1874
Frederick Bridgman: *The Diligence*
catalogue £126; bought for £105
J. Birnie Philip:
In the Vineyard, South of Spain†
catalogue £60; bought for £50
E.A. Waterlow: *A Summer Shower*
catalogue £68 5s; bought for £50

1875
None

1876
A.D. Fripp:
*Dinner Time at the Quarries – Purbeck**
catalogue £315; bought for £262 10s
Sir John Gilbert: *Richard II Resigning the Crown to Bolingbroke*
catalogue £700; bought for £665
Joseph Knight: *Showery Weather*
catalogue £200; bought for £150
Haynes Williams:
The Ancestor on the Tapestry
catalogue £550; bought for £350

INDEX

ABOUT THE AUTHOR

Alex Kidson studied at Oxford University and the Courtauld Institute of Art, London, before becoming a curator at the Walker Art Gallery Liverpool in 1982. Although his remit was all British art from the Tudor period to the present day, his chief area of specialist interest was late eighteenth-century painting. He wrote for the Walker two permanent collection catalogues of the earlier paintings at the Walker and Lady Lever Art Galleries, and he curated major monographic exhibitions devoted to George Romney (2002), George Stubbs (2006) and Joseph Wright of Derby (2007). After leaving the Walker in 2008 he was Special Projects Fellow at the Paul Mellon Centre for Studies in British Art, London where he completed a three-volume catalogue raisonné of the paintings of Romney, published by Yale University Press in 2015. He is currently editing for publication the late Hamish Miles's complete catalogue of the paintings of David Wilkie for the Paul Mellon Centre, and compiling an online dictionary of the exhibits at the Liverpool Autumn Exhibitions, for National Museums Liverpool.